Going for the Fences
The Minor League Home Run Record Book

Second Edition

Edited by
Bob McConnell

Society for American Baseball Research
Phoenix, AZ

Cover: Joe Bauman. Historical Society of Southeast New Mexico.

Published by
The Society for American Baseball Research, Inc.
4455 E. Camelback Rd. Suite D-150
Phoenix, Arizona 85015
www.sabr.org

Copyright © 2009, 2014 by The Society for American Baseball Research
Printed in the United States of America

All rights reserved.
Reproduction in whole or in part without permission is prohibited.

This POD edition is a replica of the 2009 edition and is presented without changes.

Contents

Preface	i
Introduction	ii
Players with 150+ Career Home Runs in the Minor Leagues	1
Top One Hundred Career Home Run Hitters in Minor Leagues	15
Some Interesting Facts about the Top 100 Career Home Run Hitters	16
The Interesting Case of Pete Kousagan	16
Top Ten Career Home Run Hitters Batting Right, Left, or Both	17
Top Ten Career Home Run Hitters at the End of Each Decade	18
Top Ten Career Home Run Hitters by League	20
Players with 100+ Home Runs in Each of Two Leagues	24
Buzz Arlett Hit More Than 80 Home Runs in Each of Three Leagues	24
Top Fifty Career Home Run Hitters in Organized Baseball (Major and Minor League Totals Combined)	25
Players with 100+ Career Home Runs in Both the Major Leagues and the Minor Leagues	26
Players Reaching Double Figures in Home Runs in Both the Majors and Minors During the Same Season	27
Minor League Career Home Runs for Players with 300 or More in the Major Leagues	29
Career Home Run Leaders by First Letter of Last Name	31
Players with 50+ Home Runs in a Season	32
Interesting Facts about 50+ Home Run Seasons	34
Players with 45 to 49 Home Runs in a Season in Chronological Order	36
Top Ten Season Home Run Totals by Players, Active Leagues	38
Top Ten Season Home Run Totals by Players, Defunct Leagues	41
First Players with 20 HR, 30 HR, 40 HR, 50 HR, and 60 HR Seasons	46
The Most 20 HR, 30 HR, 40 HR, 50 HR, and 60 HR Seasons	47
Top Twenty-five Career Home Run Averages	48
Players with a Home Run Average of 60.00 or Higher for a Season	49
Most Home Runs in a Season by Two Teammates	51
Most Home Runs in a Season by Three Teammates	52
Most Home Runs by a Player in Consecutive Seasons	53
Most Home Runs by a Player in Three Consecutive Seasons	55
Home Runs in a Single Season	57
Clubs with 200+ Home Runs in a Season	59
Top Season Home Run Rate by Club	60
Top Home Run Seasons by League	61
Top Season Home Run Rates by League	63
Home Runs in One Inning	64
Three Shots of Rye	66
Home Runs in One Game	67
Home Runs in a Series of Games	69
Four or More Home Runs in a Game	71
Players with Four or More Home Runs in a Game	75
Three Home Runs in a Game—Nineteenth Century	78
Players with the Highest Balance of Home Runs and Stolen Bases—Season	79
Players with the Highest Balance of Home Runs and Stolen Bases—Career	79
Best Home Run to Strikeout Ratios	80
Homerless Streaks	81
It Might Be OK to Quit While You're Ahead, but This Is Overdoing It!	83
The Evolution of the Season Home Run Record	84

Season Hone Run Record Holders	85
Home Run Logs for Home Run Record Holders	
Tony Lazzeri, 1925	86
Moose Clabaugh, 1926	88
Joe Hauser, 1930	90
Joe Hauser, 1933	92
Bob Crues, 1948	94
Joe Bauman, 1954	96
Logs of Other 60 Home Run Seasons	
Dick Stuart, 1956	98
Frosty Kennedy, 1956	100
Minor League Players with Five or More Home Run Titles	102
Players with Fourteen or More Seasons Between First and Last Home Run Titles	105
Top Minor League Home Run Hitter, Yearly Leader	106
Year-by-Year League Home Run Leaders	109
Players Who Led Two Different Leagues in the Same Season	149
Hall of Fame Players Who Have Led a Minor League in Home Runs	149
Major League Season Home Run Leaders Who Also Led a Minor League in Home Runs	150
Moses Solomon	152
Joe Hauser	152
Joe Bauman	153

Preface

I began collecting minor league home run statistics over fifty years ago. I was fascinated by players such as Joe Hauser, Buzz Arlett, Nick Cullop, Ollie Carnegie and Ab Wright. At the time there were no published career records for these players, and I became curious about their home run totals. I started to work on a few players, but that project quickly expanded to include many more sluggers. And that project led me to another: collecting data on hitters with four home runs in a game, which in turn snowballed into everything relating to minor league home runs.

Then one Christmas, in the early 1950s, my wife gave me a run (from 1920 through 1939) of *Spalding Guides* to complement the guides from later years that I already owned. That put my research into high gear. Sometime during the late 1960s, I began to correspond and exchange information with Bob Davids and Ray Nemec.

When SABR was founded, I really struck gold! Many SABR members have helped me over the years. There are four members who have been, by far, the biggest help to me: Bob Davids, Bob Hoie, Vern Luse and Ray Nemec.

Others who have helped me enormously include:

John Benesch, the expert on yearly minor league batting leaders. John supplied me with some of the information in the Yearly Home Run Leaders section, and he was kind enough to proofread that entire section.

Art Cantu, who a few years ago took on the mammoth task of compiling a year-by-year alphabetical list of every player whose name appeared in the league averages section of the yearly baseball guides. When I first heard about the project, I estimated that it would take about fifty years to complete. Art finished it in only a couple of years! This index is invaluable in searching for a player for a given year when you have no idea as to his club or even what league he appeared in.

Jerry Jackson and Lloyd Johnson have catalogued every minor league, and all the clubs in those leagues. *The Encyclopedia of Minor League Baseball* is the result of that research, and that work has proved to be an indispensable tool for me.

This work attempts to list every player with 150 or more minor league home runs. It's very easy to miss a few players. Jamie Selko has been a tremendous help in this regard; he discovered many players whom I had inadvertently overlooked.

Davis Barker is a SABR member with whom I have been corresponding for a number of years. Davis travels all over Texas (and that is a lot of travelling) to research ball players with a Texas connection. The HR-by-HR record of Moose Clabaugh, which appears here for the first time, is Davis' work. In the same vein, I would like to thank Stew Thornley for letting me publish his seminal home run log of Joe Hauser's 1933 season. I would also like to thank those others who have graciously let me publish their work in this section: Larry Gerlach and Carlos Bauer for their home run log of Tony Lazzeri; the anonymous compiler whose Bob Crues record appeared in the 1954 West Texas–New Mexico League Record Book; and, especially, statistician Bill Weiss who culled his league sheets to put together home run logs for Joe Bauman, Frosty Kennedy and Dick Stuart (with much new added data supplied by Larry Gerlach).

During the Nineteenth Century, averages were not published for many leagues, and many of the ones that did get published were very incomplete, usually omitting extra base hits. This state of affairs continued into the early part of the Twentieth Century. Ray Nemec and Vern Luse laboriously compiled league averages for many of these leagues. A few other people have compiled league averages. Included in this group are Carlos Bauer, Jack Dougherty, Bob Hoie, Reed Howard, Tony Kissel, Bill Plott, Eves Raja, Tim Rask, Bob Richardson, John Spalding, Dick Thompson and Bob Tiemann. There would be major gaps in my work without the final league averages produced by these men.

A Research tool that has been extremely useful to me over the years is a year-by-year list of every league that has its box scores in *Sporting Life* and *The Sporting News*. This information was compiled by Frank Phelps.

Other members who have been a big help are: Jack Carlson, Ray Gonzalez, Jim Holl, Joe Overfield, John Pardon, Pat Rock, Art Schott, and Frank Williams.

The following people have also helped me along the way: Bill Carle, Dick Clark, Brian Davis, Harold Dellinger, Gary Fink, Bob Gerard, Stan Grosshandler, Dave Gumley, Ralph Horton, Tom Hufford, Jerry Jackson, Dave Kemp, Herm Krabbenhoft, Jim Maywar, Kevin McCann, Bob Mitchell, Marc Okkonen, Terry O'Neil, Bill Plott, Jim Price, Owen Ricker, Willie Runquist, Steve St. Martin, John Schwartz, Jim Shearon, Tom Strother, Chris Trudeau, Alain Usereau, Ralph Winnie and Gene Wood..

On many occasions, I have referred to the three volumes of *Minor League Stars*, published by SABR, and the *Minor League Register*, published by *Baseball America*.

Ray Nemec and Bob Hoie have extensive collections of career player records which they willingly shared with me. Other SABR members who have compiled career records which were of help are: Ed Brooks, Dean Coughenour, Bill Deane, and Willie George.

I want to thank Cliff Kachline, Tom Heitz and other members of the staff at the Baseball Hall of Fame Library who have helped me so much during my many visits to Cooperstown. I also wish to thank Jean Kaufman of the Wilmington Public Library, and Nancy Parsons, of the Brandywine Branch of the New Castle County Library, for the many hundreds of reels of microfilm that they have obtained for me via inter-library loan.

Another person I would very much like to thank is Jack Dougherty, my close friend. He spent many hours going over galley proofs of the first edition of this book.

And, finally, thanks to Carlos Bauer and Bob Hoie. It is hard for me to express my gratitude to these two people. Without their encouragement, the first edition would never have seen the light of day. They have supplied so much information and made so many suggestion for *Going For the Fences*.

—Bob McConnell

Introduction

Not all home run records are created equal. Several factors are involved in determining the number of home runs that a player may be able to hit during a season. This is, of course, true in both the majors and the minors; however, the factors are much more pronounced in the minors.

The length of the schedule, obviously, can have a great effect on a player's total. Most fans will remember the famous asterisk on Maris's record of 61 home runs. The American League had just gone from a 154 games schedule to a 162 games schedule. Commissioner Ford Frick reportedly told some people that an asterisk should be placed next to the record to denote that it was set while playing during a longer schedule than the one in which Babe Ruth played when he set his record. Back in the 1920s, the Pacific Coast League had a 200-or-more-game schedule. When Tony Lazzeri set his then O.B.-record 60 home runs, he appeared in 197 games. At various times, the International and Western Leagues played long schedules, although not nearly as long as the longest of the PCL. At the other end of the spectrum, the Longhorn League played a 140-game schedule the year Joe Bauman set the all-time record of 72 in 1954.

Climatic conditions, including elevation above sea level, are factors. The barrage of home runs at Coors Field and Mile High Stadium in Denver over the last couple of years readily come to mind. During Denver's long history in the minors, more than a few players took advantage of the "light air" in the Mile High City. A few other cities offered a similar advantage.

The size of the ballpark has, naturally, always been a big factor. Infamous Hughes Stadium in Sacramento has to be the most extreme example of this *(see section "Top Ten Home Runs Per Game by Clubs" for the gory details on this park)*. Other hitters' parks have been Sulphur Dell in Nashville, Nicollet Park in Minneapolis and Oriole Park in Baltimore.

One factor not always easy to pin down is the "rabbit" in the ball. It is known that one league—and suspected in several others—was using a "juiced" baseball for a few years right after World War II. At the Winter Meetings following the 1948 season, the National Association ruled that all minor leagues must use a ball of "uniform resiliency." Therefore, it was not much of a coincidence that the Big State League had a 27% drop in home runs from 1948 to 1949, or that the West Texas-New Mexico League had a 23% fall.

The last factor is the level of competition. During the heyday of the minor leagues there were six (and for a short period, seven) classifications. The pitching was obviously better in AAA (and especially in the Open Classification PCL) than in class D.

In spite of all these factors, we are lumping all minor league home runs together. To do otherwise would make this work so complicated as to render it unintelligible.

The first professional baseball league was organized in 1871 and bore the name of National Association of Professional Baseball Players. This loosely run league operated for five years. Baseball historians are divided on whether to consider this league a "major league." Needless to say, it happened to be the only game in town.

The National League succeeded the National Association in 1876. This league has operated continuously ever since, and has been considered a major league from its inception.

The International Association was formed in 1877 to compete with the National League. Several additional leagues were formed over the next few years. At the time, the various leagues were not designated as "major" or "minor." Historians— retroactively— designated the National League as a major league, and all the others as minor leagues.

The American Association was formed in 1882 and successfully challenged the National League. The Association operated for ten years as a major league. Two additional leagues, the Union Association of 1884 and the Player's League of 1890 also operated as major leagues during the Nineteenth Century.

The number of minor leagues increased con-siderably during the latter part of the Nineteenth Century. Many of them were signatories to the National Agreement. This was an agreement which gave almost complete domination over dealings with players to the major leagues. Some leagues chose to operate independently of the National Agreement. We have arbitrarily decided to recognize all well-organized leagues during the nineteenth century, whether or not they were signatories to the National Agreement.

The American League unilaterally declared itself a major league in 1901. This, in turn, set off a war with the National League. The National Association of Professional Baseball Leagues formed in the Fall of 1901. This organization was created to give the minor leagues some protection from the warring American and National Leagues. Most recognized minor leagues joined this organization for the start of the 1902 season. The National Association remains in existence to this day and works closely with the major leagues. Collectively, the major leagues and National Association members are known as Organized Baseball. In this work, we recognize every league that has ever been a member of the National Association.

Many independent leagues have operated since the National Association was established, including some that eventually joined the National Association. Most of the well-known independent leagues of the Twentieth Century are listed in the *Yearly Home Run Leader* section and are identified as being independent leagues. The statistics for these leagues, however, are not used for any other compilations in this work. The independent leagues include the following:

American Association, 1902
California State League, 1903–1909
Colonial League, 1915
Federal League, 1913
Mexican League, 1937–1954
Pacific Coast League, 1903
Provincial League, 1935–1939, 1944–1949, 1958–1970
Tri-State League, 1904–1906
United States League, 1912–1913

Several compilations in this work use *Home Run Average*. This statistic was designed to reflect the number of home runs that a player would hit if he played a reasonably full schedule in a league with a somewhat standard number of games in its schedule. For this purpose, 600 official at bats has been selected to represent a reasonably full schedule.

The formula is as follows:

$$\text{HR Avg} = \frac{600}{\text{AB}} \times \text{HR}$$

Thus, if a player has 500 official at bats, and hits 30 home runs, then his Home Run Average will be 36.00. In other words, we assume that if a player had played a full schedule of games, he would have hit 36 home runs.

The San Francisco Missions of the Pacific Coast League (1914, 1926–1937) are referred to only as Mission. Mission is a district in San Francisco. This is similar to the case of Hollywood which is a district in Los Angeles.

When a player appeared with two clubs in a league during a single season, it is denoted by use of a slash (/) between the names of the two clubs. For example, Troy/Albany. The use of a dash (-) between two names can denote one of three things:

The club represented two cities. An example might be that of Fargo-Moorhead.

The franchise shifted from one city to another during the course of the season. For example, Charleston-Macon in 1923.

The dash could also be a city with a hyphenated name such as Wilkes-Barre or Winston-Salem.

When compiling minor league statistics, you can never be sure that your data is complete. However, we feel that the information in this volume is as complete and as accurate as possible. There is one notable exception to all the data being complete — the case of the 1910 Southern Illinois League. This five club league folded on July 9 of its initial season. As in the case with most leagues that fold during the season, no official or unofficial averages were published. Ernie Calbert and Clarence "Big Boy" Kraft, two very good home run hitters, played in the league. Only one town in the league had a daily newspaper and very few boxscores appeared on its pages. In an attempt to get information on Calbert and Kraft, we checked the weekly newspapers in the other town in the league as well as newspapers in Chicago and St. Louis, the nearest large cities. From brief game accounts, we determined that Calbert hit at least one home run and Kraft at least three.

The names used for leagues in the *Yearly Home Run Leader* section of the book require some explanation.

A number of leagues have been formed over the years and resurrected the name of a league that had previously ceased to exist. Many times these newly formed leagues have operated in an entirely different area. With a few exceptions, we have chosen to group all leagues with the same name under one listing. There are ten cases where we have subdivided the league listing in order to give a clearer picture of the territory in which the league operated. The States and Canadian Provinces are given for each subdivision. These leagues are as follows:

Bi-State League
Inter-State Association
Northwestern League
Blue Ridge League
Inter-State League
Southwestern League
Border League
Mountain States League
Tri-State League
Dixie League

Some leagues changed their names during the period of their operation while maintaining the same general organization and, basically, the same territory. These leagues are listed under their most widely known names. These leagues are listed on the following page.

League	Listed Under
Alabama State, 1940–1941, 1946–1950	Alabama-Florida
American, 1900	Western II
Arizona-Mexico, 1955–1958	Arizona-Texas
Arizona State, 1928–1930	Arizona-Texas
Arkansas State, 1934–1935	Arkansas-Missouri
Dakota, 1921–1922	South Dakota
Eastern, 1884–1887, 1892–1911	International II
Empire State, 1913	Georgia State
Florida Rookie, 1965	Gulf Coast Rookie
Gulf States, 1976	Lone Star
International Northwestern, 1919	Pacific Coast International
Mississippi–Ohio Valley, 1949–1955	Midwest II
Mississippi State, 1921	Cotton States
Naughatuck Valley, 1896	Connecticut State
New California, 1881	Pacific
New York-Pennsylvania, 1923–1937	Eastern II
Northeastern, 1934	New England
Pacific Northwest, 1901–1902	Pacific National
Panhandle-Pecos Valley, 1923	West Texas
Quebec Provincial, 1940	Provincial
Sarasota Rookie, 1964	Southern Michigan Association
South Atlantic Association, 1919–1930	Southern
South Atlantic, 1904–1917, 1936–1942, 1946–1963	Southern
South Michigan, 1906–1909	Gulf Coast Rookie
Southern, 1885–1889, 1892–1896, 1898–1899	Southern Association
Southwest International, 1951–1952	Sunset
Texas-Southern, 1895–1896	Texas
West Michigan, 1910	Michigan State
Western, 1939–1941	Nebraska State
Western International, 1922	Pacific Coast International
Western International, 1937–1942, 1946–1954	Northwest

There were, of course, other leagues that formed as the result of mergers or reorganizations, but their ancestry is not as clear cut as the leagues listed above, and , therefore, each of these leagues is listed separately.

The histories of the Eastern League, International League, New York-Pennsylvania League, South Atlantic League, Western Association and Western League are a little complicated and require some explanation.

Leagues named International operated in 1898, 1900 and 1908. Collectively they are listed as *International League I* in the *Year by Year Home Run Leaders by Leagues* section. The Eastern League organized in 1884 and with the exception of 1888 through 1891 it operated continuously under that same name until 1911. The league changed its name in 1912 to International League and has operated to the present under that name. The league, from its inception in 1884, is listed as *International League II*. A league named New York-Pennsylvania formed in 1923 and operated under that name through the 1937 season. It changed its name in 1938 to Eastern League and has operated under that name to the present. Collectively, these leagues are listed as *Eastern League II*. The International and Eastern Leagues should not be confused with leagues called International Association and Eastern Association.

The New York-Pennsylvania League of 1923–1937 is mentioned above. Another league named New York-Pennsylvania League was organized in 1957 as a full season league. This league is listed as *New York-Pennsylvania League I*. In 1967, the league changed to a short (summer) season league and has operated to the present with a short schedule. It is listed as *New York-Pennsylvania II*.

The original South Atlantic League had a long history as a strong league. The league, usually called the Sally League, operated from 1904 through 1963 with several breaks. It changed its name in 1964 to Southern League while adding two clubs and losing two. Collectively, the original South Atlantic League and the Southern League are listed as *Southern League*. A new South Atlantic League was formed in 1980, adopting five cities from the Western Carolinas League that had gone out of business the previous season. This league is listed under its own name.

The Western Association and the Western League had a mixed history during the 19th Century, moving from one territory to another and switching names. All leagues named Western Association during the 19th Century are grouped together and listed as *Western Association I*. The Western Association of 1901 was an entirely different organization and operated in a new territory. It is listed as *Western Association II*. This league operated for only one year. A new Western Association was formed in 1905 as a successor to the Missouri Valley League of 1903–04 and it operated off and on in a five-state area through 1954. This league is listed as *Western Association III*.

Several leagues calling themselves Western League operated through 1893. They are grouped together and listed as *Western League I*. Ban Johnson took over a new Western League in 1894 and this fairly strong league operated through 1900. It changed its name to American League in 1900 and declared itself a major league in 1901. This league is listed as *Western League II*. When Johnson's league changed its name in 1900, a new league adopted the name Western League. This league operated through 1937 and is listed as *Western League III*. The Class D Nebraska State League changed its name in 1939 to Western League and operated under that banner until it disbanded following the 1941 season. This three-year operation of the Western League is included under the *Nebraska State League* listing. Yet another Western League was formed in 1947 and continued through the 1958 season. This league is listed as *Western League IV*.

The California League and the California State Leagues also need some explanation. Several leagues operated under the banner of California League during the 19th Century through 1896. They are listed as *California League I*. Another California League operated from 1898 through 1902 and then became the Pacific Coast League in 1903. It is listed as *California League II*. Several leagues called themselves California State League during the 19th Century. Collectively, they are listed as *California State League I*. A new California State League organized in 1903 and operated through 1915 with one break in 1911. This league was not a member of the National Association for most of that time period. It is listed as *California State League II*. Another league operated in 1929 for one season and is listed as *California State League III*. Finally, a California League was organized in 1941 and has operated continuously to the present, except when suspending operations during World War II. It is listed as *California League III*.

Four active leagues have become short-season leagues after many years as full-season leagues. Because of the schedule differences, these leagues are divided into separate entities. The leagues in question are: *Appalachian League I (1911–1955)* & *Appalachian League II (1957–present); New York-Pennsylvania League I (1957–1966)* & *New York-Pennsylvania League II (1967–present); Northwest League I (1937–1965)* & *Northwest League II (1966–present); Pioneer League I (1939–1963)* and *Pioneer League II (1964–present)*.

GOING FOR THE FENCES

Players with 150 or More Career Home Runs in the Minor Leagues

Notes for the following table

- The *Minor* and *Major* columns indicate the total number of home runs the player hit in the minor leagues and major leagues.
- A dash "—" in the *Major* column indicates that the player did not play in the major leagues.
- The *Total* column is the total home runs hit in the major and minor leagues.
- The *Years* column includes years played in both the minors and majors.
- The *Bats* column indicates whether the player hit right-handed (R), left-handed (L) or was a switch-hitter (S).
- The *Led* column indicates the number of seasons a player led a league in home runs and includes years in which the player led the league in home runs or tied for the lead.
- The *20+, 30+, 40+* and *50+* columns show the number of seasons a player hit 20+, 30+, 40+, and 50+ home runs. The *20+* column includes years with thirty or more runs. Likewise, the *30+* column includes years with 40+ and 50+ home runs, etc. When a player appeared in more than one league during a year, his total home runs were used to determine if he had a 20+, 30+, 40+, 50+ or 60+ season.
- The *Notes* column include: Notations of 60+ home run years; years in which the player led all minor leagues in home runs (LM); four or more home runs in a game; career home runs in the Japanese Leagues (JL), Negro Leagues (NL) and pre–1955 Mexican League (ML).

Player	Minor	Major	Total	Years	Bats	Led	20+	30+	40+	50+	Notes
Abad, Fausto A. "Andy"	157	0	157	1993–2008	L	0	1	0	0	0	
Abernathy, Woodley T. "Woody"	210	—	210	1928–1940	L	2	5	3	1	0	
Adair, Marion D. "Bill"	182	—	182	1935–1956	R	1	3	0	0	0	
Adams, Elvin C. "Buster"	169	50	219	1935–1951	R	1	2	0	0	0	
Adriana, Sharnol	167	—	167	2000–2008	R	0	4	0	0	0	
Aganza, Ruben	163	—	163	1990–2005	R	0	2	0	0	0	
Aguilar, Enrique	305	—	305	1974–1998	R	0	6	1	0	0	
Aikens, Willie M.	276	110	386	1975–1991	L	2	6	4	1	0	
Airoso, Alvin K. "Kurt"	155	—	155	1996–2006	R	0	3	1	0	0	
Alcantara, Israel C.	326	6	332	1991–2007	R	3	6	1	0	0	
Alcarez, A. Luis	252	4	256	1959–1981	R	1	4	0	0	0	
Aleno, Charles	158	2	160	1937–1953	R	2	3	1	0	0	
Alexander, David D. "Dale"	159	61	220	1924–1942	R	2	2	1	0	0	4 HR G 1935
Alfaro, Jesus A.	208	—	208	1976–1994	R	0	2	0	0	0	
Alston, Walter E.	176	0	176	1935–1947	R	4	4	1	0	0	
Altobelli, Joseph S.	178	5	183	1951–1970	L	1	2	1	0	0	
Alvarez, Rogelio H. "Borrego"	337	0	337	1956–1973	R	2	7	2	0	0	
Alvarez, Ultus S.	150	—	150	1952–1964	R	0	0	0	0	0	
Alyea, Garrabrant R. "Brant"	162	38	200	1962–1973	R	0	4	2	0	0	
Ananias, Nicholas T.	157	—	157	1947–1956	R	0	3	1	0	0	
Arias, George A.	172	14	186	1993–2006	R	1	4	2	0	0	JL 2
Arlett, Russell L. "Buzz"	432	18	450	1918–1937	S	3	11	8	2	1	LM 1932, 1934; two 4 HR G 1932
Atkins, Ralph	199	—	199	1943–1955	L	2	4	2	0	0	
Avila, Ruben	151	—	151	1983–2000	R	0	2	0	0	0	
Bailey, Jeffrey T.	154	3	157	1997–2008	R	0	2	0	0	0	
Baker, Jack E.	153	1	154	1971–1978	R	3	3	1	0	0	
Balaz, John L.	177	2	179	1970–1980	R	2	4	0	0	0	
Balboni, Stephen C.	239	181	420	1978–1993	R	6	8	5	0	0	
Banks, George E.	223	9	232	1957–1968	R	1	6	2	0	0	
Barbarito, Edward R.	168	—	168	1949–1959	R	2	4	1	0	0	
Barbee, David M.	198	6	204	1925–1942	R	3	4	2	2	0	LM 1931
Barker, Kevin S.	226	6	232	1996–2008	L	0	6	0	0	0	
Barker, Raymond H.	193	10	203	1955–1967	L	0	3	0	0	0	
Barna, Herbert P. "Babe"	290	12	302	1937–1952	L	2	8	1	1	0	

MCCONNELL

Player	Minor	Major	Total	Years	Bats	Led	20+	30+	40+	50+	Notes
Barrera, Nelson E.	479	—	479	1974–2002	R	1	11	4	1	0	LM 1987
Barron, Anthony D.	208	4	212	1987–2002	R	0	3	0	0	0	
Barry, Richard D.	280	0	280	1958–1972	R	1	7	1	0	0	
Barton, Lawrence J.	299	—	299	1932–1956	L	1	2	0	0	0	
Barton, Vincent D.	158	16	174	1928–1936	L	1	3	2	0	0	
Bass, Jayson A.	187	—	187	1993–2006	L	0	4	0	0	0	
Bass, Randy W.	238	9	247	1972–1982	L	4	7	3	0	0	LM 1980; JL 202
Basso, James S.	195	—	195	1941–1957	R	0	5	1	0	0	
Batista, Rafael	176	0	176	1965–1984	L	0	2	0	0	0	JL 3
Bauman, Joe W.	337	—	337	1941–1956	L	5	6	6	5	3	LM 1946, 1952, 1953, 1954; 72 HR (1954); 4 HR G 1954
Baxes, Dimitrios S. "Jim"	228	17	245	1947–1961	R	1	6	2	0	0	
Beauchamp, James E. "Champ"	192	14	206	1958–1974	R	1	4	2	0	0	
Beck, Frederick T.	166	34	200	1905–1926	L	2	3	3	0	0	
Beeler, Joseph S. "Jodie"	186	0	186	1940–1957	R	0	3	2	0	0	4 HR G 1955
Bennett, J. Fred	197	1	198	1924–1939	R	0	5	3	0	0	
Berger, Brandon C.	177	8	185	1996–2005	R	1	1	1	1	0	
Bernier, Carlos R.	212	3	215	1948–1965	R	0	4	0	0	0	
Berroa, Geronimo E.	166	101	267	1984–2003	R	0	3	1	0	0	
Bilko, Stephen T.	313	76	389	1945–1963	R	4	7	4	2	2	LM 1957
Blackerby, George F.	154	0	154	1924–1937	R	1	2	1	0	0	
Blakesley, James T.	201	—	201	1920–1933	L	0	3	2	0	0	
Blanco, Oswaldo C. "Ossie"	160	0	160	1963–1979	R	0	0	0	0	0	
Blosser, Gregory B.	155	0	155	1989–2000	L	1	3	0	0	0	JL 3
Bodie, Frank S. "Ping"	201	43	244	1908–1928	R	1	4	3	0	0	LM 1910
Boken, Robert A.	158	6	164	1929–1947	R	0	1	0	0	0	
Boles, Howard W.	216	—	216	1945–1956	R	?	5	3	0	0	
Bolick, Frank C.	167	5	172	1987–1998	S	0	3	0	0	0	JL 92
Bollweg, Donald R.	175	11	186	1942–1956	L	1	4	0	0	0	
Bonowitz, Joseph J.	151	—	151	1918–1936	R	0	1	0	0	0	
Boone, Issac M. "Ike"	217	26	243	1920–1936	L	2	3	2	1	1	LM 1929
Boone, James A. "Dan"	214	0	214	1919–1933	R	2	5	2	1	0	
Branom, E. Dudley "Dud"	152	0	152	1920–1934	L	0	0	0	0	0	
Brant, Marshall L.	185	0	185	1975–1983	R	3	5	1	0	0	JL 25
Branyan, Russell O.	210	133	343	1994–2008	R	1	5	3	1	0	
Brazell, Craig W.	155	1	156	1998–2007	L	0	4	1	0	0	
Brazill, Frank L.	254	0	254	1918–1938	L	0	3	1	0	0	
Brief, Anthony V. "Bunny"	342	5	347	1910–1928	R	8	7	4	2	0	LM 1916, 1921, 1922
Bright, Harry J.	159	32	191	1946–1971	R	0	2	0	0	0	
Brito, Bernardo	297	5	302	1981–1997	R	6	9	0	0	0	JL 50
Brooks, Robert	160	5	165	1965–1975	R	2	3	0	0	0	
Brovia, Joseph J.	214	0	214	1940–1957	L	0	5	2	0	0	
Brown, Dermal B. "Dee"	168	13	181	1996–2008	L	0	2	0	0	0	
Browne, Byron E.	198	30	228	1963–1975	R	2	5	2	0	0	
Browne, Earl J.	183	6	189	1928–1949	L	0	2	1	0	0	
Browne, Prentice A. "Pidge"	190	1	191	1949–1962	L	1	2	1	0	0	
Bryant, Derek R.	162	0	162	1973–1988	R	1	4	2	1	0	LM 1984; 4 HR G 1985
Bullett, Scott D.	164	6	170	1988–2006	L	1	3	1	0	0	
Burge, Lester K.	182	—	182	1938–1950	L	2	4	1	0	0	LM 1941
Burgess, Thomas R.	200	2	202	1946–1963	L	0	3	0	0	0	
Burkhart, Morgan	157	5	162	1999–2006	S	1	5	1	0	0	JL 9
Burns, Glenn C.	196	—	196	1947–1955	R	0	6	2	0	0	
Burns, Russell G.	268	—	268	1940–1956	R	2	8	1	0	0	
Burton, Ellis N.	169	17	186	1955–1965	S	1	4	0	0	0	

GOING FOR THE FENCES

Player	Minor	Major	Total	Years	Bats	Led	20+	30+	40+	50+	Notes
Bynon, James H.	188	—	188	1947–1954	R	0	6	2	0	0	
Caballero, Ramiro S.	212	—	212	1955–1965	R	3	5	3	1	1	LM 1962
Calbert, Ernest E.	204	—	204	1910–1928	R	6	2	1	1	0	LM 1917
Calero, Jose L.	166	—	166	1959–1975	R	0	2	0	0	0	
Camacho, Moises "Moi"	241	—	241	1951–1975	R	0	3	0	0	0	ML 3
Camacho, Ronaldo "Ronnie"	355	—	355	1953–1975	R	2	9	3	0	0	
Camarero, Rolando	156	—	156	1961–1979	R	0	1	0	0	0	
Canada, Romel W. "Red"	190	—	190	1966–1979	L	1	4	0	0	0	
Canale, George A.	155	4	159	1986–1999	L	0	3	0	0	0	
Carlyle, H. Cleo	155	1	156	1924–1939	L	0	1	0	0	0	
Carmel, Leon J. "Duke"	198	4	202	1955–1967	L	0	4	1	0	0	
Carnegie, Oliver A.	297	—	297	1922–1945	R	2	7	4	1	0	LM 1938
Carrillo, Matias G.	370	0	370	1982–2008	L	1	9	1	0	0	LM 1993
Carswell, Frank W.	209	0	209	1941–1958	R	1	4	2	0	0	4 HR G 1947
Castañeda, Nicolas	219	—	219	1980–1995	L	0	4	1	1	1	
Castellano, Pedro O.	230	3	233	1989–2008	R	0	3	1	0	0	
Castro, Eddie	164	—	164	1988–1996	L	0	3	1	0	1	
Cearley, Wilbur R.	179	0	179	1939–1954	R	0	2	0	0	0	
Chance, Robert A. "Tony"	217	—	217	1983–2000	R	0	3	0	0	0	
Christian, Joseph L.	157	—	157	1949–1966	R	1	2	0	0	0	
Christopher, Loyd E.	179	0	179	1938–1955	R	1	3	1	0	0	
Clabaugh, John W. "Moose"	346	0	346	1923–1940	L	3	8	4	1	1	62 HR (1926); LM 1926
Clark, Daniel C.	174	5	179	1913–1930	L	1	2	2	0	0	
Colavito, Rocco D. "Rocky"	150	374	524	1951–1968	R	3	4	2	0	0	
Coleman, P. Edward "Ed"	165	40	205	1926–1940	L	1	3	1	0	0	
Coles, Charles E.	176	0	176	1950–1963	L	0	3	0	0	0	
Collins, James A. "Rip"	193	135	328	1923–1947	S	3	4	2	1	0	
Conners, Mervyn J.	400	8	408	1934–1953	R	6	12	3	1	0	
Cook, R. Clifford "Cliff"	195	7	202	1955–1964	R	2	5	3	0	0	
Cookson, Brent A.	163	0	163	1991–2004	R	0	3	0	0	0	
Coolbaugh, Michael R.	258	2	260	1990–2006	R	0	5	2	0	0	
Cortes, Hermino M.	183	—	183	1951–1964	R	0	4	1	0	0	
Cosey, Donald R.	188	0	188	1973–1990	L	0	2	0	0	0	JL 15
Cotton, John F.	170	—	170	1989–2001	L	0	1	0	0	0	
Cron, Christopher J.	172	0	172	1984–1995	R	0	4	0	0	0	
Crosby, Jerry L.	158	—	158	1940–1955	S	0	2	0	0	0	4 HR G 1953
Cross, Leonard E.	173	—	173	1943–1953	R	2	5	2	1	0	4 HR G 1948
Crues, Robert F.	232	—	232	1939–1953	R	1	5	3	2	2	69 HR (1948); LM 1948
Cruz, Henry	152	8	160	1972–1985	L	0	2	0	0	0	
Cruz, Luis A.	210	—	210	1984–1999	R	0	3	0	0	0	
Cruz, Luis I. "Ivan"	254	2	256	1989–2002	L	2	6	2	0	0	JL 25
Cruz, Nelson R.	169	22	191	1998–2008	R	1	5	1	0	0	
Cuitti, Arthur E.	184	—	184	1949–1958	R	0	4	1	1	0	
Cullop, Henry N. "Nick"	420	11	431	1920–1944	R	3	12	3	2	1	
Curry, G. Anthony	152	6	158	1957–1968	L	0	3	0	0	0	
Cust, John J. "Jack"	200	64	264	1997–2008	L	1	5	2	0	0	
Daniel, Handley J. "Jake"	152	0	152	1933–1953	L	1	2	1	0	0	
Daniels, Harold J. "Jack"	167	2	169	1946–1958	L	0	2	1	0	0	
Darkis, William A. "Willie"	220	—	220	1979–1988	R	3	7	3	0	0	
Daubach, Brian M.	160	93	253	1990–2006	L	1	4	1	0	0	
Davidson, Crawford L.	214	—	214	1948–1961	L	0	5	1	0	0	
Davis, Cecil A. "Stormy"	270	—	270	1921–1933	R	3	6	2	1	1	
Davis, Harry A.	150	7	157	1925–1950	L	0	1	0	0	0	
Davis, John W. "Wilbur"	254	0	254	1915–1937	L	2	2	1	1	1	4 HR G 1924
Davis, Nathan "Yank"	208	—	208	1909–1927	L	1	5	3	1	0	

Name										
Davis, Van A.	163	—	163	1950–1956	R	2	5	3	1	0	
Deer, Robert G. "Rob"	185	230	415	1978–1996	R	3	5	3	0	0	JL 8
Demeter, Stephen	272	0	272	1953–1972	R	0	4	0	0	0	
Denson, Andrew "Drew"	182	0	182	1984–1997	R	2	2	1	0	0	
Derry, Alva R. "Russ"	294	17	311	1937–1954	L	4	7	3	2	0	
Diaz, Juan C.	184	1	185	1996–2008	R	0	5	1	0	0	
Diaz, Luis F.	159	—	159	1985–2004	L	0	1	0	0	0	
Diaz-Rodriguez, Arsenio	217	—	217	1964–1981	R	0	1	0	0	0	
Dillon, Joseph W.	156	2	158	1997–2008	R	0	3	1	0	0	JL 2
DiMaggio, Vincent P.	273	125	398	1932–1951	R	3	7	4	1	0	
Dixon, Walter E.	208	—	208	1940–1958	R	2	6	1	0	0	
Dodd, Thomas M.	206	1	207	1980–1990	R	1	3	3	0	0	
Dominguez, David	170	—	170	1986–2001	R	0	3	0	0	0	
Dooley, Clifford M. "Mike"	157	—	157	1946–1955	R	0	3	2	0	0	
Dorsett, Brian R.	158	8	166	1983–1996	R	0	1	0	0	0	
Downs, Benjamin E.	169	—	169	1948–1959	L	1	2	1	0	0	
Dubois, Jason B.	159	10	169	2001–2008	R	0	5	1	0	0	
Dugas, Augustin J. "Gus"	191	3	194	1930–1946	L	1	4	0	0	0	
Duke, Willie E.	184	—	184	1934–1950	L	1	2	0	0	0	
Dunn, Cecil A. "Dynamite"	208	—	208	1935–1945	R	4	3	2	1	0	5 HR G 1936
Dunn, J.C.	162	—	162	1948–1961	R	2	3	0	0	0	
Dupon, Barton C.	151	—	151	1955–1962	L	1	4	1	1	0	
Durham, Albert L. "Bull"	152	—	152	1909–1916	R	5	3	1	0	0	LM 1912
Dyck, James R.	163	26	189	1941–1961	R	0	1	0	0	0	
Easter, Luscious L. "Luke"	269	93	362	1949–1964	L	2	7	4	1	0	NL 23
Easterling, Paul	257	4	261	1926–1951	R	1	3	2	0	0	
Eastham, Leo W.	184	—	184	1938–1953	L	1	4	0	0	0	
Eldred, Bradley R.	157	14	171	2002–2008	R	0	4	2	0	0	
Elliot, Lawrence L.	171	15	186	1958–1969	L	0	3	0	0	0	
Emery, Calvin W.	207	0	207	1958–1972	L	1	4	1	0	0	JL 8
Engel, Arlo W.	169	—	169	1960–1968	R	1	3	2	1	0	LM 1963
English, Charles D.	155	1	156	1931–1949	R	1	0	0	0	0	
Enos, William E.	163	—	163	1939–1951	R	1	4	3	0	0	
Espino, Hector	484	—	484	1960–1984	R	4	12	5	1	0	LM 1964, 1972
Estalella, Roberto M.	155	44	199	1934–1951	R	3	3	3	0	0	ML 29
Estrada, Hector	164	—	164	1986–2007	R	0	0	0	0	0	
Etchison, Clarence H. "Buck"	172	8	180	1939–1953	L	0	2	0	0	0	
Etten, Nicholas R.T.	187	89	276	1933–1950	L	1	4	1	1	0	
Fair, Woodrow C. "Woody"	275	—	275	1934–1952	R	2	7	1	0	0	
Fasano, Salvatore F.	152	47	199	1993–2008	R	0	3	1	0	0	
Fernandez, Miguel	186	—	186	1955–1974	S	0	3	1	0	0	
Ferrell, George S.	256	—	256	1926–1951	R	1	6	1	0	0	
Fiore, Michael G.J.	152	13	165	1963–1978	L	0	2	0	0	0	
Fisher, George A.	175	8	183	1919–1933	L	0	1	1	0	0	
Fleming, Leslie H.	280	29	309	1935–1956	L	0	8	0	0	0	
Fogg, Floyd C.	163	—	163	1945–1954	R	1	5	0	0	0	
Fortin, Joseph L.	219	—	219	1942–1956	R	0	5	3	1	0	4 HR G 1948
Franklin, Micah I.	200	2	202	1990–2000	S	0	5	1	0	0	JL 37
Freed, Roger V.	244	22	266	1966–1980	R	3	6	3	1	0	LM 1976
Freese, George W.	195	3	198	1948–1963	R	0	5	1	0	0	
Freire, Alejandro	178	1	179	1993–2006	R	1	2	0	0	0	
Fridley, James R.	210	8	218	1948–1961	R	0	5	0	0	0	
Frierson, Robert L. "Buck"	227	0	227	1937–1953	R	1	4	1	1	1	LM 1947
Frierson, W. Lewis "Lou"	186	—	186	1931–1942	L	1	3	2	1	0	5 HR G 1934
Friol, Rene	161	—	161	1954–1970	R	0	1	0	0	0	
Fuentes, Michael J.	150	0	150	1981–1987	R	1	4	2	0	0	
Fulenwider, Emmitt	186	—	186	1937–1946	R	0	5	2	1	0	

GOING FOR THE FENCES

Player	Minor	Major	Total	Years	Bats	Led	20+	30+	40+	50+	Notes
Fuller, James H.	170	11	181	1970–1978	R	2	3	3	0	0	LM 1973
Funderburk, Mark C.	222	2	224	1976–1987	R	2	6	2	0	0	
Gabler, William L.	215	0	215	1950–1961	L	1	7	1	0	0	
Gainer, Jonathan K. "Jay"	174	3	177	1990–2001	L	1	4	2	0	0	
Gainey, Telmanch "Ty"	251	1	252	1979–2000	L	2	4	1	1	0	LM 1992; JL 33
Galloway, James C.	169	0	169	1910–1929	S	1	2	1	0	0	
Garcia, David	167	—	167	1939–1957	R	1	2	0	0	0	
Garcia, Guillermo A.	197	2	199	1990–2006	R	1	4	0	0	0	
Garcia, Gustavo "Karim"	202	66	268	1993–2007	L	1	6	1	0	0	
Garcia, Humberto	203	—	203	1967–1981	R	1	3	1	0	0	
Garcia, Luis	221	—	221	1951–1966	R	0	4	0	0	0	
Garcia, Luis A.	178	—	178	1998–2008	R	1	3	1	0	0	
Garner, Horace T.	157	—	157	1951–1961	R	0	3	0	0	0	
Garrett, H. Adrian	280	11	291	1961–1976	L	4	6	1	1	0	LM 1971; JL 102
Garriott, V. Cecil	162	0	162	1936–1953	L	1	1	0	0	0	Switch-hitter, 1948–1953.
Gentile, James E.	245	179	424	1952–1968	L	1	7	3	1	0	JL 8
Getter, Richard T.	182	—	182	1947–1960	R	0	2	0	0	0	
Gibralter, Stephen B.	152	0	152	1990–2001	R	1	1	0	0	0	
Gibson, Derrick L.	161	2	163	1993–2005	R	1	2	1	0	0	
Gilbert, Andrew	206	0	206	1937–1955	R	1	3	1	0	0	
Gilbert, Harold J. "Tookie"	153	7	160	1947–1959	L	1	5	2	0	0	
Gill, John W.	289	10	299	1924–1947	L	1	3	2	1	0	
Glenn, John	153	0	153	1950–1963	R	0	0	0	0	0	
Glynn, William V.	167	10	177	1946–1958	L	0	2	0	0	0	
Goliat, Mike M.	192	20	212	1947–1961	R	0	3	0	0	0	
Gonzalez, Denio M. "Denny"	206	4	210	1981–1998	R	1	2	0	0	0	JL 9
Gonzalez, Victor R. "Raul"	167	2	169	1991–2008	R	0	0	0	0	0	
Gorinski, Robert J.	163	3	166	1970–1979	R	4	5	1	0	0	
Goss, Howard W.	184	11	195	1953–1964	R	0	4	0	0	0	
Graham, John B. "Jack"	384	38	422	1936–1954	L	3	11	6	1	0	
Grant, Charles H.	223	—	223	1941–1958	R	1	4	1	0	0	
Gravino, Frank J.	271	—	271	1940–1954	R	4	5	4	3	2	
Gray, Gary G.	217	24	241	1974–1987	R	0	3	1	0	0	
Greco, Richard A.	333	—	333	1946–1957	R	4	10	5	1	0	
Green, Gene L.	166	46	212	1952–1964	R	1	4	1	0	0	
Greene, Altar A.	228	3	231	1977–1987	L	0	5	3	0	0	
Greene, Todd A.	170	71	241	1993–2006	R	2	3	1	0	0	LM 1995
Greer, William H. "Stubby"	204	—	204	1940–1957	R	0	2	0	0	0	
Griffin, Francis A. "Pug"	171	1	172	1917–1934	R	0	4	0	0	0	
Grijak, Kevin S.	184	—	184	1991–2003	L	0	3	0	0	0	
Guerrero, Humberto	238	—	238	1954–1973	R	0	4	2	0	0	ML 1
Guettler, Kenneth A.	330	—	330	1945–1959	R	8	8	5	2	1	62 HR 1955
Guiel, Aaron C.	206	35	241	1993–2006	L	0	4	2	0	0	
Gulan, Michael W.	155	0	155	1992–2004	R	0	2	0	0	0	JL 10
Gullic, Tedd J.	370	9	379	1927–1948	R	0	10	3	0	0	
Halter, Paul C.	185	—	185	1947–1955	R	0	4	3	0	0	
Harrigan, Phillip H. "Hal"	222	—	222	1939–1951	R	3	5	3	1	0	
Harris, Anthony S. "Spencer"	258	3	261	1921–1948	L	1	2	1	0	0	
Harris, B. Gail	184	51	235	1950–1961	L	0	5	1	0	0	
Harrison, Charles W.	168	17	185	1963–1972	R	1	5	2	1	0	
Harshman, John E. "Jack"	192	21	213	1945–1961	L	2	4	3	2	0	LM 1951
Hart, Jason W.	174	0	174	1998–2006	R	1	5	1	0	0	
Hart, William W.	214	3	217	1935–1952	R	0	3	0	0	0	4 HR G 1945
Hasson, Charles E. "Gene"	177	4	181	1935–1950	L	1	2	0	0	0	
Hatcher, Christopher K.	238	0	238	1990–2002	R	1	3	2	1	0	LM 1998

Player	Minor	Major	Total	Years	Bats	Led	20+	30+	40+	50+	Notes
Hauser, Joseph J.	399	80	479	1918–1942	L	5	9	6	3	2	LM 1930, 1933; 63 HR (1930), 69 HR (1933)
Hawes, Roy L.	167	0	167	1947–1960	L	0	2	0	0	0	
Heath, Minor W. "Mickey"	288	0	288	1923–1940	L	0	6	3	0	0	
Henley, Gail C.	167	1	168	1948–1961	L	0	2	0	0	0	
Hermansen, Chad B.	173	13	186	1995–2007	R	0	4	1	0	0	
Hernandez, Leonardo J.	309	7	316	1978–1991	R	2	7	4	0	0	LM 1988, 1989
Hernandez, Rodolfo	195	0	195	1970–1991	R	0	1	0	0	0	
Herrera, Juan F. "Pancho"	321	31	352	1955–1974	R	5	9	3	1	0	LM 1969
Herrera, Roberto G.	167	—	167	1956–1975	R	0	1	0	0	0	
Hersh, Earl W.	151	0	151	1953–1961	L	0	3	0	0	0	
Heslet, Harry R. "Bud"	314	—	314	1940–1956	R	5	8	4	2	1	
Hessman, Michael S.	288	13	301	1996–2008	R	1	9	2	0	0	
Heyman, Louis W.	181	—	181	1946–1958	R	1	3	2	0	0	
Hiatt, Phillip F.	284	13	297	1990–2003	R	3	7	4	2	0	LM 1996, 2001; JL 20
Hicks, James E.	228	5	233	1959–1972	R	1	6	0	0	0	JL 33
Hicks, Melvin L.	179	—	179	1936–1951	L	1	0	0	0	0	
High, Charles E.	195	1	196	1919–1932	L	0	6	0	0	0	
Hill, Elmore "Moe"	263	—	263	1965–1980	R	5	7	4	1	0	
Hobbs, Robert	158	—	158	1945–1955	R	0	4	3	0	0	
Hoffman, Edward A. "Dutch"	191	0	191	1913–1935	L	2	1	0	0	0	
Holloway, Theodore J. "Jack"	162	—	162	1921–1931	L	2	2	1	1	0	
Holman, Ernest W.	178	—	178	1924–1938	R	0	4	0	0	0	
Holmes, Stanley C.	151	—	151	1981–1989	R	2	3	2	0	0	LM 1983
Horn, Samuel L.	220	62	282	1982–1996	L	2	5	3	0	0	LM 1993
Hosley, Timothy K.	205	12	217	1967–1982	R	1	5	0	0	0	
Howard, Charles D.	209	—	209	1963–1977	S	1	4	0	0	0	
Howard, T. Crawford	159	—	159	1940–1952	R	2	3	2	0	0	
Howell, Murray D. "Red"	229	0	229	1928–1944	R	0	5	0	0	0	
Hudgens, James P.	172	0	172	1923–1931	L	2	5	1	0	0	
Hufft, Irvin V. "Fuzzy"	237	—	237	1921–1933	L	1	5	5	0	0	
Hughes, Gabriel "Pete"	284	—	284	1937–1952	L	4	8	4	1	0	
Hunt, Arthur L. "Mike"	206	—	206	1927–1939	R	2	5	3	0	0	
Huston, Eulas D. "Bud"	161	—	161	1947–1958	R	1	2	0	0	0	
Hyzdu, Adam D.	278	19	297	1990–2006	R	1	5	2	0	0	
Ingram, Darren S.	162	—	162	1994–2003	R	0	3	0	0	0	
Jablonski, Raymond L.	215	83	298	1947–1964	R	1	5	0	0	0	
Jackson, George C.	159	4	163	1906–1932	R	0	2	0	0	0	
Jackson, Louis C.	151	1	152	1957–1968	L	0	3	1	0	0	
Jackson, William H.	181	—	181	1953–1963	R	0	4	2	0	0	
Jacobs, Raymond F.	233	0	233	1923–1942	R	0	5	1	0	0	
Jacobsen, Larry C. "Bucky"	159	9	168	1997–2007	R	2	4	1	0	0	
Jimenez, Eduardo	352	—	352	1986–2007	L	1	9	2	1	0	
Jimenez, Felix E.	173	0	173	1959–1975	R	0	1	0	0	0	
Johnson, Deron R.	162	245	407	1956–1976	R	3	6	1	0	0	
Johnson, Roy E.	216	1	217	1980–1997	L	1	3	1	0	0	LM 1991
Jok, Stanley E.	192	1	193	1947–1961	R	0	3	0	0	0	
Jolley, Smead P.	336	46	382	1922–1941	L	1	9	4	1	0	LM 1928
Jones, Clarence W.	211	2	213	1959–1978	L	1	6	1	0	0	JL 246
Jones, Grover W. "Deacon"	154	1	155	1955–1967	L	0	2	0	0	0	
Jones, Harold M.	178	2	180	1956–1964	R	1	5	2	0	0	
Jones, John W.	178	0	178	1923–1935	L	0	3	1	0	0	
Jones, Leroy L. "Cowboy"	164	—	164	1924–1941	L	0	2	1	0	0	
Jones, Mitchell C.	200	—	200	2000–2008	R	3	6	1	0	0	JL 1
Jones, Robert O.	170	20	190	1967–1987	L	0	2	0	0	0	JL 20

GOING FOR THE FENCES

Player	Minor	Major	Total	Years	Bats	Led	20+	30+	40+	50+	Notes
Jordan, Thomas J.	267	1	268	1938–1957	R	2	7	2	1	0	
Jose, Domingo "Felix"	169	54	223	1984–2007	S	0	2	1	0	0	
Joseph, Ricardo E.	157	13	170	1959–1973	R	0	1	0	0	0	
Judnich, Walter F.	202	90	292	1935–1955	L	0	4	0	0	0	
Kalin, Frank B.	167	0	167	1938–1954	R	0	1	0	0	0	
Kazak, Edward T.	153	11	164	1940–1960	R	0	1	0	0	0	
Kelleher, Francis E. "Frank"	358	3	361	1936–1954	R	3	8	2	1	0	
Keller, Charles B. "Jerry"	203	—	203	1976–1985	R	2	7	0	0	0	
Kellert, Frank W.	182	8	190	1949–1959	R	0	4	1	1	0	
Kelly, William H.	207	0	207	1920–1931	R	2	4	1	1	0	
Kennedy, Forrest E. "Frosty"	228	—	228	1948–1957	R	2	5	4	1	1	60 HR (1956)
Keyes, Stanley C.	344	—	344	1924–1940	R	5	9	3	0	0	
Kieschnick, Michael B. "Brooks"	164	16	180	1993–2005	L	1	4	0	0	0	
King, Harold	153	24	177	1965–1979	L	2	2	1	0	0	
King, John H.	197	—	197	1913–1930	L	2	4	1	0	0	
King, Kevin D.	178	—	178	1979–1988	S	1	4	1	0	0	
Kirkland, Willie C.	177	148	325	1953–1967	L	2	5	4	1	0	JL 126
Klimchock, Louis S.	150	13	163	1957–1971	L	0	1	0	0	0	
Kloza, John C.	153	0	153	1925–1936	R	0	4	1	0	0	
Knicely, Alan L.	159	12	171	1974–1987	R	1	3	2	0	0	
Knickerbocker, Austin	161	0	161	1940–1954	R	2	3	0	0	0	
Knott, Jonathan D.	155	1	156	2002–2008	R	1	5	1	0	0	
Kobesky, Edward L.	176	—	176	1937–1951	R	2	3	0	0	0	
Koegel, Peter J.	178	1	179	1966–1977	R	0	4	0	0	0	
Komminsk, Brad L.	214	23	237	1979–1993	R	1	5	2	0	0	
Koonce, Graham C.	198	0	198	1994–2007	L	2	4	1	0	0	
Kopacz, George F.	154	0	154	1960–1973	L	0	1	0	0	0	
Koranda, James B.	198	—	198	1952–1965	R	1	3	1	0	0	
Kousagan, Peter	179	—	179	1941–1954	R	2	5	1	0	0	
Kraft, Clarence O. "Big Boy"	256	0	256	1910–1924	R	6	4	4	1	1	LM 1924
Kress, Charles S.	156	1	157	1940–1959	L	0	3	0	0	0	
Kubski, Albert A.	173	—	173	1937–1957	R	1	3	1	0	0	
Laabs, Chester P.	183	117	300	1935–1950	R	2	6	2	1	0	
Laga, Michael R.	220	16	236	1980–1990	L	0	7	3	0	0	JL 35
Lahman, Calvin E.	156	—	156	1931–1939	L	2	4	1	1	0	
Lancellotti, Richard A. "Rick"	276	2	278	1977–1991	L	3	7	2	1	0	LM 1979; JL 58
Landenberger, Kenneth H.	169	0	169	1948–1958	L	0	4	1	0	0	
Larson, Brandon J.	153	8	161	1997–2007	R	0	5	0	0	0	
LeBlanc, Remy J.	179	—	179	1942–1954	R	2	4	3	2	0	
Leja, Frank J.	164	0	164	1954–1963	L	0	5	1	0	0	
Lemen, Samuel E.	153	—	153	1922–1932	L	0	2	2	0	0	
Lennon, Patrick O.	192	2	194	1986–2003	R	0	2	1	0	0	
Lennon, Robert A.	278	1	279	1945–1961	L	1	5	2	1	1	64 HR (1954)
Leon, Donny	199	—	199	1995–2008	S	1	4	1	0	0	
Leone, Justin P.	170	6	176	1999–2008	R	0	5	0	0	0	
Levan, Jesse R.	216	1	217	1944–1959	L	1	4	1	0	0	
Levy, Edward C.	238	4	242	1936–1955	R	1	3	1	0	0	
Lewis, Herman	164	—	164	1951–1959	L	1	4	0	0	0	
Lillard, R. Eugene "Gene"	345	0	345	1932–1954	R	2	8	3	2	1	LM 1935
Limmer, Louis	244	19	263	1946–1958	L	2	7	1	0	0	
Lindsey, John W.	156	—	156	1995–2008	R	0	3	1	0	0	
Lis, Joseph A.	236	32	268	1964–1979	R	2	5	4	0	0	JL 6
Little, Keith E.	264	—	264	1948–1959	R	2	6	4	3	0	LM 1955; 4 HR G 1955
Llenas, Winston E.	220	3	223	1961–1983	R	1	4	0	0	0	JL 6
Long, R. Dale	166	132	298	1944–1964	L	2	4	2	0	0	
Lopez, Lorenzo	197	—	197	1960–1980	R	0	1	0	0	0	

Player	Minor	Major	Total	Years	Bats	Led	20+	30+	40+	50+	Notes
Lopez, Mendy	156	6	162	1999–2008	R	3	1	0	0	0	
Lovullo, Salvatore A. "Torey"	157	15	172	1987–1999	S	0	1	0	0	0	
Lowe, Walter A.	154	—	154	1937–1949	R	2	4	1	0	0	
Lugo, Gabriel	210	—	210	1966–1983	R	0	4	1	0	0	
Lutz, Michael	241	—	241	1948–1960	R	1	7	1	0	0	
Lyden, Mitchell S.	163	1	164	1983–1995	R	0	2	0	0	0	
Lyons, Albert H.	159	1	160	1940–1956	R	0	4	0	0	0	
Machiria, Pablo	179	—	179	1985–2002	R	0	1	0	0	0	
Macko, Joseph J.	306	—	306	1948–1970	R	0	7	1	0	0	
Mangual, Jose M.	161	16	177	1970–1984	R	0	3	0	0	0	
Manno, Donald D.	162	1	163	1935–1951	R	2	1	1	0	0	LM 1942
Manto, Jeffery P.	243	31	274	1985–2000	R	1	6	1	0	0	
Marquez, Luis A.	186	0	186	1949–1963	R	0	4	1	0	0	NL 6
Marrero, Oreste V.	152	1	153	1987–2004	L	0	1	0	0	0	
Marshall, Rufus J. "Jim"	202	29	231	1950–1962	L	1	7	3	0	0	JL 78
Martin, Harold L.	179	—	179	1940–1954	R	2	5	2	1	0	
Martin, Herschel R.	165	28	193	1932–1953	S	0	0	0	0	0	
Martin, Robert F.	177	—	177	1942–1956	R	0	4	0	0	0	
Martinez, Domingo E.	187	2	189	1985–1999	R	0	3	0	0	0	JL 104
Martinez, Ramon "Ray"	192	—	192	1994–2008	R	0	4	1	0	0	
Mateosky, Bernard B.	192	—	192	1953–1962	R	1	5	0	0	0	
Matias, John R.	156	2	158	1963–1980	L	0	1	0	0	0	
Matthews, James W.	307	—	307	1939–1955	R	2	6	5	2	1	
McCall, Roderick J.	184	—	184	1990–1999	L	0	6	2	0	0	
McClain, Scott M.	291	2	293	1990–2008	R	0	9	3	0	0	JL 71
McDaniel, James R.	280	—	280	1950–1963	R	1	7	4	0	0	
McDaniel, Osborne C. "Chili"	177	—	177	1922–1932	L	1	3	1	0	0	
McDonald, David B.	165	1	166	1962–1974	L	1	3	0	0	0	
McGowan, Frank B.	190	6	196	1920–1939	L	0	3	1	0	0	
McGraw, Henry T. "Hank"	160	—	160	1961–1972	R	1	2	0	0	0	
McKnight, James A.	184	0	184	1955–1972	R	0	2	0	0	0	
McNulty, William F.	237	0	237	1965–1975	R	2	6	1	1	1	LM 1974
McPherson, Dallas L.	150	18	168	2001–2008	L	1	3	2	2	0	
Mead, Charles R.	193	3	196	1940–1954	L	1	3	1	0	0	
Medina, Luis M.	155	10	165	1985–1992	R	3	3	1	0	0	
Mele, Albert E. "Dutch"	244	0	244	1934–1951	L	1	4	1	0	0	
Mendez, Roberto C.	179	—	179	1992–2008	L	0	2	0	0	0	
Mere, Pedro	184	—	184	1988–2008	R	0	0	0	0	0	
Meriwether, Conklyn W. "Al"	280	—	280	1939–1954	L	4	7	5	2	0	
Meulens, Hensley F. "Bam Bam"	206	15	221	1986–2002	R	1	5	0	0	0	
Miller, Charles F. "Hack"	180	—	180	1920–1930	R	2	4	2	0	0	
Miller, D. C. "Pud"	268	—	268	1940–1953	L	3	6	3	3	2	LM 1949; 4 HR G 1949
Minor, Damon R.	182	13	195	1996–2006	L	0	6	2	0	0	
Mizeur, William F.	158	0	158	1922–1935	L	1	2	0	0	0	
Monahan, Peter G.	186	—	186	1921–1940	L	1	0	0	0	0	
Montag, Robert E.	223	—	223	1946–1959	L	2	6	1	0	0	
Montemayor, Felipe A.	245	2	247	1950–1968	L	0	4	0	0	0	ML 6
Moore, Alvin E. "Junior"	159	7	166	1971–1985	R	0	3	2	1	0	
Moore, Edward W.	185	—	185	1949–1963	R	1	4	1	0	0	
Mora, Andres	444	27	471	1971–1997	R	4	12	5	1	0	LM 1975
Morgan, Edwin W.	174	1	175	1934–1950	L	1	1	1	0	0	
Morgan, R. Barry	165	—	165	1959–1970	L	2	2	0	0	0	
Morgan, Scott A.	164	—	164	1995–2003	R	0	5	1	0	0	
Morman, Russell L.	207	10	217	1983–1999	R	1	3	1	0	0	
Morton, James L.	236	—	236	1946–1959	L	0	4	0	0	0	
Moss, Howard G.	279	0	279	1936–1952	R	4	7	4	1	1	
Mottola, Charles E. "Chad"	249	4	253	1992–2007	R	1	5	1	0	0	

GOING FOR THE FENCES

Player	Minor	Major	Total	Years	Bats	Led	20+	30+	40+	50+	Notes
Moyer, Robert R.	239	—	239	1944–1954	R	2	6	3	0	0	
Mulcahy, Lester T.	164	—	164	1941–1953	R	1	5	3	1	0	
Muller, Frederick W.	233	0	233	1928–1940	R	2	6	2	0	0	
Munson, Joseph M. N.	208	3	211	1918–1932	L	2	4	4	0	0	
Murray, Glenn E.	169	2	171	1989–2002	R	0	4	0	0	0	
Murray, James O.	152	3	155	1897–1920	R	4	1	0	0	0	
Murrell, Ivan A.	186	33	219	1963–1983	R	2	4	1	0	0	
Nagel, William T.	247	15	262	1935–1951	R	2	4	2	0	0	
Nash, Charles F. "Cotton"	185	0	185	1964–1972	R	1	5	3	0	0	
Neil, Albert R.	213	—	213	1947–1954	R	5	5	3	1	0	
Nell, Gordon T.	365	—	365	1930–1949	R	5	9	6	5	0	
Nelson, Glenn R. "Rocky"	234	31	265	1942–1962	L	3	5	4	1	0	LM 1958
Nelson, Robert A.	204	4	208	1983–1994	L	0	5	1	0	0	
Newman, John H.	152	—	152	1935–1947	R	3	3	1	0	0	
Newsom, Warren D.	182	34	216	1986–2003	L	0	4	1	0	0	
Nieman, Elmer L. "Butch"	197	37	234	1940–1951	L	5	6	1	0	0	
Norbert, Theodore J.	314	—	314	1930–1948	R	6	10	1	0	0	LM 1943
Norman, Henry W. "Bill"	295	0	295	1929–1946	R	1	6	1	0	0	
Novikoff, Louis A.	186	15	201	1937–1950	R	1	3	1	1	0	LM 1940
Nunnally, Jonathan K. "Jon"	195	42	237	1992–2006	L	0	4	0	0	0	JL 6
Oana, Henry K. "Prince"	261	1	262	1929–1951	R	3	5	2	0	0	
Obradovich, James T.	205	0	205	1967–1982	L	3	4	0	0	0	
Oglesby, James D.	180	0	180	1926–1942	L	2	0	0	0	0	
Oliver, Eugene G.	154	93	247	1956–1969	R	3	3	3	1	0	
Orteig, Raymond J.	161	—	161	1939–1958	R	0	2	0	0	0	
Ortenzio, Frank J.	181	1	182	1969–1978	R	2	3	2	1	0	JL 30
Ortiz, Alejandro	434	—	434	1981–2004	R	0	11	6	0	0	
Ortiz, Luis P.	163	—	163	1946–1958	R	0	2	0	0	0	
Osborne, Lawrence S.	190	17	207	1953–1969	L	1	2	1	0	0	
Osorio, Elias C.	217	—	217	1952–1965	L	0	3	1	0	0	
Ostrowski, John T.	218	14	232	1939–1953	R	1	5	2	0	0	
Osuna, Elpidio	214	—	214	1962–1983	R	0	1	0	0	0	
Otanez, Willis A.	231	7	238	1990–2008	R	0	4	1	0	0	
Ozark, Daniel L.	238	—	238	1942–1963	R	1	5	2	0	0	4 HR G 1956
Pagel, Karl D.	163	1	164	1976–1984	L	2	5	1	0	0	
Palmer, Isaac B. "Ike"	198	—	198	1946–1957	L	0	4	1	0	0	
Palys, Stanley F.	189	10	199	1950–1963	R	1	4	1	0	0	JL 66
Parker, Roy	222	—	222	1946–1958	L	0	5	2	1	0	
Parks, Jack W.	195	—	195	1944–1961	L	1	3	0	0	0	
Parlier, William O.	186	—	186	1963–1973	S	1	5	0	0	0	
Paschal, Benjamin E.	152	24	176	1915–1934	R	4	1	0	0	0	
Pascual, Carlos L.	199	0	199	1949–1962	R	0	4	1	0	0	
Pascucci, Valentino M.	174	2	176	1999–2008	R	2	5	1	0	0	JL 21
Peden, Leslie E.	249	1	250	1947–1964	R	0	5	0	0	0	
Peel, Homer H.	161	2	163	1923–1946	R	0	0	0	0	0	
Pellow, Kit D.	282	4	286	1996–2008	R	1	10	3	0	0	
Pemberton, Rudy H.	186	3	189	1988–2005	R	0	3	0	0	0	JL 6
Perez, Robert A.	159	8	167	1989–2008	R	0	1	0	0	0	
Perry, Melvin G. "Bob"	240	6	246	1953–1970	R	1	5	1	0	0	
Perry, Raymond L.	348	—	348	1940–1960	R	7	7	5	2	0	
Phelps, Joshua L.	187	64	251	1996–2008	R	1	5	1	0	0	
Phelps, Kenneth A.	151	123	274	1976–1991	L	1	4	1	1	0	
Phillips, Adolfo E.	153	59	212	1961–1979	R	0	2	1	0	0	
Phillips, Charles G. "J.R."	268	23	291	1988–2005	L	2	7	1	1	0	4 HR G 1997
Pickering, Calvin E.	206	14	220	1995–2005	L	0	6	2	0	0	
Pierce, Laverne J. "Jack"	395	8	403	1970–1987	R	3	9	4	2	1	LM 1986; JL 13; Switch-hit at times

MCCONNELL

Player	Minor	Major	Total	Years	Bats	Led	20+	30+	40+	50+	Notes
Pike, Jesse W.	156	1	157	1939–1952	L	1	2	1	0	0	
Pinkston, Alfred C.	250	—	250	1951–1965	L	1	6	1	0	0	
Pisoni, James P.	187	6	193	1949–1962	R	0	3	0	0	0	
Pless, Rance	153	0	153	1947–1960	R	0	2	0	0	0	
Pokel, James L.	235	—	235	1946–1958	L	3	6	3	1	0	
Poole, James R.	311	13	324	1914–1946	L	3	7	3	1	1	
Pope, David	152	12	164	1950–1961	0	2	0	0	0	0	
Posada, Leopoldo J.	160	8	168	1954–1969	R	1	3	0	0	0	
Powers, John C.	298	6	304	1949–1965	L	2	7	2	0	0	
Prather, Murl A. "Dutch"	211	—	211	1927–1951	L	2	4	0	0	0	
Prescott, George B. "Bobby"	398	0	398	1952–1970	R	2	9	5	1	0	LM 1965
Puccinelli, George L. "Pooch"	266	19	285	1927–1940	R	1	6	2	1	1	
Pyle, Thomas L.	189	—	189	1922–1938	L	1	3	0	0	0	
Queen, William E.	154	0	154	1947–1960	R	0	2	1	0	0	
Quellich, George W.	190	1	191	1923–1933	R	0	2	1	0	0	
Quinlan, Thomas R.	173	1	174	1987–1999	R	0	1	0	0	0	
Quintana, Patricio W. "Witty"	156	—	156	1951–1964	R	1	2	0	0	0	
Rabb, John A.	187	4	191	1978–1991	R	0	3	0	0	0	
Radmanovich, Ryan A.	153	2	155	1993–2003	R	0	3	0	0	0	
Rajsich, Gary L.	158	3	161	1976–1985	L	0	5	0	0	0	JL 76
Ransom, Bryan C. "Cody"	162	7	169	1998–2008	R	0	4	0	0	0	
Rapp, Earl W.	203	2	205	1940–1959	L	0	4	1	0	0	
Raven, Luis A.	184	—	184	1989–2003	R	2	5	3	0	0	
Rawlings, George R. "Reg"	183	—	183	1915–1929	R	3	3	0	0	0	
Reed, Raymond C.	183	—	183	1951–1961	R	2	5	1	0	0	LM 1960
Reid, Robert E.	153	—	153	1942–1956	L	0	1	0	0	0	
Reider, John E.	201	—	201	1923–1934	L	1	5	2	0	0	
Restovich, Michael J.	175	6	181	1998–2007	R	0	5	0	0	0	
Reyes, Juan M.	178	—	178	1976–1993	L	0	3	0	0	0	
Reynolds, Jeffrey A.	162	—	162	1980–1989	R	0	4	0	0	0	
Reynolds, Thomas D.	187	12	199	1963–1978	R	0	4	1	0	0	
Rhodes, James L. "Dusty"	179	54	233	1947–1962	L	0	3	1	0	0	
Richards, Paul R.	171	15	186	1926–1949	R	2	2	1	0	0	
Richardson, Kenneth F.	222	0	222	1934–1955	R	0	2	0	0	0	
Richardson, Virgil D.	262	—	262	1939–1954	S	0	7	3	0	0	
Riddle, Charles L. "Chase"	157	—	157	1943–1962	R	0	2	0	0	0	
Riggert, Joseph A.	172	8	180	1909–1928	R	4	1	0	0	0	
Riggs, Adam D.	158	3	161	1994–2004	R	0	3	0	0	0	JL 39
Riley, Leon F. "Lee"	248	0	248	1927–1949	L	2	3	1	0	0	
Rios, Eduardo E.	158	—	158	1991–2007	R	1	3	2	0	0	
Rivera, Andres	155	—	155	1960–1974	R	0	2	0	0	0	
Rivera, German	209	2	211	1978–1996	R	0	3	0	0	0	JL 25
Rivera, Jesus M. "Bombo"	168	10	178	1970–1988	R	0	2	0	0	0	JL 37
Rivera, Michael R.	163	11	174	1997–2008	R	2	2	1	0	0	
Rivera, Ruben M.	210	64	274	1991–2008	R	0	5	1	0	0	
Robbins, Spencer G.	151	—	151	1948–1962	R	0	3	0	0	0	
Robello, Thomas V. "Tony"	243	0	243	1932–1946	R	5	6	2	1	1	LM 1939
Roberts, David L.	244	2	246	1952–1966	L	1	4	2	0	0	JL 183
Robinson, Henry F. "Hank"	218	—	218	1943–1957	R	1	5	1	0	0	
Robles, Acuna "Javier"	207	—	207	1992–2008	R	0	4	0	0	0	
Robson, Thomas J.	197	0	197	1967–1975	R	2	4	3	1	0	JL 3
Rocco, Michael D. "Mickey"	226	30	256	1935–1952	L	0	6	0	0	0	
Rodgers, Frank	217	—	217	1927–1946	R	1	3	1	0	0	
Rodriguez, Fernando "Boi"	265	—	265	1987–2005	L	1	5	2	0	0	
Rodriguez, Guillermo	207	—	207	1977–1994	R	0	6	1	0	0	
Rodriguez, H. Oscar	244	—	244	1951–1969	R	0	3	0	0	0	

Player	Minor	Major	Total	Years	Bats	Led	20+	30+	40+	50+	Notes
Rohrmeier, Daniel	177	0	177	1987–2002	R	0	3	1	0	0	
Rohwer, Ray	196	3	199	1921–1931	L	0	4	3	1	0	
Rollin, Rondal J.	155	—	155	1980–1987	R	1	3	2	0	0	
Romero, Marco A.	235	—	235	1986–2005	R	1	4	1	0	0	
Rosburg, Russell C.	156	—	156	1949–1957	R	1	3	1	0	0	
Roser, John W. J. "Bunny"	213	0	213	1920–1939	L	3	5	1	0	0	
Ruiz, Randy R.	167	1	168	1999–2008	R	0	4	0	0	0	
Rushing, Gary L.	180	—	180	1956–1964	R	1	5	1	0	0	
Russell, Ewell A. "Reb"	200	21	221	1911–1930	L	0	4	2	0	0	
Saenz, Ricardo	295	—	295	1983–2007	R	0	5	0	0	0	
Salvent, Aldo F.	160	—	160	1952–1962	R	2	4	1	0	0	
Sanchez, Alejandro	251	8	259	1978–1994	R	1	5	1	0	0	
Sanchez, Gerardo	204	—	204	1983–2003	R	0	2	0	0	0	
Sanchez, Orlando	204	0	204	1974–1993	L	0	3	0	0	0	
Sanchez, Roberto G.	153	—	153	1953–1965	R	1	1	1	0	0	
Sanders, Reginald J.	194	3	197	1968–1979	R	0	3	0	0	0	
Sandoval, Jose L.	238	—	238	1990–2008	R	0	4	0	0	0	
Sanicki, Edward R.	160	3	163	1946–1952	R	2	5	3	0	0	
Sanner, Roy D. "Tex"	220	—	220	1941–1957	L	1	5	3	1	0	
Santomauro, Maurice A.	224	—	224	1944–1957	R	0	6	1	1	0	
Saucedo, Roberto	217	—	217	1997–2008	R	2	5	2	0	0	
Sauer, Henry J. "Hank"	150	288	438	1937–1959	R	0	2	1	1	1	
Sawatski, Carl E.	202	58	260	1945–1963	L	4	6	2	1	0	
Schall, Eugene D. "Gene"	154	2	156	1991–2002	R	0	2	0	0	0	
Schino, Stanley	178	—	178	1927–1940	R	1	2	0	0	0	
Schmees, George E.	169	0	169	1946–1958	L	0	4	0	0	0	
Schmidt, Robert A. "Joe"	189	—	189	1937–1954	R	1	2	1	0	0	
Schulmerich, E. Wesley	164	27	191	1927–1941	R	1	3	0	0	0	
Seabol, Scott A.	181	1	182	1996–2007	R	0	3	2	0	0	
See, Ralph L. "Larry"	240	0	240	1980–1995	R	0	4	1	0	0	
Seeley, C.E. "Ed"	191	—	191	1922–1933	R	1	5	0	0	0	
Seerey, J. Patrick	156	86	242	1941–1951	R	3	4	3	1	0	
Segrist, Kal H.	156	0	156	1951–1961	R	0	3	0	0	0	
Selby, William F.	189	11	200	1992–2005	L	0	4	0	0	0	
Sepkowski, Theodore W.	194	0	194	1942–1955	L	2	3	2	1	0	
Serena, William R.	182	48	230	1946–1957	R	1	5	1	1	1	
Sessi, Walter A.	253	1	254	1937–1955	L	1	6	1	1	0	
Shearer, Ray S.	204	0	204	1950–1962	R	1	4	1	0	0	
Sheely, Earl H.	197	48	245	1911–1934	R	4	4	1	0	0	LM 1918, 1919
Shepherd, Ronald W.	168	2	170	1979–1993	R	0	1	1	0	0	
Shetler, Vernon G. "Moose"	205	—	205	1936–1954	L	1	5	0	0	0	
Shiver, Ivey M. "Chick"	172	2	174	1929–1936	R	0	3	1	0	0	
Shoals, Leo C. "Muscle"	362	—	362	1937–1955	L	7	9	5	1	1	
Shuba, George T.	153	24	177	1944–1957	L	1	3	0	0	0	
Silverio, Tomas R.	180	0	180	1965–1981	L	0	2	0	0	0	
Simmons, Nelson B.	201	11	212	1981–2000	S	0	3	1	0	0	
Simms, Michael H.	196	36	232	1985–1999	R	1	4	1	0	0	
Simon, Randall C.	156	49	205	1992–2007	L	0	0	0	0	0	
Simononis, Alphonsus J.	165	—	165	1939–1951	R	2	3	0	0	0	
Simpson, Halbert M.	263	—	263	1936–1957	L	0	7	1	0	0	
Simpson, Harry L. "Suitcase"	162	73	235	1949–1964	L	1	4	2	0	0	NL 4
Sinovic, Richard J.	176	—	176	1947–1958	R	0	2	0	0	0	
Skidmore, Robert R. "Roe"	153	0	153	1966–1975	R	1	2	0	0	0	
Small, Norman W.	336	—	336	1934–1953	R	7	7	6	1	0	
Smith, Charles L. "Bubba"	308	—	308	1991–2003	R	4	9	4	0	0	
Smith, Demond L.	155	—	155	1990–2008	S	0	0	0	0	0	
Smith, Earl L.	212	9	221	1911–1935	S	1	4	1	0	0	

Player	Minor	Major	Total	Years	Bats	Led	20+	30+	40+	50+	Notes
Smith, Elmer J.	227	70	297	1911–1933	L	4	5	2	2	0	LM 1927
Smith, Robert E.	168	21	189	1992–2006	R	0	2	0	0	0	
Snider, Van V.	218	1	219	1982–1996	L	1	4	1	0	0	
Snyder, Earl C.	220	1	221	1998–2007	R	0	6	1	0	0	
Solaita, Tolia "Tony"	167	50	217	1965–1979	L	1	3	1	1	0	LM 1968; JL 155
Solano, Claudio	211	—	211	1945–1967	R	3	5	4	3	0	ML 38
Sommers, Jesus M.	265	—	265	1966–1996	R	0	2	0	0	0	
Soto, Carlos	272	—	272	1972–1991	R	1	5	0	0	0	
Soufas, Harry C.	174	—	174	1937–1950	R	2	4	1	0	0	
Stafford, Dean L.	277	—	277	1946–1955	R	3	7	4	1	0	
Stankey, Lawrence J.	158	—	158	1952–1963	L	0	4	1	1	0	
Stark, Matthew S.	164	0	164	1983–1999	R	0	1	1	0	0	
Steels, James E.	153	0	153	1980–1994	L	0	3	1	0	0	
Stevens, Edward L.	257	28	285	1941–1961	L	0	5	0	0	0	
Stevens, Macolm J. "Mal"	183	—	183	1938–1951	L	2	4	2	0	0	
Stevens, R.C.	191	8	199	1952–1963	R	1	3	1	0	0	LM 1960
Stockstill, David A.	242	—	242	1978–1993	L	0	5	1	0	0	
Stokes, James D.	196	—	196	1942–1956	L	0	4	1	0	0	
Stone, John L.	186	—	186	1938–1952	R	2	6	1	0	0	
Storti, Lindo T.	292	9	301	1927–1945	S	0	10	4	0	0	
Stratton, Robert V.	197	—	197	1996–2006	R	1	5	2	0	0	
Streza, John	150	—	150	1938–1956	R	1	1	1	0	0	
Stroble, Frederick E.	183	—	183	1935–1948	R	3	3	0	0	0	
Stroner, James M.	177	0	177	1923–1939	R	2	3	1	1	0	
Stroughter, Stephen L.	156	1	157	1971–1983	L	0	1	0	0	0	
Stuart, Richard L.	222	228	450	1951–1969	R	3	5	5	2	1	LM 1956; 66 HR (1956); JL 49
Stubing, Lawrence G. "Moose"	192	0	192	1956–1977	L	1	3	1	0	0	
Sturdy, Guy R.	203	1	204	1920–1940	L	1	4	1	1	0	
Sullivan, Russell G.	186	5	191	1948–1957	L	1	3	2	0	0	
Swann, Pedro A.	182	1	183	1991–2007	L	0	1	0	0	0	
Taitt, Douglas J. "Paco"	158	4	162	1925–1947	L	2	1	0	0	0	
Tanner, John W. "Jack"	165	—	165	1945–1953	R	4	5	1	0	0	
Tasby, Willie	180	46	226	1950–1965	R	1	5	0	0	0	
Tatum, James R.	152	3	155	1985–2000	R	0	1	0	0	0	
Taylor, Joe C.	264	9	273	1951–1963	R	0	8	1	0	0	
Taylor, William M.	186	7	193	1947–1961	L	0	4	1	0	0	
Tedesco, Joseph G. "Rocky"	176	—	176	1946–1960	R	0	2	0	0	0	
Tellez, Alonso	235	—	235	1978–2004	R	0	1	0	0	0	
Thomas, James G. "Gorman"	164	268	432	1969–1986	R	2	4	3	1	1	
Thomas, Juan D.	194	—	194	1992–2004	R	0	5	0	0	0	
Thompson, Albert B.	169	—	169	1965–1976	R	2	3	1	0	0	
Thompson, Ryan O.	174	52	226	1987–2007	R	0	3	0	0	0	JL 3
Thorpe, Benjamin R. "Bob"	195	3	198	1946–1961	R	1	3	0	0	0	
Throneberry, Marvin E.	201	53	254	1952–1964	L	4	5	4	2	0	
Tillman, Kerry J. "Rusty"	175	2	177	1979–1995	R	0	2	0	0	0	
Timmons, Osborne L.	195	20	215	1991–2005	R	1	4	0	0	0	JL 14
Tolentino, Jose F.	162	1	163	1983–1997	S	0	1	0	0	0	JL 1
Torres, A. Raymundo "Ray"	332	—	332	1976–1998	R	0	10	2	0	0	
Tracy, Andrew M.	231	20	251	1996–2008	L	0	8	2	0	0	
Traylor, Robert W. "Woody"	159	—	159	1934–1946	L	2	4	1	0	0	
Truby, Christopher J.	179	23	202	1993–2007	R	0	4	1	0	0	
Tucker, Leonard W.	236	—	236	1953–1963	R	0	7	2	1	1	
Tucker, Oliver D.	239	1	240	1921–1935	L	1	7	0	0	0	
Turgeon, Eugene J. "Pete"	179	0	179	1920–1934	R	1	3	0	0	0	

GOING FOR THE FENCES

Player	Minor	Major	Total	Years	Bats	Led	20+	30+	40+	50+	Notes
Valdez, Baltazar	211	—	211	1976–1994	R	0	4	1	0	0	
Valenzuela, Benjamin B. "Benny"	154	0	154	1951–1971	R	0	3	0	0	0	ML 3
Valenzuela, Horacio	167	—	167	1982–1998	L	0	1	0	0	0	
Valenzuela, Mario	166	—	166	1996–2008	R	0	5	1	0	0	
Vargas, Hediberto	269	0	269	1982–1998	R	1	6	2	0	0	
Vazquez, Jorge A.	150	—	150	1999–2008	R	0	3	2	0	0	
Vergez, Jean L. "Johnny"	179	52	231	1926–1943	R	0	3	1	1	0	
Vidal, Jose N.	251	3	254	1958–1975	R	1	4	2	1	0	JL 2
Villanueva, Hector B.	184	25	209	1985–2001	R	1	3	1	0	0	
Vitiello, Joseph D.	154	26	180	1991–2004	R	0	1	0	0	0	
Vizcarra, Roberto	232	—	232	1986–2008	R	0	2	0	0	0	
Wagner, Leon L.	154	211	365	1954–1971	L	2	3	1	1	1	
Walker, Cleotha "Chico"	154	17	171	1976–1994	S	0	0	0	0	0	
Walters, Ferdinand R.	151	—	151	1959–1968	R	0	4	0	0	0	
Walton, Daniel J.	238	28	266	1965–1980	R	2	6	2	1	0	LM 1977; JL 9; Switch-hitter 1974–1980
Ward, John F. "Jay"	241	0	241	1956–1971	R	0	6	0	0	0	JL 14
Warner, James A.	240	—	240	1942–1954	R	1	7	4	1	0	4 HR-G 1949
Warren, Bennie L.	166	33	199	1931–1954	R	0	3	0	0	0	
Washburn, James R. "Mule"	188	—	188	1913–1932	R	1	3	2	1	0	
Washington, Sloane V. "Vern"	200	9	209	1931–1950	L	0	4	1	0	0	
Weatherspoon, Charles B.	231	—	231	1955–1969	R	2	4	2	0	0	
Weintraub, Phillip	194	32	226	1926–1945	L	0	3	1	0	0	
Wellman, Robert J.	219	1	220	1946–1959	R	4	6	2	1	0	
Wentzel, Stanley A.	223	0	223	1940–1957	R	2	4	0	0	0	
Werden, Percival W. "Perry"	169	26	195	1885–1908	R	6	2	2	2	0	LM 1886, 1894, 1895; 4 HR G 1895
Werhas, John C.	151	2	153	1960–1973	R	0	1	0	0	0	JL 8
West, Max E.	230	77	307	1935–1954	L	3	5	5	2	0	
West, Walter M. "Max"	161	0	161	1923–1934	R	0	2	0	0	0	
White, Derrick R.	232	3	235	1991–2008	R	0	3	0	0	0	JL 7
Whiteman, George	162	1	163	1905–1929	R	1	1	0	0	0	
Wieczorek, Chester J.	180	—	180	1936–1947	R	0	4	1	0	0	
Williams, Edward L.	222	39	261	1983–2001	R	0	5	0	0	0	JL 5
Williams, Fred "Pap"	151	0	151	1935–1955	R	0	2	1	0	0	
Williams, Leonard D.	158	—	158	1952–1959	R	1	3	2	2	0	
Williams, Marvin	205	—	205	1950–1961	R	2	5	2	1	0	ML 39; NL 8
Williams, Wiley W.	186	—	186	1946–1957	R	1	5	0	0	0	
Williams, William	154	0	154	1952–1969	R	0	0	0	0	0	
Willingham, Thomas H. "Hugh"	165	1	166	1929–1952	R	1	3	1	0	0	
Wilson, Archibald C. "Archie"	194	0	194	1947–1961	R	0	3	1	0	0	
Wilson, George W.	275	3	278	1942–1962	L	1	5	2	0	0	JL 27
Wilson, James G.	197	0	197	1982–1994	R	2	5	1	0	0	JL 1
Wilson, Nesbit C. "Neb"	329	—	329	1940–1960	R	4	8	3	1	0	
Wilson, Richard C.	285	—	285	1944–1960	R	4	7	4	2	0	
Wilson, Thomas L.	153	15	168	1991–2006	R	0	3	0	0	0	
Wilson, William D.	228	32	260	1947–1961	R	3	6	3	0	0	
Wingard, Ernest J.	150	7	157	1924–1941	L	0	1	0	0	0	
Winsett, J. Thomas	220	8	228	1929–1952	L	1	4	1	1	1	LM 1936
Winters, Matthew L.	190	2	192	1978–1989	L	2	5	0	0	0	JL 138
Withrow, Raymond W. "Corky"	211	0	211	1956–1966	R	1	5	2	0	0	
Witt, Kevin T.	269	15	284	1994–2006	L	3	7	2	0	0	JL 4
Witte, Jerome C. "Jerry"	308	4	312	1937–1952	R	3	7	4	2	1	
Wood, Jason	180	5	185	1991–2008	R	0	3	0	0	0	

MCCONNELL

Player	Minor	Major	Total	Years	Bats	Led	20+	30+	40+	50+	Notes
Wood, Kenneth L.	169	34	203	1941–1956	R	0	3	1	0	0	
Woodson, Tracy M.	155	5	160	1984–1996	R	0	1	0	0	0	
Workman, Charles T. "Chuck"	231	50	281	1937–1951	L	4	4	2	2	1	
Wright, Albert O. "Ab"	323	9	332	1928–1946	R	3	8	3	0	0	4 HR G 1940
Yan, Julian	364	—	364	1986–2007	R	2	7	3	0	0	
Yaryan, Clarence E. "Yam"	213	2	215	1917–1940	R	5	2	1	1	0	LM 1920
Yordy, Harold E.	186	—	186	1920–1931	R	3	3	1	0	0	
York, Anthony B.	158	0	158	1933–1956	R	0	0	0	0	0	
Young, Ernest W.	319	27	346	1990–2007	R	0	9	2	0	0	
Zambrano, Roberto J.	213	—	213	1985–2004	R	0	4	1	0	0	
Zinter, Alan M.	250	3	253	1989–2006	S	0	5	0	0	0	

Top One Hundred Career Home Run Hitters in Minor Leagues

#	Player	HR		#	Player	HR
1.	Hector Espino	484		58.	Mickey Heath	288
2.	Nelson Barrera	479			**Mike Hessman**	**288**
3.	Andres Mora	444		60.	Dick Wilson	285
4.	Alejandro Ortiz	434		61.	Phil Hiatt	284
5.	Buzz Arlett	432			Pete Hughes	284
6.	Nick Cullop	420		**63.**	**Kit Pellow**	**282**
7.	Merv Conners	400		64.	Richard Barry	280
8.	Joe Hauser	399			Les Fleming	280
9.	Bobby Prescott	398			Adrian Garrett	280
10.	Jack Pierce	395			Jim McDaniel	280
11.	Jack Graham	384			Al Merriwether	280
12.	**Matias Carrillo**	**370**		69.	Howie Moss	279
	Tedd Gullic	370		70.	Adam Hyzdu	278
14.	Gordon Nell	365			Bob Lennon	278
15.	Julian Yan	364		72.	Dean Stafford	277
16.	Muscle Shoals	362		73.	Willie Aikens	276
17.	Frank Kelleher	358			Rick Lancellotti	276
18.	Ronnie Camacho	355		75.	Woody Fair	275
19.	Eduardo Jiminez	352			George Wilson	275
20.	Ray Perry	348		77.	Vince DiMaggio	273
21.	Moose Clabaugh	346		78.	Steve Demeter	272
22.	Gene Lillard	345			Carlos Soto	272
23.	Stan Keyes	344		80.	Frank Gravino	271
24.	Bunny Brief	342		81.	Stormy Davis	270
25.	Rogelio Alvarez	337		82.	Luke Easter	269
	Joe Bauman	337			Heriberto Vargas	269
27.	Smead Jolley	336			Kevin Witt	269
	Norm Small	336		85.	Russ Burns	268
29.	Dick Greco	333			Pud Miller	268
30.	Ray Torres	332			Charles "J.R." Phillips	268
31.	Ken Guettler	330		88.	Tom Jordan	267
32.	Neb Wilson	329		89.	George Puccinelli	266
33.	Israel Alcantara	326		90.	Keith Little	265
34.	Ab Wright	323			"Boi" Rodriguez	265
35.	Pancho Herrera	321			Jesus Sommers	265
36.	Ernest Young	319		93.	Joe Taylor	264
37.	Bud Heslet	314		94.	Moe Hill	263
	Ted Norbert	314			Hal Simpson	263
39.	Steve Bilko	313		96.	Virgil Richardson	262
40.	Jim Poole	311		97.	Prince Oana	261
41.	Leo Hernandez	309		98.	Mike Coolbaugh	258
42.	Bubba Smith	308			Spencer Harris	258
	Jerry Witte	308		100.	Paul Easterling	257
44.	Jim Matthews	307			Ed Stevens	257
45.	Joe Macko	306				
46.	Enrique Aguilar	305				
47.	Larry Barton	299				
48.	Johnny Powers	298				
49.	Bernardo Brito	297				
	Ollie Carnegie	297				
51.	Bill Norman	295				
	Ricardo Saenz	295				
53.	Russ Derry	294				
54.	Lin Storti	292				
55.	**Scott McClain**	**291**				
56.	Babe Barna	290				
57.	John Gill	289				

Bold indicates a player active during the 2008 season

Some Interesting Facts about the Top 100 Career Home Run Hitters

- Hector Espino became the career home run leader during the 1977 season and he continues to be the leader 32 years later. Buzz Arlett moved to the top of the list in 1933 and held the title for 44 years until passed by Espino.

- Thirteen of the players on the list hit all or most of their round trippers south of the border in the Mexican League. The Mexican League joined Organized Baseball in 1955 and all of the homers by the 13 players were hit after that time.

- You would think that virtually any player who is good enough to make the top 100 list would get at least one shot in the big leagues. That has not been the case. Forty-two of the players on the list never appeared in a major league game.

- Joe Bauman played for only nine years in the minor leagues. Although he slugged 337 home runs in those few years, he never managed to get a real shot in Triple A, let alone the majors.

- Twenty-two of the players on the list played all or most of their careers prior to World War II.

- Vince DiMaggio hit the most major league home runs of anyone on the list (125). He is followed by Willie Aikens (110), Luke Easter (93) and Joe Hauser with (80).

- Scott McClain hit 71 home runs in the Japanese Leagues in addition to his minor league total.

- Prince Oana won 80 games in the minors and 3 in the majors as a pitcher.

The Interesting Case of Pete Kousagan

Pete Kousagan holds the record for hitting home runs in the largest number of individual leagues. Pete was an outfielder-first baseman who hit 179 home runs in sixteen different leagues during an eleven-year minor league career. He began his career in 1941, and finished up in 1954. He spent three years in military service during World War II. His home run totals in each league are as follows:

- Border League   53
- California League   23
- Cotton States League   18
- Northern League   18
- Eastern Shore League   17
- Three I League   12
- New England League   9
- Inter-State League   8
- Ohio State League   4
- Pony League   4
- Central League   3
- Tri-State League   3
- Canadian-American League   2
- Pennsylvania State Association 2
- Piedmont League   2
- West Texas-New Mexico League 1

Five players hit home runs in thirteen different leagues during the course of their careers. They are Larry Barton, Wilbur Davis, Jim Poole, Dutch Prather, and John Streza.

The most home runs hit by a player who spent his entire minor league career in one league is 230 by Max West in the Pacific Coast League. He is followed by Ray Rohwer with 196, also in the Pacific Coast League. Reg Rawlings rounds out the top three with 183 homers in the Blue Ridge League.

Top Ten Career Home Run Hitters, Batting Right, Left, or Both

Top Ten Career Home Run Hitters, Right-Handed Batters

1. Hector Espino   484
2. Nelson Barrera   479
3. Andres Mora   444
4. Alejandro Ortiz   434
5. Nick Cullop   420
6. Merv Connors   400
7. Bobby Prescott   398
8. Jack Pierce   395
9. Tedd Gullic   370
10. Gordon Nell   365

Top Ten Career Home Run Hitters, Left-Handed Batters

1. Joe Hauser   399
2. Jack Graham   384
3. Matias Carrillo   370
4. Leo "Muscle" Shoals   362
5. Eduardo Jiminez   349
6. John "Moose" Clabaugh 346
7. Joe Bauman   337
8. Smead Jolley   336
9. Jim Poole   311
10. Larry Barton   299

Top Ten Career Home Run Hitters, Switch-Hitters

1. Russell "Buzz" Arlett 432
2. Lin Storti   292
3. Virgil Richardson   262
4. Alan Zinter   250
5. Earl Smith   212
6. Charles Howard   209
7. Nelson Simmons   201
8. Micah Franklin   200
9. Rip Collins   193
10. Miguel Fernandez   186
    Bill Parlier   186

Top Ten Career Home Run Hitters at the End of Each Decade

The lists include both active and retired players.

Through 1900 Season

1. Perry Werden — 151
2. Count Campau — 132
3. Ed Breckinridge — 120
4. Dan Lally — 116
5. Joe Katz — 104
6. Joe Werrick — 102
7. Lew Whistler — 97
8. Bill Klusman — 96
9. Joe Strauss — 95
10. Buck Freeman — 92

Through 1910 Season

1. Perry Werden — 169
2. Count Campau — 137
3. Buck Freeman — 127
4. Dan Lally — 121
5. Ed Breckinridge — 120
   Truck Eagan — 120
   Lew Whistler — 120
8. Joe Katz — 106
9. Joe Werrick — 102
10. Frank Weikart — 99

Through 1920 Season

1. Perry Werden — 169
2. Albert Durham — 152
3. Jim Murray — 152
4. Count Campau — 137
5. Frank Huelsman — 133
6. Buck Freeman — 127
7. Truck Eagan — 123
8. Dan Lally — 122
9. Ed Breckinridge — 120
   Lew Whistler — 120

Through 1930 Season

1. Bunny Brief — 342
2. Big Boy Kraft — 256
3. Buzz Arlett — 251
4. Stormy Davis — 234
5. Jim Poole — 210
6. Yank Davis — 208
7. Bill Kelly — 207
8. Fuzzy Hufft — 205
9. Ernie Calbert — 204
10. Joe Munson — 202

Through 1940 Season

1. Buzz Arlett — 432
2. Nick Cullop — 416
3. Joe Hauser — 374
4. Moose Clabaugh — 346
5. Stan Keyes — 344
6. Bunny Brief — 342
7. Smead Jolley — 312
8. Jim Poole — 294
9. Tedd Gullic — 293
10. Yank Davis — 288
    Mickey Heath — 288

Through 1950 Season

1. Buzz Arlett — 432
2. Nick Cullop — 420
3. Joe Hauser — 399
4. Tedd Gullic — 370
5. Gordon Nell — 365
6. Moose Clabaugh — 346
7. Stan Keyes — 344
8. Bunny Brief — 342
9. Smead Jolley — 336
10. Ab Wright — 323

Through 1960 Season

1. Buzz Arlett — 432
2. Nick Cullop — 420
3. Merv Connors — 400
4. Joe Hauser — 399
5. Jack Graham — 384
6. Tedd Gullic — 370
7. Gordon Nell — 365
8. Muscle Shoals — 362
9. Ray Perry — 348
10. Moose Clabaugh — 346

Through 1970 Season

1. Buzz Arlett — 432
2. Nick Cullop — 420
3. Merv Connors — 400
4. Joe Hauser — 399
5. Bobby Prescott — 398
6. Jack Graham — 384
7. Tedd Gullic — 370
8. Gordon Nell — 365
9. Muscle Shoals — 362
10. Ray Perry — 348

Through 1980 Season

1. Hector Espino 473
2. Buzz Arlett 432
3. Nick Cullop 420
4. Merv Connors 400
5. Joe Hauser 399
6. Bobby Prescott 398
7. Jack Graham 384
8. Tedd Gullic 370
9. Gordon Nell 365
10. Muscle Shoals 362

Through 1990 Season

1. Hector Espino 484
2. Buzz Arlett 432
3. Nick Cullop 420
4. Merv Connors 400
5. Joe Hauser 399
6. Bobby Prescott 398
7. Jack Pierce 395
8. Jack Graham 384
9. Andres Mora 376
10. Tedd Gullic 370

Through 2000 Season

1. Hector Espino 484
2. Nelson Barrera 470
3. Andres Mora 444
4. Buzz Arlett 432
5. Nick Cullop 420
6. Merv Connors 400
7. Joe Hauser 399
8. Bobby Prescott 398
9. Jack Pierce 395
10. Alejandro Ortiz 389

Top Career Home Run Hitters by League

Players usually do not stay in one league very long with today's minor league setup. This, however, was not always the case. During the first half or so of the 20th Century, it was not uncommon for a player to spend many years in one league, especially in the higher minors. Thus, these players had the opportunity to rack up impressive career batting stats. Among today's leagues, the Mexican League is the only one that retains that continuity of personnel. Players, mostly Mexican natives, tend to spend long careers in the league and have the opportunity to post impressive numbers.

This compilation is divided into two parts. The first lists the top fifteen career home run hitters for each of six leagues, four of which are still active. These leagues have had a long history as strong minor leagues and have produced players with good career home run totals. An argument could be made for including the Eastern League II in this group. However, the league never had a player with 100 career home runs.

The second part lists the top career home run hitter for many other leagues, along with other players who had significant totals in a given league.

Part I

American Association

1. Bunny Brief — 276
2. Joe Hauser — 266
3. Ted Gullic — 247
4. Nick Cullop — 206
5. Lin Storti — 202
6. Bill Norman — 176
7. Earl Smith — 171
8. Spencer Harris — 166
   Reb Russell — 166
10. Babe Barna — 165
11. Ab Wright — 159
12. George Wilson — 156
13. Marv Throneberry — 139
14. Mickey Heath — 137
15. Mike Laga — 132

International League

1. Ollie Carnegie — 258
2. Rocky Nelson — 203
3. Luke Easter — 195
4. Ed Stevens — 188
5. Pancho Herrera — 187
6. Mike Hessman — 178
7. Howie Moss — 172
   George Puccinelli — 172
9. Russ Derry — 162
   Mike Goliat — 162
11. Steve Demeter — 159
12. Bill Kelly — 157
13. Chad Mottola — 152
    George Quellich — 152
15. Woody Abernathy — 147

Mexican League

1. Nelson Barrera — 455
2. Hector Espino — 453
3. Alejandro Ortiz — 434
4. Andres Mora — 419
5. Eduardo Jiminez — 352
6. Matias Carrillo — 330
7. Ronnie Camacho — 317
8. Ray Torres — 311
9. Enrique Aguilar — 305
10. Ricardo Saenz — 295
11. Jack Pierce — 294
12. Carlos Soto — 264
13. Jesus Sommers — 241
14. Marco Romero — 235
15. Jose Sandoval — 233

Surprisingly, Hector Espino, the all-time minor league career home run leader, did not head the Mexican League. He played in a lower classification Mexican League at the start of his career and hit 28 home runs. Later he played in the International League and hit three home runs.

Pacific Coast League

1. Buzz Arlett — 251
2. Frank Kelleher — 234
3. Max West — 230
4. Smead Jolley — 217
5. Ted Norbert — 205
6. Ray Jacobs — 198
7. Ray Rohwer — 196
   Fred Muller — 196
9. Mike Hunt — 179
10. Earl Sheely — 174
    Gene Lillard — 174
    Joe Brovia — 174
    Steve Bilko — 174
14. Fuzzy Hufft — 166
15. Bernardo Brito — 164

Southern Association

1. Ralph Atkins — 142
2. Bob Montag — 113
3. Joe Hutchinson — 107
4. Hal Simpson — 106
5. Bob Lennon — 103
6. Roy Hawes — 101
   Chuck Workman — 101
8. Babe Barna — 93
   Floyd Fogg — 93
10. Eddie Rose — 90
    Bob Thorpe — 90
12. George Shuba — 87
13. Jim Poole — 86
14. Willie Duke — 85
15. Frank Brazill — 83
    Jesse Levan — 83
    John Powers — 83

Texas League

1. Paul Easterling — 223
2. Jerry Witte — 174
3. Russ Burns — 172
4. Big Boy Kraft — 170
5. Joe Macko — 141
6. Moose Stubing — 138
   Pete Turgeon — 138
8. Mike Lutz — 133
9. Jim Galloway — 112
10. Bud Heslet — 111
11. Hack Miller — 109
12. Ernie Holman — 108
13. Homer Peel — 105
14. Keith Little — 104
    Del Pratt — 104

Part II

Alabama–Florida League

1. Neb Wilson — 104

Appalachian League I

1. Muscle Shoals — 132

Arizona–Texas League

1. Claudio Solano — 197
2. Humberto Barbon — 117
3. Humberto Guerrero — 101

Bi–State League

1. Taylor Sanford — 104

Big State League

1. Dean Stafford — 260
2. Moe Santomauro — 136
3. Albert McCarty — 123
4. Roy Sanner — 118
5. Buck Frierson — 110

Blue Ridge League

1. Reg Rawlings — 183

California League III

1. Dick Wilson — 200
2. Ray Perry — 112

Carolina League

1. Woody Fair — 123

Coastal Plain League

1. Harry Soufas — 133

Eastern League I

1. John Roser — 145
2. Harold Yordy — 124
3. Walter Simpson — 96

Eastern League II

1. Horace McBride — 93
2. Albert Thompson — 91
3. Ray Flood — 85
4. Don Manno — 82
5. Israel Alcantara — 80
   Adam Hyzdu — 80

Evangeline League

1. Remy LeBlanc — 122
2. Robert Dunn — 121

Far West League

1. Ray Perry — 143

Florida State League

1. Ed Levy — 101

Georgia State League

1. Van Davis — 163
2. Parnell Ruark — 106

Longhorn League

1. Joe Bauman — 221
2. Robert Martin — 140

Mexican Center League

1. Ramiro Caballero — 134

Middle Atlantic League

1. Walter Alston — 128

Midwest League

1. Moe Hill — 201

North Carolina State League

1. Norm Small — 279
2. Harold Harrigan — 114

Northern League

1. Frank Gravino — 140

Northwest League I

1. Charles Mead — 147
2. Dick Greco — 145
3. Herman Lewis — 119
4. Pete Hughes — 111

Piedmont League

1. George Ferrell — 175
2. Dan Boone — 169
   Ken Guettler — 169
4. Molly Cox — 142
5. Crawford Davidson — 126

Pioneer League I

1. Walt Lowe — 145
2. Tony Robello — 106

Southeastern League

1. Neb Wilson — 113
2. Fred Stroble — 102

South Atlantic League (pre-1964)

1. Wiley Williams — 120

Southern League (1964–present)

1. Mark Funderburk — 117

Three I League

1. Bill Mizeur — 102
2. Horace Garner — 100

Virginia League

1. Stan Stack — 103

West Texas–New Mexico League

1. Gordon Nell — 270
2. Virgil Richardson — 230
3. Emmitt Fulenwider — 178
4. Joe Fortin — 168
5. Ike Palmer — 167
6. Bob Crues — 162
7. Jim Matthews — 138
8. Paul Halter — 136
9. Les Mulcahy — 126

Western Association III

1. Butch Nieman — 145
2. Frank Reiger — 117

Western League III

1. Yank Davis — 173
2. Mule Washburn — 119
3. Lee Riley — 115
4. Jim Blakesley — 114
5. Joe Munson — 106

Western League IV

1. Jim McDaniel — 117

Players with 100+ Home Runs in Each of Two Leagues

- **Jack Graham**
  133 Pacific Coast League
  120 International League

- **Mickey Heath**
  137 American Association
  103 Pacific Coast League

- **Frank Kelleher**
  234 Pacific Coast League
  107 International League

- **Jim Matthews**
  138 West Texas—New Mexico
  119 Big State League

- **Ray Perry**
  143 Far West League
  20 California League

- **Bobby Prescott**
  199 Mexican League
  11 Pacific Coast League

Buzz Arlett Hit More Than 80 Home Runs in Each of Three Leagues

- 251 Pacific Coast League
- 93 International League
- 81 American Association

These leagues were all top classification leagues.

Top Fifty Career Home Run Hitters in Organized Baseball (Major and Minor League Totals Combined)

Rank	Player	Major	Minor	Total
1.	Hank Aaron	755	31	786
2.	Barry Bonds	762	20	782
3.	Babe Ruth	714	1	715
4.	Willie Mays	660	12	672
5.	Sammy Sosa	609	35	644
6.	Frank Robinson	586	54	640
7.	Ken Griffey, Jr.	611	27	638
8.	Harmon Killebrew	573	63	636
9.	Mark McGwire	583	48	631
10.	Willie McCovey	521	105	626
11.	Reggie Jackson	563	40	603
12.	Rafael Palmeiro	569	28	597
13.	Manny Ramirez	527	68	595
14.	Carlos Delgado	469	125	594
15.	Jim Thome	541	52	593
16.	Alex Rodriguez	553	36	589
17.	Ted Williams	521	66	587
18.	Mike Schmidt	548	34	582
19.	Mickey Mantle	536	44	580
20.	Fred McGriff	493	84	577
21.	Eddie Murray	504	66	570
22.	Eddie Mathews	512	56	568
23.	Gary Sheffield	499	60	559
24.	Lou Gehrig	493	61	554
25.	Jimmie Foxx	534	11	545
	Frank E. Thomas	521	24	545
27.	Willie Stargell	475	67	542
28.	Jose Canseco	462	67	529
29.	Rocky Colavito	374	150	524
30.	Ernie Banks	512	—	512
31.	Mel Ott	511	—	511
32.	Stan Musial	475	32	507
33.	Juan Gonzalez	434	72	506
34.	Mike Piazza	427	69	496
35.	Andres Galarraga	399	96	495
36.	Billy Williams	426	66	492
37.	Cal Ripken, Jr.	431	56	487
38.	Dave Kingman	442	43	485
39.	Hector Espino	—	484	484
40.	Nelson Barrera	—	479	479
	Andre Dawson	438	41	479
	Joe Hauser	80	399	479
43.	Tony Perez	379	97	476
44.	Carl Yastrzemski	452	22	474
45.	Andres Mora	27	444	471
46.	Greg Vaughn	355	115	470
47.	Frank Howard	382	84	466
48.	Dave Winfield	465	—	465
49.	Joe Carter	396	66	462
50.	Jim Rice	382	78	460
	Larry Walker	383	77	460

There are only four players on this list who were primarily minor leaguers: Hector Espino, Nelson Barrera, Joe Hauser and Andres Mora. A list such as this, compiled prior to World War II, would have contained many more minor league players. Times change. There are few career minor league players anymore except in the Mexican League. Note that three of the four players mentioned above spent most of their careers in the Mexican League. Almost every minor league club is now a major league farm club. If a player can't cut it in a few years, he is let go to make room for a new prospect.

Ernie Banks, Mel Ott and Dave Winfield never played in the minor leagues. Hector Espino and Nelson Barrera never played in the major leagues.

Players with 100+ Career Home Runs in Both the Major and Minor Leagues

Seventy-nine players have hit at least 100 home runs in both the majors and the minors. The first player to accomplish this feat was Gavvy Cravath in 1921. He was followed by Tilly Walker in 1928, Tony Lazzeri in 1933 and Rip Collins in 1936.

Dick Stuart is the only player to reach the 200 level in each category. The best balance is by Dick Gernert with 103 in the majors and 102 in the minors, and by Don Hurst with 115 in the majors and 114 in the minors. Willie McCovey has, by far, the most major league home runs of any player on the list with 521. He is followed by Carlos Delgado with 431 and Rocky Colavito with 374. Willie Aikens has the most minor league home runs with 276. He is followed closely by Vince DiMaggio with 273. Six players—Wally Berger, Cecil Fielder, Willie Horton, Derrek Lee, Dan Pasqua and George Selkirk—barely made the list, each with 100 in the minors.

Player	Majors	Minors	Player	Majors	Minors
Willie Aikens	110	276	Tony Lazzeri	178	135
Steve Balboni	181	239	Derrek Lee	238	100
Wally Berger	242	100	Jim Lemon	164	130
Geronimo Berroa	101	172	Danny Litwhiler	107	104
Zeke Bonura	119	132	Don Lock	122	137
Russell Branyan	121	198	Dale Long	132	166
Greg Brock	110	129	Greg Luzinski	307	113
Dolf Camilli	239	141	Mike Marshall	148	102
Rocky Colavito	374	150	Carmelo Martinez	108	120
Rip Collins	135	193	Charlie Maxwell	148	131
Gavvy Cravath	119	108	Lee May	354	103
Glenn Davis	190	106	Willie McCovey	521	105
Rob Deer	230	185	Minnie Minoso	186	114
Carlos Delgado	431	125	Walt Moryn	101	140
Don Demeter	163	134	Ron Northey	108	125
Vince DiMaggio	125	273	Dan Pasqua	117	100
Mike Easler	118	134	Ken Phelps	123	151
Nick Esasky	122	112	Rip Repulski	106	101
Cecil Fielder	319	100	Bob Robertson	115	130
Jim Gentile	179	245	Bill Robinson	166	115
Dick Gernert	103	102	Hank Sauer	288	150
Travis Hafner	142	114	George Scott	271	103
Ken Harrelson	131	103	George Selkirk	108	100
Jim Ray Hart	170	106	Richie Sexson	294	105
Woody Held	179	109	Lee Stevens	144	146
Babe Herman	181	122	Dick Stuart	228	222
Jim Hickman	159	116	Danny Tartabull	262	102
Glenallen Hill	186	128	Fernando Tatis	101	103
Willie Horton	325	100	Frank J. Thomas	286	101
Don Hurst	115	114	Gorman Thomas	268	164
John Jaha	141	112	Lee Thomas	106	110
Bob Johnson	288	123	Greg Vaughn	355	115
Cliff Johnson	196	127	Leon Wagner	211	154
Deron Johnson	245	162	Tilly Walker	118	110
Mack Jones	133	102	Gary Ward	130	101
Jim King	117	135	Fred Whitfield	108	114
Willie Kirkland	148	177	Preston Wilson	189	109
Ron Kittle	176	127	Rudy York	277	135
Paul Konerko	276	106	Richie Zisk	207	129
Chet Laabs	117	183			

GOING FOR THE FENCES

Players Reaching Double Figures in Home Runs in Both the Majors and Minors During the Same Season

Year	Player	Minor League Club	HR	Major League Club	HR
1922	Reb Russell	Minneapolis, American Association	17	Pittsburgh, NL	12
1928	Chuck Klein	Fort Wayne, Central League	26	Philadelphia, NL	11
1931	Vince Barton	Los Angeles, Pacific Coast League	17	Chicago, NL	13
1949	Dino Restelli	San Francisco, Pacific Coast League	10	Pittsburgh, NL	12
1950	Monte Irvin	Jersey City, International League	10	New York, NL	15
1951	Mickey Mantle	Kansas City, American Association	11	New York, AL	13
1952	Dusty Rhodes	Nashville, Southern Association	18	New York, NL	10
1955	Gail Harris	Minneapolis, American Association	17	New York, NL	12
1956	Rocky Colavito	San Diego, Pacific Coast League	12	Cleveland, AL	21
1958	Dick Stuart	Salt Lake City, Pacific Coast League	31	Pittsburgh, NL	16
	Leon Wagner	Phoenix, Pacific Coast League	17	San Francisco, NL	13
1959	Willie McCovey	Phoenix, Pacific Coast League	29	San Francisco, NL	13
1962	Don Lock	Richmond, International League	13	Washington, AL	12
1965	Roger Repoz	Toledo, International League	14	New York, AL	12
1969	Greg Goossen	Vancouver, Pacific Coast League	18	Seattle, AL	10
1977	Andres Mora	Rochester, International League	11	Baltimore, AL	13
1979	Jim Morrison	Oklahoma City, American Association	22	Chicago, AL	14
1982	Glenn Wilson	Evansville, American Association	10	Detroit, AL	12
1983	Nick Esasky	Indianapolis, American Association	14	Cincinnati, NL	12
1984	Joe Carter	Iowa, American Association	14	Cleveland, AL	13
	Eric Davis	Wichita, American Association	14	Cincinnati, NL	10
	Jim Presley	Salt Lake City, Pacific Coast League	13	Seattle, AL	10
1986	Jim Traber	Rochester, International League	12	Baltimore, AL	13
1987	Sam Horn	Pawtucket, International League	30	Boston, AL	14
	Rafael Palmeiro	Iowa, American Association	11	Chicago, NL	14
1989	Matt Williams	Phoenix, Pacific Coast League	26	San Francisco, NL	18
1990	Sam Horn	Rochester, International League	9	Baltimore, AL	14
		Hagerstown, Eastern League	1		
	Kevin Maas	Columbus, American Association	13	New York, AL	21
1991	Brian Hunter	Richmond, International League	10	Atlanta, NL	12
	Chito Martinez	Rochester, International League	20	Baltimore, AL	13
	Dean Palmer	Oklahoma City, American Association	22	Texas, AL	15
	Phil Plantier	Pawtucket, International League	16	Boston, AL	11
1993	Ryan Thompson	Norfolk, International League	12	New York, NL	11
1994	Eddie Williams	Las Vegas, Pacific Coast League	20	San Diego, NL	11
1996	Tony Clark	Toledo, International League	14	Detroit, AL	27
1997	Jon Nunnally	Omaha, American Association	15	Kansas City, AL	1
				Cincinnati, NL	13
1998	Richie Sexson	Buffalo, International League	21	Cleveland, AL	11
	Shane Spencer	Columbus, International League	18	New York, AL	10
	Bubba Trammell	Durham, International League	16	Tampa Bay, AL	12
1999	Erubiel Durazo	El Paso, Texas League	14	Arizona, NL	11
		Tucson, Pacific Coast League	10		
	Craig Paquette	Norfolk, International League	15	St. Louis, NL	10
2000	Russell Branyan	Buffalo, International League	21	Cleveland, AL	16
	Chris Richards	Memphis, Pacific Coast League	10	St. Louis, NL	1
				Baltimore, AL	13
	Andy Tracy	Ottawa, International League	10	Montreal, NL	11
2001	Adam Dunn	Louisville, International League	20	Cincinnati, NL	19
		Chattanooga, Southern League	12		
2002	Carlos Pena	Sacramento, Pacific Coast League	10	Oakland / Detroit, AL	19
2003	Miguel Cabrera	Carolina, Southern League	10	Florida, NL	12

Players Reaching Double Figures in Home Runs in Both the Majors and Minors During the Same Season (cont.)

Year	Player	Minor League Club	HR	Major League Club	HR
2004	Russell Branyan	Richmond, International League	1	Milwaukee, NL	11
		Buffalo, International League	25		
	John Buck	New Orleans, Pacific Coast League	12	Kansas City, AL	12
	John Mabry	Memphis, Pacific Coast League	12	St. Louis, NL	13
	Justin Morneau	Rochester, International League	22	Minnesota, AL	19
	Marcus Thames	Toledo, International League	24	Detroit, AL	10
	David Wright	Binghamton, Eastern	10	New York, NL	14
		Norfolk, International	8		
2005	Victor Diaz	Norfolk, International League	10	New York, NL	12
	Brad Eldred	Altoona, Eastern League	13	Pittsburgh, NL	12
		Indianapolis, International League	15		
	Jeff Francoeur	Mississippi, Southern League	13	Atlanta, NL	14
	Jonny Gomes	Durham, International League	14	Tampa Bay, AL	21
	Ryan Howard	Scranton-Wilkes-Barre, International Lg.	16	Philadelphia, NL	22
	Mike Jacobs	Binghamton, Eastern League	25	New York, NL	11
	Carlos Pena	Toledo, International League	12	Detroit, AL	18
	Richie Weeks	Nashville, Pacific Coast League	12	Milwaukee, NL	13
2006	Luke Scott	Round Rock, Pacific Coast League	20	Houston, NL	10
	Chad Tracy	Spokane, Northwest League	11	Arizona, NL	20
2007	Rick Ankiel	Memphis, Pacific Coast League	32	St. Louis, NL	11
	Ryan Braun	Nashville, Pacific Coast League	10	Milwaukee, NL	34
	Joshua Fields	Charlotte, International League	10	Chicago, AL	23
2008	Mike Aviles	Omaha, Pacific Coast League	10	Kansas City, AL	10
	Russell Branyan	Nashville, Pacific Coast League	12	Milwaukee, NL	12
	Jay Bruce	Louisville, International League	10	Cincinnati, NL	21
	Chris Davis	Frisco, Texas League	13	Texas, AL	17
		Oklahoma, Pacific Coast League	10		
	Matt Joyce	Toledo, International League	13	Detroit, AL	12
	Ian Stewart	Colorado Springs, Pacific Coast League	19	Colorado, NL	10
	Fernando Tatis	New Orleans, Pacific Coast League	12	New York, NL	11

Russell Branyan accomplished the feat three times and Sam Horn twice.

Three players reached double figures in two minor leagues plus the majors in the same season. They are Erubiel Durazo in 1999, Adam Dunn in 2001, Brad Eldred in 2005, and Chris Davis in 2008.

Willie McCovey led the Pacific Coast League in home runs in 1959 and Dean Palmer led the American Association in home runs in 1991.

GOING FOR THE FENCES

Minor League Career Home Runs for Players with 300 or More in the Major Leagues

Player	Minor	Major	Total	Player	Minor	Major	Total
Hank Aaron	31	755	786	Frank Howard	84	382	466
Joe Adcock	32	336	368	Reggie Jackson	40	563	603
Dick Allen	82	351	433	Andruw Jones	66	371	437
Moises Alou	43	332	375	Chipper Jones	42	408	450
Jeff Bagwell	6	449	455	David Justice	71	305	376
Harold Baines	40	384	424	Al Kaline	—	399	399
Ernie Banks	—	512	512	Jeff Kent	42	377	419
Don Baylor	72	338	410	Harmon Killebrew	63	573	636
Albert Belle	39	381	420	Ralph Kiner	27	369	396
Johnny Bench	47	389	436	Dave Kingman	43	442	485
Yogi Berra	22	358	380	Chuck Klein	28	300	328
Barry Bonds	20	762	782	Greg Luzinski	113	307	420
Bobby Bonds	83	332	415	Fred Lynn	27	306	333
George Brett	25	317	342	Mickey Mantle	44	536	580
Jay Buhner	84	310	394	Edgar Martinez	46	309	355
Ellis Burks	38	352	390	Tino Martinez	48	339	387
Jeromy Burnitz	87	315	402	Eddie Mathews	56	512	568
Jose Canseco	67	462	529	Lee May	103	354	457
Gary Carter	41	324	365	Willie Mays	12	660	672
Joe Carter	66	396	462	Willie McCovey	105	521	626
Norm Cash	41	377	418	Fred McGriff	84	493	577
Vinny Castilla	50	320	370	Mark McGwire	48	583	631
Orlando Cepeda	77	379	456	Johnny Mize	81	359	440
Ron Cey	90	316	406	Dale Murphy	48	398	446
Jack Clark	68	340	408	Eddie Murray	66	504	570
Rocky Colavito	150	374	524	Stan Musial	32	475	507
Chili Davis	71	350	421	Graig Nettles	69	390	459
Andre Dawson	41	438	479	Mel Ott	—	511	511
Carlos Delgado	125	469	594	Rafael Palmeiro	28	569	597
Joe DiMaggio	74	361	435	Dave Parker	48	339	387
Jim Edmonds	30	382	412	Lance Parrish	56	324	380
Darrell Evans	40	414	454	Tony Perez	97	379	476
Dwight Evans	37	385	422	Mike Piazza	69	427	496
Cecil Fielder	100	319	419	Boog Powell	59	339	398
Steve Finley	13	304	317	Albert Pujols	19	319	338
Carlton Fisk	46	376	422	Manny Ramirez	68	527	595
George Foster	40	348	388	Jim Rice	78	382	460
Jimmie Foxx	11	534	545	Cal Ripken, Jr.	56	431	487
Gary Gaetti	66	360	426	Frank Robinson	54	586	640
Andres Galarraga	96	399	495	Alex Rodriguez	36	553	589
Ron Gant	63	321	384	Babe Ruth	1	714	715
Lou Gehrig	61	493	554	Reggie Sanders	35	305	340
Jason Giambi	29	396	425	Ron Santo	18	342	360
Troy Glaus	37	304	341	Mike Schmidt	34	548	582
Juan Gonzalez	72	434	506	Richie Sexson	105	306	411
Luis Gonzalez	38	354	392	Gary Sheffield	60	499	559
Shawn Green	18	328	346	Ruben Sierra	58	306	364
Hank Greenberg	75	331	406	Roy Sievers	57	318	375
Ken Griffey, Jr.	27	611	638	Al Simmons	23	307	330
Vladimir Guerrero	59	392	451	Reggie Smith	49	314	363
Todd Helton	26	310	336	Duke Snider	43	407	450
Gil Hodges	8	370	378	Sammy Sosa	35	609	644
Rogers Hornsby	8	301	309	Willie Stargell	67	475	542
Willie Horton	100	325	425	Darryl Strawberry	79	335	414

Minor League Career Home Runs for Players with 300 or More in the Major Leagues (cont.)

Player	Minor	Major	Total
Frank Thomas	24	521	545
Jim Thome	52	541	593
Greg Vaughn	115	355	470
Mo Vaughn	50	328	378
Larry Walker	77	383	460
Billy Williams	66	426	492
Matt Williams	58	378	436
Ted Williams	66	521	587
Dave Winfield	—	465	465
Carl Yastrzemski	22	452	474

Career Home Run Leaders by First Letter of Last Name

This is a whimsical compilation of career home run leaders based on the first letter of each player's last name. A similar compilation has been done for major leaguers and fans seem to get a charge out of it.

There has never been an "X" player in the majors. Joe Xavier, who played from 1985 through 1990, is the only known "X" player to have ever homered in the minor leagues.

In spite of the fact that very few modern players pile up high career totals, nine players have cracked the Alphabetical List recently. They are Ingram, Inglin, Jiminez, Ortiz, Rodriguez, Yan, Young, Zinter and Zambrano.

	Top Player	HR	Runner-up	HR
A	Buzz Arlett	432	Rogelio Alvarez	337
B	Nelson Barrera	479	Bunny Brief	342
C	Nick Cullop	420	Merv Connors	400
D	Russ Derry	294	Vince DiMaggio	273
E	Hector Espino	484	Luke Easter	269
F	Les Fleming	280	Woody Fair	275
G	Jack Graham	384	Tedd Gullic	370
H	Joe Hauser	399	Pancho Herrera	321
I	Darron Ingram	162	Jeff Inglin	142
J	Eduardo Jimenez	352	Smead Jolley	336
K	Frank Kelleher	358	Stan Keyes	344
L	Gene Lillard	345	Bob Lennon	278
M	Andres Mora	444	Jim Matthews	307
N	Gordon Nell	365	Ted Norbert	314
O	Alejandro Ortiz	434	Prince Oana	261
P	Bobby Prescott	398	Jack Pierce	395
Q	George Quellich	190	Tom Quinlan	173
R	Boi Rodriguez	265	Virgil Richardson	262
S	Muscle Shoals	362	Norm Small	336
T	Ray Torres	332	Joe Taylor	264
U	Dixie Upright	149	Ed Urban	120
V	Hediberto Vargas	269	Jose Vidal	251
W	Neb Wilson	329	Ab Wright	323
X	Joe Xavier	12		
Y	Julian Yan	364	Ernie Young	319
Z	Alan Zinter	250	Roberto Zambrano	213

Players with 50+ Home Runs in a Season

HR Avg is the rate of home runs per 600 at bats. See Introduction for more detailed explanation of Home Run Average.

HR	Player	Club	League	Class	Year	HR Avg	B	Pos
72	Joe Bauman	Roswell	Longhorn League	C	1954	86.75	L	1B
69	Joe Hauser	Minneapolis	American Association	AA	1933	72.63	L	1B
69	Bob Crues	Amarillo	West Texas-New Mexico	C	1948	73.27	R	OF
66	Dick Stuart	Lincoln	Western League	A	1956	75.72	R	OF*
64	Bob Lennon	Nashville	Southern Association	AA	1954	63.05	L	OF
63	Joe Hauser	Baltimore	International League	AA	1930	61.26	L	1B
62	Moose Clabaugh	Tyler	East Texas League	D	1926	83.78	L	1B*
62	Ken Guettler	Shreveport	Texas League	AA	1956	77.34	R	OF
60	Tony Lazzeri	Salt Lake City	Pacific Coast League	AA	1925	50.70	R	SS
60	Frosty Kennedy	Plainview	Southwestern League	B	1956	64.06	R	1B*
59	Ramiro Cabellero	Guanajuato	Mexican Center League	C	1962	83.69	R	1B*
58	Tony Robello	Pocatello	Pioneer League	C	1939	68.64	R	1B
58	Buck Frierson	Sherman-Denison	Big State League	B	1947	52.73	R	OF
57	Pud Miller	Wichita Falls	Big State League	B	1947	61.84	R	OF
57	Bill Serena	Lubbock	West Texas-New Mexico	C	1947	67.59	R	SS
56	Gene Lillard	Los Angeles	Pacific Coast League	AA	1935	52.34	R	3B
56	Frank Gravino	Fargo-Moorhead	Northern League	C	1954	67.07	R	OF
56	Steve Bilko	Los Angeles	Pacific Coast League	Open	1957	62.69	R	1B
55	Big Boy Kraft	Fort Worth	Texas League	A	1924	56.80	R	1B
55	Ike Boone	San Francisco Mission	Pacific Coast League	AA	1929	41.56	L	OF
55	Pud Miller	Gladewater (3)	East Texas League	C	1949	67.35	R	OF
		Lamesa (52)	West Texas-New Mexico	C				
55	Muscle Shoals	Reidsville	Carolina League	B	1949	65.87	L	1B
55	Steve Bilko	Los Angeles	Pacific Coast League	Open	1956	55.28	R	1B
55	Heriberto Vargas	Guanajuato	Mexican Center League	A	1966	68.61	R	1B*
55	Bill McNulty	Sacramento	Pacific Coast League	AAA	1974	62.74	R	3B
54	Nick Cullop	Minneapolis	American Association	AA	1930	62.91	R	OF
54	Buzz Arlett	Baltimore	International League	AA	1932	62.79	S	OF
54	Jack Pierce	Leon	Mexican League	AAA	1986	68.21	L	1B*
53	George Puccinelli	Baltimore	International League	AA	1935	54.64	R	OF
53	Howie Moss	Baltimore	International League	AAA	1947	60.23	R	OF*
53	Jesse McClain	Harlingen	Rio Grande Valley League	C	1950	54.64	R	2B*
53	Joe Bauman	Artesia	Longhorn League	C	1953	68.68	L	1B
53	Nick Castaneda	San Luis Potosi	Mexican League	AAA	1986	80.30	L	DH
52	Pat Wright	Fort Wayne	Central League	B	1930	57.35	L	1B
52	Bob Crues	Amarillo	West Texas-New Mexico	C	1947	56.42	R	OF
52	Cal Felix	Las Vegas	Sunset League	C	1947	51.15	R	OF
52	Chuck Workman	Nashville	Southern Association	AA	1948	56.42	L	OF
52	Frank Gravino	Fargo-Moorhead	Northern League	C	1953	66.24	R	OF
51	Stormy Davis	Okmulgee	Western Association	C	1924	45.27	R	OF
51	Wilbur Davis	Okmulgee	Western Association	C	1924	47.08	L	1B
51	Gus Suhr	San Francisco	Pacific Coast League	AA	1929	38.98	L	1B
51	Bud Heslet	Visalia	California League	C	1956	58.40	R	OF*
51	Len Tucker	Pampa	Southwestern League	B	1956	54.16	R	OF
51	Leon Wagner	Danville	Carolina League	B	1956	56.35	L	OF
51	Gorman Thomas	Sacramento	Pacific Coast League	AAA	1974	64.56	R	OF
50	Ed Kalluna	Sherman (6)	Lone Star League	D	1929	69.61	L	1B
		Midland (44)	West Texas League	D				
50	Jim Poole	Nashville	Southern Association	A	1930	50.85	L	1B

GOING FOR THE FENCES

HR	Player	Club	League	Class	Year	HR Avg	B	Pos
50	Tom Winsett	Columbus	American Association	AA	1936	55.97	L	OF
50	Hank Sauer	Syracuse	International League	AAA	1947	55.35	R	OF
50	Jerry Witte	Dallas	Texas League	AA	1949	52.91	R	1B
50	Manuel Salvatierra	Austin (1)	Big State League	B	1950	61.22	R	OF
		Laredo (49)	Rio Grande Valley League	C				
50	Joe Bauman	Artesia	Longhorn League	C	1952	63.97	L	1B
50	Jim Matthews	Amarillo	West Texas-New Mexico	C	1953	63.42	R	OF*
50	Pedro Hernandez	Guanajuato	Mexican Center League	A	1966	57.69	R	C
50	Ron Kittle	Edmonton	Pacific Coast League	AAA	1982	63.56	R	OF

* Did not play full time at primary position.

To put league classifications in proper perspective, the following are the ranges over the years:

1908–1935: AA, A, B, C, D
1936–1942, 1944–1945: AA, A1, A, B, C, D
1943: AA, A1, A, B, C, D, E
1946–1951, 1958–1962: AAA, AA, A, B, C, D
1952–1957: Open, AAA, AA, A, B, C, D
1963-Present: AAA, AA, A, Rookie

Interesting Facts about 50+ Home Run Seasons

- First accomplished in 1924. Three players hit more than 50 home runs that season, including teammates Stormy Davis and Wilbur Davis (no relation) of Okmulgee of the Western Association.

- Accomplished by teammates Heriberto Vargas and Pedro Hernandez of Guanajuato in 1966 and by Bill McNulty and Gorman Thomas of Sacramento in 1974.

- Hitting 50 or more home runs has been accomplished on 55 occasions by 48 different players. Joe Bauman reached the milestone three times while Joe Hauser, Bob Crues, Pud Miller, Frank Gravino and Steve Bilko each reached it twice.

- Thirty-one of the players batted right-handed, sixteen batted left and one (Buzz Arlett) was a switch-hitter.

- Outfielders accomplished the feat twenty-seven times, twenty-one times by first baseman, twice by shortstops and once each by a second baseman (Jesse McClain), catcher (Pedro Hernandez) and a designated hitter (Nick Castaneda)

- The Pacific Coast League leads all leagues in achieving the mark with nine instances. Both the International League and West Texas-New Mexico League did it five times and it was done three times each in the American Association, Southern Association, Texas League, Longhorn League and Mexican Center League.

- Hitting fifty home runs has been accomplished nineteen times at the highest classification (at the time) of minor leagues.

- Ed Kallina reached the fifty mark while leading the West Texas League in 1929 with 44 home runs after having tied for the lead in the Lone Star League with six that same year. The Lone Star League folded early in the season of 1929.

- Manuel Salvatierra also hit fifty while playing in two leagues in 1950 and Pud Miller improved his total from 52 to 55 as the result of playing in a second league in 1949.
- Pud Miller's 52 home runs for Lamesa in 1949 was one more than the total for all his teammates combined.

- Joe Bauman hit 72 home runs for Roswell in 1954 and the rest of his team hit 71. His closest competition on the team was Jim Day with fourteen.

- Clarence "Big Boy" Kraft, Bud Heslet, Frank Gravino and Pedro Hernandez retired from professional baseball following their fifty home run seasons.

- Dick Stuart hit 40 of his 66 home runs for Lincoln of the Western League in 1956 in just two months, June (23) and July (17). Stuart's 23 home runs in June were the most ever hit in one month in the entire history of Organized Baseball.

- The following players hit 50 or more home runs yet did not lead their respective leagues in home runs:
    Gus Suhr – 1929 Pacific Coast League
    Bob Crues – 1947 West Texas-New Mexico League
    Pud Miller – 1947 Big State League
    Len Tucker – 1956 Southwestern League
    Pedro Hernandez – 1956 Mexican Center League
    Gorman Thomas – 1974 Pacific Coast League
    Nick Castaneda – 1986 Mexican League

- The feat of hitting fifty home runs has been accomplished four times by players on the Baltimore roster and three times each by players with Los Angeles, Nashville, Amarillo and Guanajuato.

- The ten best home run averages by players hitting fifty or more home runs have been:
    Joe Bauman, 86.75 (1954)
    Moose Clabaugh, 83.78 (1926)
    Ramiro Caballero, 83.69 (1962)
    Nick Castaneda, 80.30 (1986)
    Ken Guettler, 77.34 (1956)
    Dick Stuart, 75.72 (1956)
    Bob Crues, 73.27 (1948)
    Joe Hauser, 72.63 (1933)
    Ed Kallina, 69.61 (1929)
    Joe Bauman, 68.68 (1953)

- The poorest home run averages of those who hit fifty or more home runs:
    Gus Suhr, 38.98 (1929)
    Ike Boone, 41.56 (1929)
    Stormy Davis, 45.27 (1924)
    Wilbur Davis, 47.08 (1924)
    Tony Lazzeri, 50.70 (1925)
    Jim Poole, 50.85 (1930)
    Cal Felix, 51.15 (1947)
    Gene Lillard, 52.34 (1935)
    Buck Frierson, 52.73 (1947)
    Jerry Witte, 52.91 (1949)

- Joe Bauman reached the fifty home run mark in three consecutive years. Bob Crues, Frank Gravino and Steve Bilko each did it two years in a row.

- Six different leagues had at least one player with fifty home runs in 1956.

- 1947 and 1956 had the most players reaching fifty home runs in a single season with seven.

- The number of players who hit fifty home runs in each decade:
  - 1950's—17
  - 1940's—12
  - 1930's—10
  - 1920's—8
  - 1960's—3
  - 1980's—3
  - 1970's—2

- Twenty of the forty-eight players on the list never played in the major leagues. Eight others on the list reached the majors but did not manage to hit a big-league home run.

- For those who did reach the majors, Gorman Thomas had the most home runs in a major league season with 45 in 1979. Dick Stuart hit 42 in 1963. Hank Sauer hit 41 in 1954. Leon Wagner had 37 in 1962. Ron Kittle homered 35 times in 1983. Joe Hauser hit 27 in 1924 and Chuck Workman knocked out 25 homers in 1945.

- The best major league career totals were by:
  - Hank Sauer—288
  - Gorman Thomas—268
  - Dick Stuart—228
  - Leon Wagner—211
  - Tony Lazzeri—178
  - Ron Kittle—176

- The sixty home run mark has been reached only ten times in the minor leagues.

- Fourteen of the players on the list had minor league career total of 300 homers or more. Buzz Arlett heads the list with 432. He is followed by Nick Cullop with 420 and Joe Hauser with 399.

- On the flip side, Pedro Hernandez had only 71 career home runs in the minors. Ed Kallina had a mere 80, and Cal Felix hit 97. None of these players ever reached the major leagues. Hernandez is the real mystery man. He played only two years and then dropped completely out of sight after his big year in 1966.

- Pat Wright and Jesse McClain each hit nineteen home runs in their second best season. Fifteen additional players hit fewer than thirty home runs in their second best season.

- An obituary for Frosty Kennedy stated that he waited until his last at bat of the 1956 season to reach the magic 60 home run mark. This makes a great story, however, it didn't quite happen like that. He did wait until his last game (September 6 at San Angelo) but he connected in the third inning. He came to the plate three more times in the game. He was the leadoff batter for Plainview in that game. Obviously, the manager wanted to give him as many opportunities as possible in his final game of the season to reach the sixty home run mark.

Players with 45 to 49 Home Runs in a Season in Chronological Order

Year	HR	Player	Club	League
1895	45	Perry Werden	Minneapolis	Western League
1923	49	Moses Solomon	Hutchinson	Southwestern League
1924	48	Mule Washburn	Tulsa	Western League
1926	49	Guy Sturdy	Tulsa	Western League
1926	46	Elmer Smith	Portland	Pacific Coast League
1928	45	Smead Jolley	San Francisco	Pacific Coast League
1929	46	Dan Boone	High Point	Piedmont League
1929	46	John Vergez	Oakland	Pacific Coast League
1929	45	Clay Parrish	Greensboro	Piedmont League
1930	45	Ken Strong	New Haven	Eastern League
			Hazleton	New York-Penn League
1931	47	Dave Barbee	Hollywood	Pacific Coast League
1931	45	Gordon Nell	Muskogee	Western Association
			Minneapolis	American Association
1932	49	Joe Hauser	Minneapolis	American Association
1934	48	Buzz Arlett	Birmingham	Southern Association
			Minneapolis	American Association
1934	45	Frank Demaree	Los Angeles	Pacific Coast League
1936	48	Cal Lahman	Jamestown	Northern League
1936	47	Cecil Dunn	Alexandria	Evangeline League
1938	45	Ollie Carnegie	Buffalo	International League
1939	46	Vince DiMaggio	Kansas City	American Association
1939	45	Emmitt Fullenwider	Lake Charles	Evangeline League
			Lamesa	West Texas-New Mexico
1946	48	Joe Bauman	Amarillo	West Texas-New Mexico
1946	46	Jerry Witte	Toledo	American Association
1947	49	Gordon Nell	Borger	West Texas-New Mexico
1948	48	Jack Graham	San Diego	Pacific Coast League
1949	48	Max West	San Diego	Pacific Coast League
1949	45	Ray Perry	Redding	Far West League
1949	45	Carl Sawatski	Nashville	Southern Association
1950	46	Pat Seerey	Memphis	Southern Association
			Colorado Springs	Western League
1951	47	Jack Harshman	Nashville	Southern Association
1952	47	Merv Connors	Amarillo	West Texas-New Mexico
1952	47	Dean Stafford	Paris/Tyler	Big State League
1952	45	Les Mulcahy	Amarillo	West Texas-New Mexico
1952	45	Roy Sanner	Texarkana	Big State League
1952	45	Walt Sessi	Brownsville	Gulf Coast League
1952	45	Marv Williams	Chihuahua	Arizona-Texas League
1953	48	Bob Featherstone	Lubbock	West Texas-New Mexico
1953	45	Harold Martin	Hot Springs	Cotton States League
			Beaumont	Texas League
1954	47	Claudio Solano	Cananea	Arizona-Texas League
1954	45	Richard Hogan	Tucson	Arizona-Texas League
1954	45	Ted Sepkowski	Wellsville	PONY League
1955	48	Keith Little	Corpus Christi	Big State League
			Columbus	International League
1955	46	Joe Bauman	Roswell	Longhorn League

Year	HR	Player	Club	League
1956	49	Allen Weygandt	Topeka	Western League
1956	46	Art Cuitti	Amarillo	Western League
1956	45	Claudio Solano	Cananea	Arizona-Mexico League
1957	47	Bob Wellman	Graceville	Alabama-Florida League
			Savannah	South Atlantic League
1957	45	Dick Stuart	Hollywood	Pacific Coast League
			Atlanta	Southern Association
			Lincoln	Western League
1964	49	Hector Espino	Monterey	Mexican League
			Jacksonville	International League
1966	46	Dave Duncan	Modesto	California League
1968	49	Tony Solaita	High Point-Thomasville	Carolina League
1982	46	Ken Phelps	Wichita	American Association
1986	46	Willie Aikens	Puebla	Mexican League
1992	47	Ty Gainey	Mexico City Reds	Mexican League
1998	46	Chris Hatcher	Omaha	Pacific Coast League
2000	45	Eduardo Jimenez	Saltillo	Mexican League
2004	46	Ryan Howard	Reading	Eastern League
			Scranton-Wilkes Barre	International League

Perry Werden hit 45 home runs for Minneapolis in the Western League in 1895. This was an unheard of total for that time. Thirty-seven of his home runs came at his home park. Stew Thornley, the expert on ballparks in Minneapolis, estimates that both foul lines only measured about 250 feet at Athletic Park.

Jack Graham of the San Diego Padres, who led the Pacific Coast League in home runs in 1948 with 48, had 46 home runs when he was beaned by Red Adams of the Los Angeles Angels in the second game of a July 25 doubleheader at Wrigley Field. With two months left on the schedule, Graham had had an excellent chance to better Tony Lazzeri's league record of sixty. Even though the Padres rushed Graham back into the lineup a month later, he was only able to hit two more homers the rest of the season.

Top Ten Season Home Run Totals by Players, Active Leagues
Leagues in this section are listed by classification.

AAA—International League II

Rank	HR	Year	Player, Club
1.	63	1930	Joe Hauser, Baltimore
2.	54	1932	Buzz Arlett, Baltimore
3.	53	1935	George Puccinelli, Baltimore
	53	1947	Howie Moss, Baltimore
5.	50	1947	Hank Sauer, Syracuse
6.	45	1938	Ollie Carnegie, Buffalo
7.	44	1926	Bill Kelly, Buffalo
8.	43	1958	Rocky Nelson, Toronto
9.	42	1936	Woody Abernathy, Baltimore
	42	1949	Russ Derry, Rochester

AAA—Mexican League

Rank	HR	Year	Player, Club
1.	54	1986	Jack Pierce, Leon
2.	53	1986	Nick Castaneda, San Luis Potosi
3.	47	1992	Ty Gainey, Mexico City Reds
4.	46	1964	Hector Espino, Monterrey
	46	1986	Willie Aikins, Puebla
6.	45	2000	Eduardo Jimenez, Saltillo
7.	42	1987	Nelson Barrera, Mex. C. Reds
8.	41	1966	Bobby Prescott, Poza Rica
	41	1967	Elrod Hendricks, Jalisco
	41	1984	Derek Bryant, Tampico
	41	1985	Andres Mora, Nuevo Laredo

AAA—Pacific Coast League

Rank	HR	Year	Player, Club
1.	60	1925	Tony Lazzeri, Salt Lake City
2.	56	1935	Gene Lillard, Los Angeles
	56	1957	Steve Bilko, Los Angeles
4.	55	1929	Ike Boone, Mission
	55	1956	Steve Bilko, Los Angeles
	55	1974	Bill McNulty, Sacramento
7.	51	1929	Gus Suhr, San Francisco
	51	1974	Gorman Thomas, Sacramento
9.	50	1982	Ron Kittle, Edmonton
10.	48	1948	Jack Graham, San Diego
	48	1949	Max West, San Diego

AA—Eastern League II

Rank	HR	Year	Player, Club
1.	41	1930	Ken Strong, Hazleton
	41	1979	Rick Lancellotti, Buffalo
3.	40	1981	Ron Kittle, Glen Falls
4.	39	2004	Mitch Jones, Trenton
5.	38	1962	Ken Harrelson, Binghamton
	38	1973	Tom Robson, Pittsfield
	38	1999	Chris Norton, Portland
8.	37	1997	Matt Raleigh, Binghamton
	37	1999	Andy Tracy, Harrisburg
	37	2004	Ryan Howard, Reading

AA—Southern League

Rank	HR	Year	Player, Club
1.	42	1981	Tim Laudner, Orlando
2.	39	1987	Rondal Rollin, Birmingham
3.	37	1971	Ken Hottman, Charlotte
	37	1982	Mike Fuentes, Memphis
	37	1987	Tom Dodd, Charlotte
6.	36	1987	Geronimo Berroa, Knoxville
7.	35	1973	Terry Clapp, Asheville
8.	34	1980	Steve Balboni, Nashville
	34	1982	Brian Dayett, Nashville
	34	1985	Mark Funderburk, Orlando
	34	1996	Derrick Lee, Memphis

AA—Texas League

Rank	HR	Year	Player, Club
1.	62	1956	Ken Guettler, Shreveport
2.	55	1924	Big Boy Kraft, Fort Worth
3.	50	1949	Jerry Witte, Dallas
4.	43	1930	Larry Bettencourt, Wichita Falls
5.	42	1954	Bus Clarkson, Beaumont/Dallas
6.	41	1925	Ed Konetchy, Fort Worth
	41	1953	Bud Heslet, Shreveport
	41	1954	Frank Kellert, San Antonio
	41	1956	Don Demeter, Fort Worth
	41	1963	Arlo Engel, El Paso

A—California League III

Rank	HR	Year	Player, Club
1.	51	1956	Bud Heslet, Visalia
2.	46	1966	Dave Duncan, Modesto
3.	44	1956	Dick Greco, Modesto
	44	1962	Larry Daniels, Bakersfield
5.	43	2005	Richard Wood, Cucamonga
6.	42	1962	Dick Simpson, San Jose
7.	40	1951	Dick Wilson, Modesto
	40	1958	Bart Dupon, Bakersfield
	40	1963	Jose Vidal, Reno
	40	1964	Ollie Brown, Fresno

A—Carolina League

Rank	HR	Year	Player, Club
1.	55	1949	Muscle Shoals, Reidsville
2.	51	1956	Leon Wagner, Danville
3.	49	1968	Tony Solaita, High Pt.-Thom.
4.	41	1946	Gus Zernial, Burlington
5.	38	1949	Woody Fair, Danville
	38	1954	Jim Pokel, Fayetteville
7.	35	1948	Russ Sullivan, Danville
	35	1949	Emile Showfety, Greensboro
	35	1960	Ed Oliveres, Winston-Salem
10.	34	1981	Gerald Davis, Salem
	34	1997	Dan Peoples, Kinston

GOING FOR THE FENCES

A—Florida State League

Rank	HR	Year	Player, Club
1.	33	1950	Ed Levy, Sanford
	33	1971	Jim Fuller, Miami
3.	32	2004	Brandon Sing, Daytona
4.	30	1992	Carlos Delgado, Dunedin
5.	29	2000	Rob Stratton, St. Lucie
	29	2008	Ryan Strieby, Lakeland
7.	28	2005	Andrew Wilson, St. Lucie
8.	27	1972	Jack Baker, Winter Haven
	27	2000	Kevin Mench, Charlotte
	27	2005	Matthew Kemp, Vero Beach
	27	2008	Brian Dopirak, Dunedin

A—Midwest League

Rank	HR	Year	Player, Club
1.	42	1982	Jeff Jones, Cedar Rapids
2.	41	1977	Moe Hill, Wisconsin Rapids
3.	39	2004	Brian Dopirak, Lansing
4.	38	1999	Aaron McNeal, Michigan
5.	35	1981	Glen Walker, Wausau
	35	1986	Luis Medina, Waterloo
7.	34	1978	Bill Foley, Burlington
	34	1994	Matt Raleigh, Burlington
	34	1995	Jesus Ibarra, Burlington
10.	33	1987	Greg Vaughn, Beloit
	33	1997	Joe Freitas, Peoria
	33	2004	Kevin Collins, Lansing

A—New York-Pennsylvania League II

Rank	HR	Year	Player, Club
1.	23	1982	John Hennell, Utica
2.	22	1982	Dave Cochrane, Little Falls
	22	1982	Rolando Roomes, Geneva
	22	1983	Don Jacoby, Utica
	22	1999	Dan Grummitt, Hudson Valley
6.	21	1969	Larry Mansfield, Williamsport
	21	1977	Tim Glass, Batavia
8.	20	1982	Wesley Kent, Niagara Falls
9.	19	1976	Gary Holle, Newark
	19	1981	Bob Gilles, Little Falls
	19	1982	Jason Felice, Little Falls
	19	1984	Bernardo Brito, Batavia

A—Northwest League II

Rank	HR	Year	Player, Club
1.	25	1980	Willie Darkis, Central Oregon
2.	21	1996	Steve Hacker, Eugene
3.	20	1998	Jason Hart, South Oregon
4.	19	1996	Rob Zachman, Everett
5.	18	1996	Kit Pellow, Spokane
6.	17	11 players tied	

A—South Atlantic League

Rank	HR	Year	Player, Club
1.	40	1996	Russell Branyan, Columbus
2.	39	1987	Mike Simms, Asheville
	39	2008	Michael Stanton, Greensboro
4.	37	1998	Marcus Giles, Macon
5.	36	2005	Joe Koshansky, Asheville
6.	33	1997	Steve Hacker, Macon
7.	32	1995	Derrick Gibson, Asheville
	32	1995	Ron Wright, Macon
	32	2004	Jon Benick, Hickory
10.	30	2001	Jason Kinchen, Greensboro
	30	2004	Ian Stewart, Asheville
	30	2005	Matt Miller, Asheville
	30	2007	Ryan Royster, Columbus

R—Appalachian League II

Rank	HR	Year	Player, Club
1.	24	1960	Joy Gritts, Wytheville
	24	2004	Mitch Einerston, Greenville
3.	22	1990	Paul Russo, Elizabethton
4.	20	1964	Ross Moschetto, Johnson City
	20	1965	Richard Hense, Wytheville
6.	19	1974	Fay Thompson, Covington
	19	1991	Manuel Ramirez, Burlington
8.	18	Nine players tied	

R—Arizona Rookie League

Rank	HR	Year	Player, Club
1.	16	2003	Wladimir Balentien, Mariners
2.	14	2007	Andrew D'Alessio, Giants
3.	13	1999	Luis Garcia, Mexico
4.	12	1999	Joel Noboa, Diamondbacks
5.	11	1997	Jesus Basabe, Athletics
6.	10	2004	Miguel Vega, Royals
7.	9	Ten players tied	

R—Gulf Coast Rookie League

Rank	HR	Year	Player, Club
1.	13	1996	Derrick Bly, Cubs
	13	2000	Bryan Barnowski, Red Sox
	13	2000	Tony Bianco, Red Sox
4.	12	1998	Juan Rivera, Yankees
5.	11	1995	Gary Coffee, Royals
	11	2006	Christopher Carlson, Tigers
	11	2008	Abner Abreu, Indians
8.	10	Eight players tied	

Top Ten Season Home Run Totals by Players, Active Leagues (cont.)

Leagues in this section are listed by classification.

R—Pioneer League II

Rank	HR	Year	Player, Club
1.	23	1997	Greg Morrison, Medicine Hat
2.	21	1977	Mike Zouras, Lethbridge
3.	20	1968	Steve Garvey, Ogden
	20	1978	Ed Packard, Idaho Falls
	20	1979	Willie Darkis, Helena
	20	1982	Cecil Fielder, Butte
	20	1983	Tom Krupa, Calgary
	20	2007	Brandon Waring, Billings
9.	19		Five players tied

Dominican Summer League

Rank	HR	Year	Player, Club
1.	19	1996	Julio Silvestre, Mariners
2.	18	1994	Jose Amado, Mariners
	18	1994	Carlos Soriano, Mets
	18	1994	Miguel Tejada, Athletics
5.	16	1994	Jose Luis Castro, Mariners
6.	15	1993	Carlos Adolfo, Expos
	15	1995	Ignacio Suero, Blue Jays
	15	1996	Henry de la Cruz, Cubs-Padres
9.	14	1992	Lorenzo de la Cruz, Blue Jays E.
	14	1994	Miguel Jiminez, Mariners
	14	1996	Danny Cabrera, Mets

GOING FOR THE FENCES

Top Ten Season Home Run Totals by Players, Defunct Leagues
This list includes all defunct leagues that operated for a long period of time, plus other well-known leagues.

Alabama–Florida League

Rank	HR	Year	Player, Club
1.	40	1956	Neb Wilson, Donaldsonville
2.	37	1955	Charles Grant, Donaldsonville
3.	32	1941	Forrest Austin, Tallassee
	32	1955	Neb Wilson, Crestview
5.	31	1940	Gordon Goodell, Tallassee
	31	1954	John Streza, Ft. Walton Beach
	31	1955	Charles Tulner, Ft. Walton Beach
8.	30	1940	John Ostrowski, Troy
	30	1957	Bob Wellman, Graceville
10.	27	1953	Charles Quimby, Ft. Walt./Grvl.
	27	1957	Bob Zuccarini, Pensacola

American Association

Rank	HR	Year	Player, Club
1.	69	1933	Joe Hauser, Minneapolis
2.	54	1930	Nick Cullop, Minneapolis
3.	50	1936	Tom Winsett, Columbus
4.	49	1932	Joe Hauser, Minneapolis
5.	46	1939	Vince DiMaggio, Kansas City
	46	1946	Jerry Witte, Toledo
	46	1982	Ken Phelps, Wichita
8.	43	1935	Johnny Gill, Minneapolis
	43	1938	Ted Williams, Minneapolis
10.	42	1921	Bunny Brief, Kansas City
	42	1936	Chet Laabs, Milwaukee
	42	1956	Marv Thronberry, Denver
	42	1976	Roger Freed, Denver

Appalachian League I

Rank	HR	Year	Player, Club
1.	33	1955	Mike Coppola, Wytheville
	33	1955	Muscle Shoals, Kingsport
3.	32	1947	Muscle Shoals, Kingsport
4.	31	1947	Homer Moore, Bluefield
5.	30	1951	Muscle Shoals, Kingsport
6.	27	1953	Dick Stanton, Johnson City
	27	1955	Harry Keister, Johnson City
8.	26	1950	Don Boring, Elizabethton
	26	1953	William Hopkins, Johnson City
	26	1954	Bob Quinn, Pulaski

Arizona–Texas League

Rank	HR	Year	Player, Club
1.	47	1954	Claudio Solano, Cananea
2.	45	1952	Marv Williams, Chihuahua
	45	1954	Richard Hogan, Tuscon
	45	1956	Claudio Solano, Cananea
5.	39	1956	Arnaldo Bachelier, Nogales
	39	1956	John Haley, Tuscon
7.	38	1947	Pete Hughes, Phoenix
	38	1955	Humberto Barbon, Nogales/Yuma
9.	37	1949	Gene Clough, Bisbee-Douglas
	37	1954	Bill Jackson, Phoenix
	37	1955	Ralph Wilcox, Phoenix

Big State League

Rank	HR	Year	Player, Club
1.	58	1947	Buck Frierson, Sherman-Denison
2.	57	1947	Pud Miller, Wichita Falls
3.	47	1952	Dean Stafford, Paris/Tyler
	47	1955	Keith Little, Corpus Christi
5.	45	1952	Roy Sanner, Texarkana
6.	40	1947	Larry Drake, Sherman-Denison
	40	1947	Jim Matthews, Wichita Falls
8.	39	1947	Milan Vucelich, Greenville
	39	1950	Johnny Powers, Waco
	39	1952	Bob Moyer, Temple
	39	1953	Albert Neil, Wichita Falls

Cotton States League

Rank	HR	Year	Player, Club
1.	41	1953	Harold Martin, Hot Springs
2.	40	1930	Ralph Winegarner, El Dorado
3.	32	1939	Al Gardella, Hot Springs
4.	29	1936	Milt Stroner, El Dorado
	29	1941	Merv Connors, Texarkana
	29	1953	Bill Adair, El Dorado
7.	28	1929	Stormy Davis, Lake Charles
	28	1954	Pelham Austin, El Dorado
9.	27	1947	Floyd Fogg, Clarkesdale
	27	1951	Pete Konyar, Pine Bluff
	27	1953	Lou Schaufele, Jackson
	27	1954	Frank Walenga, El Dorado

Top Ten Season Home Run Totals by Players, Defunct Leagues (cont.)

This list includes all defunct leagues that operated for a long period of time, plus other well-known leagues.

East Texas League

Rank	HR	Year	Player, Club
1.	62	1926	Moose Clabaugh, Tyler
2.	41	1925	Jack Holloway, Tyler
3.	38	1938	Tony Robello, Jacksonville
4.	35	1924	Pete Daniels, Marshall
5.	31	1923	Lillard Belcher, Marshall/Paris
	31	1925	Moose Clabaugh, Paris
	31	1938	Lou Frierson, Marshall/Kilgore
8.	30	1926	Randy Moore, Longview
	30	1946	Frank Sacka, Paris
10.	28	1924	Jack Holloway, Tyler
	28	1925	George Watkins, Marshall
	28	1937	Tony Robello, Jacksonville

Eastern League I

Rank	HR	Year	Player, Club
1.	44	1923	Walter Simpson, Springfield
2.	41	1929	Bruce Caldwell, New Haven
3.	38	1924	John Roser, Worcester
	38	1931	Bruce Caldwell, New Haven
5.	37	1924	Lou Gehrig, Hartford
6.	33	1923	Harry Damrau, Springfield
7.	30	1929	Harold Yordy, Albany
8.	27	1928	John Roser, Hartford
9.	25	1924	Walter Simpson, Springfield
	25	1929	Joe Cicero, Pittsfield
	25	1929	John Roser, Hartford

Eastern Shore League

Rank	HR	Year	Player, Club
1.	33	1948	Norm Zauchin, Milford
2.	31	1938	Bill Phillips, Federalsburg
3.	29	1939	Henry Schluter, Dover
	29	1946	Don Marshall, Dover
	29	1947	Ducky Detweiler, Federalsburg
6.	28	1938	Jim Conlan, Salisbury
	28	1938	Henry Schluter, Pocomoke City
	28	1939	Francis Walsh, Centerville
	28	1947	John Werner, Dover
10.	27	1923	Charles Tolson

Evangeline League

Rank	HR	Year	Player, Club
1.	47	1936	Cecil Dunn, Alexandria
2.	42	1951	Remy LeBlanc, New Iberia
	42	1953	Al Meriwether, Crowley
	42	1954	Remy LeBlanc, New Iberia
5.	39	1950	Robert Dunn, Hammond
6.	38	1936	Frank Narbut, Rayne
7.	37	1954	Roy Sanner, Port Arthur
8.	34	1936	Arthur Bartelli, Rayne
	34	1948	Roy Sanner, Houma
10.	33	1936	Dan Pavlovic, Rayne
	33	1951	Bob Akenhead, Hammond
	33	1952	Al Meriwether, Crowley
	33	1954	Roger McKee, Baton Rouge

Georgia–Florida League

Rank	HR	Year	Player, Club
1.	32	1958	Bob Boyer, Albany
2.	30	1956	Bob Wellman, Moultrie
3.	29	1951	Glenn Eury, Moultrie
4.	27	1948	Ken Rhyne, Moultrie
5.	26	1937	Tom Corbett, Thomasville
	26	1957	Jim Hickman, Albany
	26	1962	Glen Clark, Dublin
8.	24	1947	Ken Rhyne, Moultrie
	24	1956	Charles Riddle, Albany
10.	23	1956	Don Whitcomb, Brunswick

Inter-State League

Rank	HR	Year	Player, Club
1.	37	1947	Ed Sanicki, Wilmington
2.	30	1944	John Cappa, Allentown
	30	1946	Ed Sanicki, Wilmington
	30	1952	Lou Heyman, Wilmington
5.	29	1952	Jack Tanner, Salisbury
6.	28	1946	Ed Sudol, Allentown
7.	27	1942	Tom Koval, Allentown
	27	1949	Jim Lemon, Harrisburg
9.	25	1947	Frank Heckinger, Allentown
	25	1947	Bob McLean, Allentown
	25	1948	Maurice Cunningham, Trenton

Kitty League

Rank	HR	Year	Player, Club
1.	34	1940	Edward Urban, Owensboro
2.	33	1939	John Newman, Owensboro
3.	32	1946	Ray Fletcher, Owensboro
4.	31	1946	Paul Zubak, Mayfield
5.	30	1939	Vern Stephens, Mayfield
	30	1941	Melvin Merkle, Jackson
7.	28	1946	Elmer Rambert, Cairo
	28	1950	Ned Waldrop, Fulton
9.	27	1940	Newt Parker, Jackson
	27	1940	Joe Polcha, Jackson

Longhorn League

Rank	HR	Year	Player, Club
1.	72	1954	Joe Bauman, Roswell
2.	53	1953	Joe Bauman, Artesia
3.	50	1952	Joe Bauman, Artesia
4.	46	1955	Joe Bauman, Roswell
5.	44	1950	Tom Jordan, Roswell
6.	43	1954	Lewis Hull, Artesia/Midland
7.	39	1955	Alfredo Jimenez, Midland
8.	38	1953	Glenn Burns, San Angelo
9.	37	1947	Bob Cowsar, Sweetwater
	37	1954	Bob Hobbs, Carlsbad/San Angelo

Middle Atlantic League

Rank	HR	Year	Player, Club
1.	38	1931	Frank Welch, Beckley
2.	36	1949	Joe Beran, Johnstown
3.	35	1936	Walter Alston, Huntington
	35	1938	Frank Silvanic, Akron
5.	34	1937	Frank Scalzi, Springfield
	34	1951	Rudy York, Oil City/New Castle
7.	31	1930	Hal Stricklin, Charloi
8.	29	1930	Bill Pritchard, Johnstown
	29	1932	Fred Sington, Beckley
	29	1937	Hugh Alexander, Springfield

New England League

Rank	HR	Year	Player, Club
1.	34	1894	Buck Freeman, Haverhill
2.	30	1948	Jim Pokel, Portland
3.	25	1893	Abe Lizotte, Lewiston
	25	1896	Ed Breckinridge, Brockton
	25	1896	George Yeager, Pawtucket
	25	1947	Ralph Atkins, Lynn
7.	24	1933	Amit Savard, Lowell
	24	1947	Clint Dahlberg, Lowell/Fall River
	24	1947	Pete Shurman, Providence
10.	22	1894	John Anderson, Worcester/Haver.
	22	1946	Lucien Belanger, Lawrence

New York-Pennsylvania League I

Rank	HR	Year	Player, Club
1.	37	1962	Bob Guindon, Olean
	37	1964	Bill Schlesinger, Wellsville
3.	36	1961	Roberto Sanchez, Batavia
	36	1964	Danny Napoleon, Auburn
5.	35	1961	Arthur Blunt, Batavia
6.	32	1958	Ray Withrow, Wellsville
	32	1962	Brant Alyea, Geneva
	32	1963	Byron Browne, Batavia
9.	30	1963	Bob Sturges, Auburn
10.	29	1963	Tom DeHart, Geneva
	29	1965	Lewis Dorsch, Wellsville

North Carolina State League

Rank	HR	Year	Player, Club
1.	41	1949	Norm Small, Mooresville
2.	40	1951	Pud Miller, Hickory
3.	37	1951	Norm Small, Hickory
4.	33	1948	Harold Harrigan, Salisbury
	33	1948	Norm Small, Mooresville
	33	1951	Len Cross, Statesville
7.	32	1942	Norm Small, Mooresville
	32	1948	Otis Stephens, Hickory
	32	1950	Ken Rhyne, Statesville
	32	1950	Norm Small, Mooresville

Northern League

Rank	HR	Year	Player, Club
1.	56	1954	Frank Gravino, Fargo-Moorhead
2.	52	1953	Frank Gravino, Fargo-Moorhead
3.	48	1936	Cal Lahman, Jamestown
4.	37	1936	Chester Wieczorek, Duluth
5.	36	1934	Gus Koch, Fargo-Moorhead
6.	35	1959	Harold Jones, Minot
	35	1959	Dave Nicholson, Aberdeen
8.	33	1954	Dave Roberts, Aberdeen
9.	32	1952	Frank Gravino, Fargo-Moorhead
10.	31		Five players tied

Northwest League I

Rank	HR	Year	Player, Club
1.	43	1949	Jim Warner, Wenatchee
2.	40	1946	Bill Barisoff, Bremerton
3.	37	1939	Morry Abbott, Tacoma
	37	1946	Dick Adams, Wenatchee
	37	1964	John Warner, Tri-City
6.	36	1947	Jack Harshman, Victoria
	36	1950	Dick Greco, Tacoma
	36	1956	Vince Moreci, Yakima
9.	34	1941	Pete Hughes, Spokane
10.	33	1947	Frank Mullens, Vancouver
	33	1948	Bill Wilson, Wenatchee
	33	1949	Dick Greco, Tacoma
	33	1964	Clarence Jones, Salem

Piedmont League

Rank	HR	Year	Player, Club
1.	46	1929	Dan Boone, High Point
2.	45	1929	Clay Parrish, Greensboro
3.	41	1955	Ken Guettler, Portsmouth
4.	40	1939	Russ Derry, Norfolk
5.	39	1930	Tom Wolfe, Durham
6.	38	1928	Dan Boone, High Point
	38	1936	Jim Bryan, Norfolk
	38	1938	Bobby Estalella, Charlotte
	38	1939	Ken Sears, Norfolk
10.	37	1930	Jack Lindley, Durham

Top Ten Season Home Run Totals by Players, Defunct Leagues (cont.)

This list includes all defunct leagues that operated for a long period of time, plus other well-known leagues.

Pioneer League I

Rank	HR	Year	Player, Club
1.	58	1939	Tony Robello, Pocatello
2.	41	1939	Pete Hughes, Ogden
3.	40	1961	Bobby Sanders, Magic Valley
4.	37	1960	Ray Reed, Boise
	37	1962	Hank Allen, Magic Valley
	37	1962	Felix DeLeon, Billings
7.	36	1939	Walt Lowe, Boise
8.	35	1958	Chuck Weatherspoon, Missoula
	35	1963	Alex Johnson, Magic Valley
10.	33	1962	Adolfo Phillips, Magic Valley

Pony League

Rank	HR	Year	Player, Club
1.	45	1954	Ted Sepkowski, Wellsville
2.	37	1953	Ted Sepkowski, Wellsville
3.	32	1956	George Lewis, Corning
4.	29	1941	John Newman, Jamestown
5.	28	1947	Jim Pokel, Bradford
6.	27	1942	John Newman, Jamestown
	27	1951	Ray Reed, Wellsville
8.	25	1940	Lawrence Mancini, Olean
	25	1951	Bill Hudacsek, Olean
	25	1956	Sheldon Brodsky, Hornell

South Atlantic League

Before changing name to Southern League in 1964.

Rank	HR	Year	Player, Club
1.	39	1927	Bob Barrett, Knoxville
	39	1930	Jim Hudgens, Graeenville
3.	36	1962	Dick Means, Charlotte/Asheville
4.	35	1926	Roy Moore, Greenville
5.	33	1928	Tilly Walker, Greenville
	33	1951	Dick Greco, Montgomery
7.	32	1927	Tex Shirley, Greenville
	32	1959	Cliff Cook, Savannah
9.	29	1925	Pete Daniels, Greenville
	29	1929	Frank Welch, Greenville

Southeastern League

Rank	HR	Year	Player, Club
1.	39	1939	Prince Oana, Jackson
2.	35	1950	Neb Wilson, Pensacola
3.	34	1927	Clay Parrish, Columbus
4.	33	1946	Roy Pinkston, Gadsden
5.	31	1950	Arthur Seguso, Meridian
6.	28	1926	Clay Parrish, Columbus
	28	1927	Jack Kloza, Albany
8.	27	1947	Bill Johnson, Gadsden
9.	26	1938	Prince Oana, Jackson
	26	1939	Arthur Bartelli, Anniston

Southern Association

Rank	HR	Year	Player, Club
1.	64	1954	Bob Lennon, Nashville
2.	52	1948	Chuck Workman, Nashville
3.	50	1930	Jim Poole, Nashville
4.	47	1951	Jack Harshman, Nashville
5.	45	1949	Carl Sawatski, Nashville
6.	42	1948	Charley Gilbert, Nashville
	42	1949	Babe Barna, Nashville
8.	40	1930	Jay Partridge, Nashville
9.	39	1954	Bob Montag, Atlanta
	39	1956	Johnny Powers, New Orleans

Three I League

Rank	HR	Year	Player, Club
1.	38	1955	John Romano, Waterloo
2.	37	1958	Frank Howard, Green Bay
3.	35	1954	Ed Barbarito, Quincy
4.	33	1942	Pat Seerey, Cedar Rapids
5.	32	1954	Roger Maris, Keokuk
6.	31	1957	Jim Koranda, Cedar Rapids
7.	30	1926	Al Maderas, Springfield
	30	1930	Moose Clabaugh, Quincy
	30	1953	Marv Throneberry, Quincy
10.	29	1940	Chuck Workman, Cedar Rapids
	29	1953	Ed Barbarito, Quincy
	29	1957	Jim Johnston, Peoria

Virginia League

Rank	HR	Year	Player, Club
1.	44	1926	Stan Stack, Richmond
2.	38	1925	Blackie Carter, Richmond
3.	35	1926	Dave Robertson, Norfolk
4.	34	1951	Ken Hatcher, Petersburg/Emporia
5.	33	1924	Ed Konetchy, Petersburg
6.	32	1950	Ken Hatcher, Petersburg
7.	31	1942	Wes Ferrell, Lynchburg
	31	1948	Morris Aderholt, Emporia
	31	1951	Harold Martin, Emporia
10.	30	1926	Ed Mooers, Richmond
	30	1950	Gordon Giebel, Suffolk

West Texas-New Mexico League

Rank	HR	Year	Player, Club
1.	69	1948	Bob Crues, Amarillo
2.	57	1947	Bill Serena, Lubbock
3.	52	1947	Bob Crues, Amarillo
	52	1949	Pud Miller, Lamesa
5.	50	1953	Jim Matthews, Amarillo
6.	49	1947	Gordon Nell, Borger
7.	48	1946	Joe Bauman, Amarillo
	48	1953	Bob Featherstone, Lubbock
9.	47	1952	Merv Connors, Amarillo
10.	45	1952	Les Mulcahy, Amarillo

Western Association III

Rank	HR	Year	Player, Club
1.	51	1924	Stormy Davis, Okmulgee
	51	1924	Wilbur Davis, Okmulgee
3.	44	1931	Gordon Nell, Muskogee
4.	43	1917	Ernie Calbert, Muskogee
5.	41	1924	Lee Dempsey, Hutchinson
6.	39	1924	Sam Lemen, Hutchinson
7.	38	1939	Harry Goorabian, Topeka
8.	37	1953	Joe Beran, Hutchinson
	37	1954	Al Kubski, Blackwell
10.	36	1923	Chili McDaniel, Enid
	36	1926	John Reider, Springfield
	36	1928	Paul Richards, Muskogee

Western League III

Rank	HR	Year	Player, Club
1.	49	1926	Guy Sturdy, Tulsa
2.	48	1924	Mule Washburn, Tulsa
3.	42	1924	Yank Davis, Tulsa
	42	1928	Jim Stroner, Wichita
5.	41	1920	Yam Yaryan, Wichita
6.	40	1924	Nick Cullop, Omaha
7.	39	1926	Jim Blakesley, Omaha
	39	1928	Joe Munson, Tulsa
9.	38	1924	Fred Beck, Wichita
	38	1931	Stan Keyes, Des Moines

Western League IV

Rank	HR	Year	Player, Club
1.	66	1956	Dick Stuart, Lincoln
2.	49	1956	Al Weygandt, Topeka
3.	46	1956	Art Cuitti, Amarillo
4.	44	1950	Pat Seerey, Colorado Springs
5.	43	1957	Len Williams, Topeka
6.	42	1956	Lawrence Stankey, Pueblo
7.	41	1957	Jim Pokel, Topeka
8.	40	1955	Willie Kirkland, Sioux City
9.	37	1956	Dick DiTusa, Colorado Springs
	37	1958	Dan Lynk, Sioux City

Western Carolinas League

Rank	HR	Year	Player, Club
1.	43	1948	Floyd Yount, Newton-Conover
2.	35	1966	Luis Lagunas, Thomasville
3.	34	1948	George DePillo, Newton-Conover
4.	33	1969	Earl Williams, Greenwood
5.	32	1965	Bob Robertson, Gastonia
6.	31	1979	Hediberto Vargas, Shelby
7.	28	1974	John Guarnaccia, Spartanburg
8.	27	1950	Bob Featherstone, Lenoir
	27	1966	Charles Howard, Gastonia
	27	1969	Dalton Renfroe, Shelby

Jim Pokel made the Top Ten list in four different leagues: Pony, New England, Carolina and Western IV.

First Players with 20 HR, 30 HR, 40 HR, 50 HR, and 60 HR Seasons

First 20 Home Run Seasons

Year	HR	Player
1887	28	Walt Andrews
1889	27	Charlie Reilly
1889	25	John Carroll
1889	25	Joe Werrick
1889	23	Bill Joyce
1889	22	Lew Whistler
1889	20	Elmer Cleveland
1890	21	John Carroll
1892	20	Ed Breckinridge
1893	25	Abe Lizotte

First 30 Home Run Seasons

Year	HR	Player
1894	43	Perry Werden
1894	34	Henry Hines
1894	33	Joe Strauss
1894	32	Frank Burrell
1894	31	Buck Freeman
1894	31	Bill Klusman
1895	45	Perry Werden
1895	37	Dan Lally
1895	32	Joe Werrick
1897	31	Jimmy Williams

First 40 Home Run Seasons

Year	HR	Player
1894	43	Perry Werden
1895	45	Perry Werden
1917	43	Ernie Calbert
1920	41	Yam Yaryan
1921	42	Bunny Brief
1922	40	Bunny Brief
1923	49	Moses Solomon
1923	44	Walt Simpson
1923	43	Paul Strand
1924	55	Big Boy Kraft

First 50 Home Run Seasons

Year	HR	Player
1924	55	Big Boy Kraft
1924	51	Stormy Davis
1924	51	Wilbur Davis
1925	60	Tony Lazzeri
1926	62	Moose Clabaugh
1929	55	Ike Boone
1929	51	Gus Suhr
1929	50	Ed Kallina
1930	63	Joe Hauser
1930	54	Nick Cullop

First 60 Home Run Seasons

Year	HR	Player
1925	60	Tony Lazzeri
1926	62	Moose Clabaugh
1930	63	Joe Hauser
1933	69	Joe Hauser
1948	69	Bob Crues
1954	72	Joe Bauman
1954	64	Bob Lennon
1956	66	Dick Stuart
1956	62	Ken Guettler
1956	60	Frosty Kennedy

The Most 20 HR, 30 HR, 40 HR, 50 HR, and 60 HR Seasons

The Most 20 HR Seasons

Number	Player
12	Merv Conners
12	Nick Cullop
12	Hector Espino
12	Andres Mora
11	Buzz Arlett
11	Jack Graham
10	Nelson Barrera
10	Dick Greco
10	Tedd Gullic
10	Ted Norbert
10	Alejandro Ortiz
10	Kit Pellow
10	Lin Storti
10	Ray Torres

The Most 30 HR Seasons

Number	Player
8	Buzz Arlett
6	Joe Bauman
6	Jack Graham
6	Joe Hauser
6	Gordon Nell
6	Alejandro Ortiz
6	Norm Small

The Most 40 HR Seasons

Number	Player
5	Joe Bauman
5	Gordon Nell
3	Frank Gravino
3	Joe Hauser
3	Keith Little
3	Pud Miller
3	Claudio Solano

The Most 50 HR Seasons

Number	Player
3	Joe Bauman
2	Steve Bilko
2	Bob Crues
2	Frank Gravino
2	Joe Hauser
2	Pud Miller

The Most 60 HR Seasons

Number	Player
2	Joe Hauser

Top Twenty-five Career Home Run Averages

HR Average is the rate of home runs per 600 at bats. See Introduction for more detailed explanation of Home Run Average. Minimum of 200 home runs.

Rank	HR Avg	HR	Player
1	58.39	337	Joe Bauman
2	48.52	222	Dick Stuart
3	43.28	232	Bob Crues
4	41.50	271	Frank Gravino
5	41.05	239	Steve Balboni
6	40.41	365	Gordon Nell
7	40.33	268	Pud Miller
8	40.01	202	Carl Sawatski
9	39.90	220	Willie Darkis
10	39.71	212	Ramiro Caballero
11	38.89	269	Luke Easter
12	38.06	284	Pete Hughes
13	37.31	272	Willie Aikens
14	37.25	399	Joe Hauser
15	37.00	238	Randy Bass
16	36.68	330	Ken Guettler
17	36.53	216	Nick Castaneda
18	36.39	244	Roger Freed
19	36.03	201	Marv Throneberry
20	35.36	333	Dick Greco
21	35.33	264	Keith Little
22	35.29	280	Al Meriwether
23	35.11	313	Steve Bilko
24	35.01	243	Tony Robello
25	35.00	236	Len Tucker

Notes

- Joe Bauman's home run average of 58.39 is nothing short of amazing. For every 600 at bats during his career, he hit more than 58 home runs. To put it in another perspective, if we compress Joe Bauman's 3,463 at bats into about six full seasons, he would have averaged more than 58 home runs per year. And he outdistanced his next rival on the list by an average of nearly ten home runs.

- Dick Stuart, the number two hitter on the list, is somewhat of a surprise. Stuart does not readily come to mind when thinking of great minor league home run hitters, though he did have that great 1956 season.

- Although the era of great home run hitting in the minors ended more than thirty years ago, there are several fairly recent players that made the list. Steve Balboni, Willie Aikens and Nick Castaneda all played in the 1990s; while Willie Darkis, Randy Bass and Roger Freed played as recently as the 1980s.

- For comparison, the major league list is headed up by, of course, Babe Ruth with an average of slightly more than 51. And seven other players (200 HR minimum) have reached the 40 mark.

GOING FOR THE FENCES

Players with a Home Run Average of 60.00 or Higher for a Season

HR Avg is the rate of home runs per 600 at bats. See Introduction for a more detailed explanation of Home Run Average. A minimum of 30 home runs is required for this list. Averages are carried out to more than two decimal places to resolve ties in ranking. Several players on this list played in more than one league during the season. Only the league in which they hit thirty or more home runs is included.

Rank	HR Avg	HR	Year	Player	Club, League
1.	99.06	35	2000	Alex Cabrera	El Paso, Texas League
2.	86.75	72	1954	Joe Bauman	Roswell, Longhorn League
3.	83.78	62	1926	Moose Clabaugh	Tyler, East Texas League
4.	83.69	59	1962	Ramiro Caballero	Guanajuato, Mexican Center League
5.	80.30	53	1986	Nick Castaneda	San Luis Potosi, Mexican League
6.	80.21	52	1949	Pud Miller	Lamesa, West Texas-New Mexico League
7.	77.47	47	1955	Keith Little	Corpus Christi, Big State League
8.	77.34	62	1956	Ken Guettler	Shreveport, Texas League
9.	75.97	49	1950	Manuel Salvatierra	Laredo, Rio Grande Valley League
10.	75.75	66	1956	Dick Stuart	Lincoln, Western League
11.	75.51	37	1950	Andy Gilbert	Springfield, Ohio-Indiana League
12.	74.18	45	1949	Ray Perry	Redding, Far West League
13.	73.27	69	1948	Bob Crues	Amarillo, West Texas-New Mexico League
14.	72.63	69	1933	Joe Hauser	Minneapolis, American Association
15.	71.93	44	1929	Ed Kallina	Midland, West Texas
16.	70.78	44	1950	Pat Seerey	Colorado Springs, Western League
17.	70.23	35	2004	Calvin Pickering	Omaha, Pacific Coast League
18.	69.63	47	1992	Ty Gainey	Mexico City Reds, Mexican League
19.	69.47	33	2005	Jorge Vazquez	Angelopolis, Mexican League
20.	69.30	41	1984	Derek Bryant	Tampico, Mexican League
21.	68.99	33	1934	Joe Hauser	Minneapolis, American Association
22.	68.68	53	1953	Joe Bauman	Artesia, Longhorn League
23.	68.64	58	1939	Tony Robello	Pocatello, Pioneer League
24.	68.61	55	1966	Heriberto Vargas	Guanajuato, Mexican Center
25.	68.21	54	1986	Jack Pierce	Leon, Mexican League
26.	68.01	45	1952	Marvin Williams	Chihuahua, Arizona-Texas League
27.	67.59	57	1947	Bill Serena	Lubbock, West Texas-New Mexico League
28.	67.07	56	1954	Frank Gravino	Fargo-Moorhead, Northern League
29.	66.24	52	1953	Frank Gravino	Fargo-Moorhead, Northern League
30.	65.87	55	1949	Muscle Shoals	Reidsville, Carolina League
31.	65.59	45	1954	Ted Sepkowski	Wellsville, Pony League
32.	65.42	35	1987	Hediberto Vargas	Aguascalientes, Mexican League
33.	64.91	37	1936	John Clements	Tiffin, Ohio State League
34.	64.90	45	2000	Eduardo Jimenez	Salitllo, Mexican League
35.	64.56	51	1974	Gorman Thomas	Sacramento, Pacific Coast League
36.	64.18	43	1948	Floyd Yount	Newton-Conover, Western Carolinas League
37.	64.06	60	1956	Frosty Kennedy	Plainview, Southwestern League
38.	63.97	50	1952	Joe Bauman	Artesia, Longhorn League
39.	63.56	50	1982	Ron Kittle	Edmonton, Pacific Coast League
40.	63.42	50	1953	Jim Matthews	Amarillo, West Texas-New Mexico League
41.	63.32	42	1976	Roger Freed	Denver, American Association
42.	63.05	64	1954	Bob Lennon	Nashville, Southern Association
43.	62.96	49	1968	Tony Solaita	High Point-Thomasville, Carolina League
44.	62.91	54	1930	Nick Cullop	Minneapolis, American Association
45.	62.87	46	1966	Dave Duncan	Modesto, California League
46.	62.79	54	1932	Buzz Arlett	Baltimore, International League
47.	62.74	55	1974	Bill McNulty	Sacramento, Pacific Coast League
48.	62.69	56	1957	Steve Bilko	Los Angeles, Pacific Coast League
49.	62.65	45	1949	Carl Sawatski	Nashville, Southern Association
50.	62.63	31	1968	Brandt Alyea	Buffalo, International League
51.	62.02	46	1986	Willie Aikens	Puebla, Mexican League

Players with a Home Run Average of 60.00 or Higher for a Season (cont.)

Rank	HR Avg	HR	Year	Player	Club, League
52.	62.02	40	1952	Len Cross	Big Stone Gap, Mountain States League
53.	61.84	57	1947	Pud Miller	Wichita Falls, Big State League
54.	61.80	48	1936	Cal Lahman	Jamestown, Northern League
55.	61.70	40	1981	Ron Kittle	Glens Falls, Eastern League
56.	61.64	49	1956	Al Weygandt	Topeka, Western League
57.	61.34	32	1982	Steve Balboni	Columbus, International League
58.	61.33	37	1949	Vince DiMaggio	Pittsburg, Far West League
59.	61.26	63	1930	Joe Hauser	Baltimore, International League
60.	61.10	39	2000	Roberto Zambrano	Cancun, Mexican League
61.	60.96	38	1931	Frank Welch	Beckley, Middle Atlantic League
62.	60.93	46	1955	Joe Bauman	Roswell, Longhorn League
63.	60.93	46	1982	Ken Phelps	Wichita, American Association
64.	60.89	48	1948	Jack Graham	San Diego, Pacific Coast League
65.	60.55	44	2001	Phil Hiatt	Las Vegas, Pacific Coast League
66.	60.23	53	1947	Howie Moss	Baltimore, International League

- Joe Bauman made the list four times. Joe Hauser is on the list three times and Frank Gravino, Ron Kittle and Pud Miller each made it twice.
- Tony Lazzeri is the only player with sixty or more homers in a season who didn't make the list. He had 60 home runs in 710 at bats in 1925 for a HR Avg of 50.70.
- Bob Seeds started the 1938 season with Newark in the strong International League and hit 28 home runs, two short of qualifying for this list. He played in 59 games and had 230 at bats to give him a HR Avg of 73.04. Newark was the top farm club of the New York Yankees and the Yankees were loaded with good hitters so they sold Seeds to the New York Giants in June.
- Alex Cabrera, playing for El Paso of the Texas League, went on a tear early in the 2000 season. He hit 35 home runs in only 212 at bats for an amazing 99.06 HR Avg. His home run total was good enough to lead the league. Cabrera started the season with Tucson of the Pacific Coast League and was demoted to El Paso at the end of April. In 53 games with El Paso, he hit .382 and had 82 runs batted in to go with his 35 homers. During a six game stretch from May 9 through May 14, he was 16 for 27 with nine home runs, twelve runs, twenty runs batted in and a batting average of .593. He had at least two hits and a homer in each of the six games. During one period during the spree he hit five home runs in six at bats.

He was brought up to the Arizona Diamondbacks in late June and it appeared that he was going to tear National League pitching apart. His first at bat came as a pinch-hitter on June 26 and he hit a homer run. He received a start the next day and tripled in his first at bat of the game making him only the second player in major league history to hit a homer and a triple in his first two at bats. After one week, Alex was hitting .571 with four homers and thirteen runs batted in. He was injured in early July and spent two weeks on the disabled list. After a two game rehabilitation assignment in the Arizona Rookie League, he returned to the Diamondbacks lineup. Shortly thereafter, he went into a slump. After going 2 for 22, he was sent to Tucson. A week later he returned to the Diamondbacks where he finished the season. He hit five home runs while with Arizona. Adding his totals for the Pacific Coast and Arizona Rookie Leagues drops his minor league season HR Avg to 79.32.

Cabrera started his minor league career in 1991 and played in seven different leagues prior to 1999 without showing any great home run power. He spent the 1999 season playing in Taiwan. Arizona sold him to Seibu of the Japan Central League in December of 2000. He played for Seibu in 2001 and we have no record of him playing anywhere after that.

Most Home Runs in a Season by Two Teammates

Total HR	Year	Player, HR	Player, HR	Team, League
106	1974	Bill McNulty, 55	Gorman Thomas, 51	Sacramento, Pacific Coast League
105	1966	Heriberto Vargas, 55	Pedro Hernandez, 50	Guanajuato, Mexican Center League
102	1924	Stormy Davis, 51	Wilbur Davis, 51	Okmulgee, Western Association
98	1947	Buck Frierson, 58	Larry Drake, 40	Sherman-Denison, Big State League
98	1948	Bob Crues, 69	Paul Halter, 29	Amarillo, West Texas-New Mexico
98	1956	Frosty Kennedy, 60	Russ Burns, 38	Plainview, Southwestern League
97	1930	Joe Hauser, 63	Johnny Gill, 34	Baltimore, International League
97	1947	Pud Miller, 57	Jim Matthews, 40	Wichita Falls, Big State League
94	1929	Ike Boone, 55	Fuzzy Hufft, 39	Mission, Pacific Coast League
94	1948	Chuck Workman, 52	Charles Gilbert, 42	Nashville, Southern Association
93	1925	Tony Lazzeri, 60	Les Sheehan, 33	Salt Lake City, Pacific Coast League
92	1952	Merv Connors, 47	Les Mulcahy, 45	Amarillo, West Texas-New Mexico
91	1932	Buzz Arlett, 54	Frank McGowan, 37	Baltimore, International League
91	1933	Joe Hauser, 69	Spencer Harris, 22	Minneapolis, American Association
91	1962	Ramiro Caballero, 59	Guillermo Frayde, 32	Guanajuanto, Mexican Center League
90	1924	Mule Washburn, 48	Yank Davis, 42	Tulsa, Western League
90	1930	Jim Poole, 50	Jay Partridge, 40	Nashville, Southern Association
90	1947	Bob Crues, 52	Joe Bauman, 38	Amarillo, West Texas-New Mexico
90	1956	Dick Stuart, 66	Bill Jackson, 24	Lincoln, Western League
88	1930	Pat Wright, 52	Cowboy Jones, 36	Fort Wayne, Central League
87	1949	Carl Sawatski, 45	Babe Barna, 42	Nashville, Southern Association
87	1953	Joe Bauman, 53	Les Mulcahy, 34	Artesia, Longhorn League
86	1929	Gus Suhr, 51	Smead Jolley, 35	San Francisco, Pacific Coast League
86	1947	Bill Serena, 57	Virgil Richardson, 29	Lubbock, West Texas-New Mexico
86	1954	Joe Bauman, 72	Jim Day, 14	Roswell, Longhorn
85	1929	John Vergez, 46	Buzz Arlett, 39	Oakland, Pacific Coast League
85	1947	Calvin Felix, 52	Olin Kelly/Ken Myers, 33	Las Vegas, Sunset League
85	1956	Ken Guettler, 62	Les Peden, 23	Shreveport, Texas League

Most Home Runs in a Season by Three Teammates

HR	Year	Club	League	Players	HR
140	1974	Sacramento	Pacific Coast League	Bill McNulty Gorman Thomas Sixto Lezcano	55 51 34
135	1947	Sherman-Denison	Big State League	Buck Frierson Larry Drake Don Stokes	58 40 37
134	1924	Okmulgee	Western Association	Stormy Davis Wilbur Davis Bill Stellbauer	51 51 32
134	1947	Wichita Falls	Big State League	Pud Miller Jim Matthews Al McCarty	57 40 37
134	1956	Plainview	Southwestern League	Frosty Kennedy Russ Burns Bob Brown	60 38 36
134	1966	Guanajuato	Mexican Center League	Heriberto Vargas Pedro Hernandez Saul Mendoza	55 50 29
129	1930	Baltimore	International League	Joe Hauser Johnny Gill Vince Barton	63 34 32
120	1949	Nashville	Southern Association	Carl Sawatski Babe Barna Harold Gilbert	45 42 33
119	1932	Baltimore	International League	Buzz Arlett Frank McGowan Frank Packard	54 37 28
119	1952	Amarillo	West Texas-New Mexico League	Merv Connors Les Mulcahy Bob Hobbs	47 45 27
119	1962	Guanajuato	Mexican Center League	Ramiro Caballero Guillermo Frayde Elpidio Osuna	59 32 28
118	1947	Las Vegas	Sunset League	Calvin Felix Olin Kelly Ken Myers	52 33 33
117	1925	Salt Lake City	Pacific Coast League	Tony Lazzeri Les Sheehan Lefty O'Doul	60 33 24
117	1930	Fort Wayne	Central League	Pat Wright Cowboy Jones John Reider	52 36 29
116	1948	Nashville	Southern Association	Chuck Workman Charles Gilbert Smokey Burgess	52 42 22
116	1948	Amarillo	West Texas-New Mexico League	Bob Crues Paul Halter Doug Lewis	69 29 18

Most Home Runs by a Player in Consecutive Seasons

Total HR	Player	Year	HR	Club, League
125	Joe Bauman	1953	53	Artesia, Longhorn League
		1954	72	Roswell, Longhorn League
121	Bob Crues	1947	52	Amarillo, West Texas-New Mexico League
		1948	69	Amarillo, West Texas-New Mexico League
118	Joe Hauser	1932	49	Minneapolis, American Association
		1933	69	Minneapolis, American Association
111	Steve Bilko	1956	55	Los Angeles, Pacific Coast League
		1957	56	Los Angeles, Pacific Coast League
111	Dick Stuart	1956	66	Lincoln, Western League
		1957	31	Lincoln, Western League
			8	Atlanta, Southern Association
			6	Hollywood, Pacific Coast League
108	Frank Gravino	1953	52	Fargo-Moorhead, Northern League
		1954	56	Fargo-Moorhead, Northern League
104	Tony Lazzeri	1924	28	Lincoln, Western League
			16	Salt Lake City, Pacific Coast League
		1925	60	Salt Lake City, Pacific Coast League
103	Ken Guettler	1955	41	Portsmouth, Piedmont League
		1956	62	Shreveport, Texas League
96	Tony Robello	1938	38	Jacksonville, East Texas League
		1939	58	Pocatello, Pioneer League
95	Moose Clabaugh	1925	31	Paris, East Texas League
			1	Decatur, Three I League
			1	Ardmore, Western Association
		1926	62	Tyler, East Texas League
95	Bob Lennon	1954	64	Nashville, Southern Association
		1955	31	Minneapolis, American Association
94	Jack Pierce	1985	40	Leon, Mexican League
		1986	54	Leon, Mexican League
93	Buzz Arlett	1932	54	Baltimore, International League
		1933	39	Baltimore, International League
93	Chuck Workman	1948	52	Nashville, Southern Association
		1949	41	Minneapolis, American Association
91	Howie Moss	1946	38	Baltimore, International League
		1947	53	Baltimore, International League
90	Frosty Kennedy	1955	30	Yuma, Arizona-Mexico League
		1956	60	Plainview, Southwestern League
90	Ron Kittle	1981	40	Glens Falls, Eastern League
		1982	50	Edmonton, Pacific Coast League

Most Home Runs by a Player in Consecutive Seasons (cont.)

Total HR	Player	Year	HR	Club, League
89	Jim Matthews	1952	39	Clovis, West Texas-New Mexico League
		1953	50	Amarillo, West Texas-New Mexico League
87	Big Boy Kraft	1923	32	Fort Worth, Texas League
		1924	55	Fort Worth, Texas League
86	Buck Frierson	1947	58	Sherman-Denison, Big State League
		1948	24	Sherman-Denison, Big State League
			4	Dallas, Texas League
86	Pud Miller	1947	57	Wichita Falls, Big State League
		1948	29	Texarkana, Big State League
85	Stormy Davis	1923	34	Okmulgee, Western Association
		1924	51	Okmulgee, Western Association
83	Jim Poole	1929	33	Atlanta/Nashville, Southern Association
		1930	50	Nashville, Southern Association
83	Gene Lillard	1934	27	Los Angeles, Pacific Coast League
		1935	56	Los Angeles, Pacific Coast League
82	Jerry Witte	1949	50	Dallas, Texas League
		1950	30	Houston, Texas League
			2	Rochester, International League
80	Bill McNulty	1973	25	Tidewater, International League
		1974	55	Sacramento, Pacific Coast League

Most Home Runs by a Player in Three Consecutive Seasons

Total HR	Player	Year	HR	Club, League
175	Joe Bauman	1952	50	Artesia, Longhorn League
		1953	53	Artesia, Longhorn League
		1954	72	Roswell, Longhorn League
151	Joe Hauser	1932	49	Minneapolis, American Association
		1933	69	Minneapolis, American Association
		1934	33	Minneapolis, American Association
150	Bob Crues	1946	29	Lamesa/Amarillo, West Texas-New Mexico League
		1947	52	Amarillo, West Texas-New Mexico League
		1948	69	Amarillo, West Texas-New Mexico League
148	Steve Bilko	1955	37	Los Angeles, Pacific Coast League
		1956	55	Los Angeles, Pacific Coast League
		1957	56	Los Angeles, Pacific Coast League
145	Frank Gravino	1952	32	Fargo-Moorhead, Northern League
			5	Cedar Rapids, Three I League
		1953	52	Fargo-Moorhead, Northern League
		1954	56	Fargo-Moorhead, Northern League
144	Dick Stuart	1955	32	Billings, Pioneer League
			1	Mexico City Tigers, Mexican League
		1956	66	Lincoln, Western League
		1957	31	Lincoln, Western League
			8	Atlanta, Southern Association
			6	Hollywood, Pacific Coast League
141	Buzz Arlett	1932	54	Baltimore, International League
		1933	39	Baltimore, International League
		1934	41	Minneapolis, American Association
			7	Birmingham, Southern Association
141	Pud Miller	1947	57	Wichita Falls, Big State League
		1948	29	Texarkana, Big State League
		1949	52	Lamesa, West Texas-New Mexico League
			3	Gladewater, East Texas League
129	Jack Pierce	1984	35	Leon, Mexican League
		1985	40	Leon, Mexican League
		1986	54	Leon, Mexican League
127	Frosty Kennedy	1954	35	Amarillo, West Texas-New Mexico League
			1	Burlington, Three I League
			1	Oklahoma City, Texas League
		1955	30	Yuma, Arizona-Mexico League
		1956	60	Plainview, Southwestern League
126	Gene Lillard	1933	43	Los Angeles, Pacific Coast League
		1934	27	Los Angeles, Pacific Coast League
		1935	56	Los Angeles, Pacific Coast League

Most Home Runs by a Player in Three Consecutive Seasons (cont.)

Total HR	Player	Year	HR	Club, League
125	Tony Lazzeri	1923	14	Peoria, Three I League
			7	Salt Lake City, Pacific Coast League
		1924	28	Lincoln, Western League
			16	Salt Lake City, Pacific Coast League
		1925	60	Salt Lake City, Pacific Coast League
124	Tony Robello	1937	28	Jacksonville, East Texas League
		1938	38	Jacksonville, East Texas League
		1939	58	Pocatello, Pioneer League
124	Howie Moss	1946	38	Baltimore, International League
		1947	53	Baltimore, International League
		1948	33	Baltimore, International League
122	Ken Guettler	1954	19	Portsmouth, Piedmont League
		1955	41	Portsmouth, Piedmont League
		1956	62	Shreveport, Texas League
120	Jerry Witte	1949	50	Dallas, Texas League
		1950	30	Houston, Texas League
			2	Rochester, International League
		1951	38	Houston, Texas League
120	Jim Matthews	1951	31	Texarkana, Big State League
		1952	39	Clovis, West Texas-New Mexico League
		1953	50	Amarillo, West Texas-New Mexico League
119	Big Boy Kraft	1922	32	Fort Worth, Texas League
		1923	32	Fort Worth, Texas League
		1924	55	Fort Worth, Texas League
119	Bob Lennon	1953	24	Nashville, Southern Association
		1954	64	Nashville, Southern Association
		1955	31	Minneapolis, American Association

Home Runs in a Single Season

- The Cordele club of the Georgia-Florida League hit one home run in 1952. Ralph Betcher drove one out in the club's 73rd game. Cordele played in 139 games with 4,679 official at bats. The eight-club league hit a total of 186 home runs— therefore, somebody must've been hittin'em!

- Ed Konetchy hit 41 home runs at age 40. His big year came in 1925 while playing for Fort Worth in the Texas League.

- Bill Serena was the talk of the minor league world in 1947 when clubbed 57 home runs (in only 137 games) for Lubbock of the West Texas-New Mexico League. That would have been enough of a season for anyone, but Serena didn't stop there. He went on to hit another thirteen round-trippers in ten playoff games, leading Lubbock to the league championship.

- Lou Limmer hit 29 home runs for St. Paul in the American Association in 1950, with only one of them coming at his home field, Lexington Park. The park measured 365 feet down the right field line. Limmer's lone blast at home came on August 10th, and traveled some 400 feet.

- Amazingly, in the dead ball era of 1895, a pitcher by the name of Chick Fraser (Minneapolis, Western League) hit fifteen home runs.

- Batters only racked up only 58 home runs in the 1906 Pacific Coast League (the year of the earthquake), but eleven of them were hit by pitchers, including three by San Francisco hurler Nick Williams, and two by Benny Henderson of Portland. Both were always considered good-hitting pitchers. In fact, Berkeley graduate Nick Williams became a catcher later on when his arm gave out. He also discovered the Waner brothers . . .but that's another story. . . .

- When Bud Heslet set the season home record for the California League in 1956 with 51, he never hit more than one in any game.

- Clarence "Big Boy" Kraft had nine two-home run games for Fort Worth in the Texas League in 1924 when he 55 HR.

- Rip Repulski of Columbus hit only nine home runs in 1951, but homered in all eight American Association parks. Box scores in *The Sporting News* gave both players 23 homers. After much debate it was decided to use the official figures of 22.

- Winnepeg of the Northern League had eleven grand slam home runs in 1958. Bobby Moegle and Jim Schaffer led the way with three each.

- Frank Roth is credited in several publications with 36 home runs in 1901 while playing for Evansville in the Three I League. This was the top figure that year for all minor leagues. A careful check of all box scores and game stories revealed that his correct total was only 27. This was still the top total for the minors.

- When Bob Crues tied the minor league record of 69 home runs in 1948, he added a couple more during the playoffs. The fences at Gold Sox Park in Amarillo that year measured 324 feet down both foul lines, and a short 360 to dead center.

- Ike Boone hit 55 home runs for the San Francisco Mission of the Pacific Coast League in 1929, and his brother, Dan, hit 46 for High Point of the Piedmont League. This total of 101 is the highest for two brothers in the same year.

- In 1907, Walter "Rosy" Carlisle of the Los Angeles Angels of the Pacific Coast League hit 10 of his league-leading thirteen home runs at Rec Park in San Francisco, which included the first three-home run game in Coast League history on August 18th. He only hit 2 home runs at home at Chutes Park, and another at Portland's Vaughn Street Grounds.

- Carl Sawatski of the Nashville club set a Southern Association record with five grand slam home runs during the 1949 season, and, to top it off, added another one during the Dixie Series against Tulsa.

- Jack Harshman hit six grand slam home runs for Nashville in 1951 to break the Southern Association record of five, which had been set only two years earlier by Carl Sawatski, who also played for Nashville.

Home Runs in a Single Season (cont.)

- Chuck Weatherspoon of Wilson in the Carolina League hit seven grand slam home runs in 1961. Two of them came in one game on May 2nd.

- Indianapolis of the American Association had thirteen grand slam home runs in 1995. Number eleven came on July 26th, but the club only managed to hit two more the rest of the way. Steve Gibralter hit three, and Dave McCarty and Chad Mottola hit two apiece.

- Ray Perry won his seventh consecutive home run title in 1954. His streak started with the Far West League from 1948 through 1951, then the Cotton States League in 1952 and the California League for the final two years. The seven titles tie him with Bunny Brief. Butch Nieman had previously held the consecutive record with five (through 1951).

- Phoenix of the Pacific Coast League hit home runs in 42 consecutive home games during the 1959 season. George Brunet of Portland stopped the streak on July 22nd when he allowed only five singles.

- The official averages of for the 1920 International League credit Frank Brower and Mike Konnick, both playing for Reading, with 22 home runs to tie for the league lead. Joe Herring, a baseball researcher from Reading, has discovered that both Brower and Konnick hit 23 homers. These figures have been verified by a second source. It is amazing that errors were made on the leading home run hitters and that with the corrections they are still tied for the leadership.

- Adam Dunn hit 51 home runs in 2001, including nineteen for the Cincinnati Reds. He hit twelve for Chattanooga of the Southern League and twenty for Louisville of the International League before moving up to the majors. He was the second player to reach double digits in the majors and two minor leagues during a single season. Erubiel Durazo hit eleven for the Arizona Diamondbacks, fourteen for El Paso of the Texas League and ten for Tucson of the Pacific Coast League in 1999. Dunn was 21 years old at the end of the season. That made him the second youngest player to hit fifty home runs in professional ball during a single season. Calvin Felix was four days younger (assuming that the season ended on the same day for both) when he hit 52 in the 1947 Sunset League.

- Indianapolis of the American Association hit thirteen grand slam home runs in 1995. This may be a minor league record. Steve Gibralter led the team with three followed by Dave McCarty and Chad Mottola with two apiece. Jerry Brooks, Brian Dorsett, Keith Gordon, Brian Hunter, Keith Mitchell and Craig Worthington each hit one.

Clubs with 200+ Home Runs in a Season

Rank	HR	HR/G	Year	Club	League
1	305	2.12	1974	Sacramento	Pacific Coast League
2	271	1.94	1947	Las Vegas	Sunset League
3	258	1.65	1947	Sherman-Denison	Big State League
4	245	1.70	1956	Plainview	Southwestern League
5	244	1.98	1962	Guanajuato	Mexican Center League
6	241	1.54	1955	Minneapolis	American Association
7	235	1.56	1957	Topeka	Western League
8	234	1.52	1947	Texarkana	Big State League
9	233	1.68	1966	Guanajuato	Mexican Center League
10	232	1.38	1932	Baltimore	International League
11	231	1.38	1930	Baltimore	International League
	231	1.64	1999	Omaha	Pacific Coast League
13	225	1.62	1955	Pampa	West Texas-New Mexico League
14	220	1.79	1895	Minneapolis	Western League
15	217	1.55	2007	Lancaster	California League
	217	1.41	1939	Minneapolis	American Association
17	216	1.53	1952	Amarillo	West Texas-New Mexico League
18	215	1.50	1998	Omaha	Pacific Coast League
19	214	1.53	1948	Amarillo	West Texas-New Mexico League
	214	1.65	1956	Cananea	Arizona-Mexico League
21	213	1.37	1947	Wichita Falls	Big State League
	213	1.50	1953	Amarillo	West Texas-New Mexico League
23	212	1.34	1936	Minneapolis	American Association
	212	1.51	1956	Pampa	Southwestern League
	212	1.81	2000	Mexico City Reds	Mexican League
26	210	1.50	1947	Lubbock	West Texas-New Mexico League
27	209	1.47	1996	Pawtucket	International League
28	208	1.48	1956	Lincoln	Western League
	208	1.33	1961	Arkansas	Pacific Coast League
30	207	1.48	1930	Fort Wayne	Central League
	207	1.48	1947	Amarillo	West Texas-New Mexico League
	207	1.48	1955	Amarillo	West Texas-New Mexico League
	207	1.48	1963	El Paso	Texas League
34	206	1.45	1998	Buffalo	International League
35	205	1.46	1947	Borger	West Texas-New Mexico League
	205	1.33	1958	Phoenix	Pacific Coast League
37	204	1.03	1923	Salt Lake City	Pacific Coast League
38	203	1.59	1986	Monclova	Mexican League
	203	1.45	2005	High Desert	California League
40	202	1.28	1924	Okmulgee	Western Association
	202	1.25	1929	Tulsa	Western League
	202	1.31	1935	Baltimore	International League
	202	1.31	1949	Minneapolis	American Association
	202	1.20	1956	Los Angeles	Pacific Coast League
	202	1.47	1994	Winston-Salem	Carolina League
	202	1.44	2002	Edmonton	Pacific Coast League
47	201	1.45	1971	Visalia	California League
	201	1.36	1972	Eugene	Pacific Coast League
49	200	1.45	1996	Jacksonville	Southern League

The 200 home run mark has been reached nine times by clubs in the Pacific Coast League, but only two times in the pre–1958 National League invasion of the territory. Interestingly, only one coastal team, Los Angeles, is on the list. Two of the PCL clubs on the list, Omaha and Arkansas, are half way across the country.

The defunct West Texas-New Mexico League had clubs reach the mark six times, five of them by Amarillo. The Minneapolis club is on the list four times while playing in hitter friendly Nicollet Park. Baltimore surpassed the 200 mark three times over a six year period (1930–1936) while playing in another hitter friendly park, Oriole Park.

The 1947 season was the biggest year ever, with seven clubs racking up more than 200 homers apiece. The second biggest year was 1956 when five clubs did it. Surprisingly, only two Mexican League clubs are on the list despite the high totals achieved by individual batters in recent seasons.

Top Season Home Run Rate by Club

Minimum of 200 home runs. Rate carried out to more than two decimal places to break ties where applicable.

Rank	HR/G	HR	Year	Club	League
1.	2.12	305	1974	Sacramento	Pacific Coast League
2.	1.98	244	1962	Guanajuato	Mexican Center League
3.	1.94	271	1947	Las Vegas	Sunset League
4.	1.81	212	2000	Mexico City Reds	Mexican League
5.	1.79	220	1895	Minneapolis	Western League
6.	1.70	245	1956	Plainview	Southwestern League
7.	1.68	233	1966	Guanajuato	Mexican Center League
8.	1.65	258	1947	Sherman-Denison	Big State League
9.	1.65	214	1956	Cananea	Arizona-Mexico League
10.	1.64	231	1999	Omaha	Pacific Coast League

The top team on the list, Sacramento, returned to the Pacific Coast League in 1974 after an absence of fourteen years. The club had to scramble to obtain a playing field and Hughes Stadium was selected. Hughes had been built in 1928 as a track and football stadium. When the baseball field was laid out, right field measured a reasonable 330 feet down the line. However, left field turned out to be an absurdly short 232 feet down the line. In an attempt to cut down on cheap home runs, a 40-foot screen was erected from the left field foul pole to the power alley in left-centerfield. Nevertheless, it still took little more than a pop fly to clear the left field fence.

Sacramento hit 305 home runs that season and 250 of them were hit at Hughes. Visiting batters chipped in with another 241 for a grand total of 491 homers at Hughes Stadium. On two occasions, fourteen home runs were hit in a game. Right-handed hitting Bill McNulty led the league that season with 55 homers, 44 of which were hit at home. He was followed by teammate Gorman Thomas with 51 home runs.

Top Home Run Seasons by League

Eight Club Leagues

Rank	HR	League	Year
1.	1,410	West Texas- New Mexico	1947
2.	1,220	Arizona-Mexico League	1956
3.	1,217	West Texas- New Mexico	1948
4.	1,210	West Texas- New Mexico	1955
5.	1,205	Western League	1956
6.	1,200	West Texas- New Mexico	1947
7.	1,158	American Association	1997
8.	1,147	Western Association	1924
9.	1,145	Pacific Coast League	1929
10.	1,138	Pacific Coast League	1950
11.	1,136	West Texas- New Mexico	1953
12.	1,113	American Association	1996
13.	1,110	American Association	1955
14.	1,107	Pacific Coast League	1974
15.	1,092	International League	1962
16.	1,073	American Association	1987
17.	1,059	American Association	1956
18.	1,056	American Association	1993
19.	1,045	International League	1949
20.	1,037	International League	1948
	1,037	Carolina League	1994

Twelve Club Leagues

Rank	HR	League	Year
1.	1,611	Pacific Coast League	1964
2.	1,490	Eastern League	2004
3.	1,459	Eastern League	1999
4.	1,439	Eastern League	2005
5.	1,428	Pacific Coast League	1965
6.	1,407	Eastern League	2001
7.	1,371	Eastern League	2008
8.	1,312	Eastern League	2007
9.	1,293	Eastern League	2002
10.	1,275	Pacific Coast League	1966
11.	1,246	Eastern League	2006
12.	1,194	Eastern League	2000
13.	1,163	Eastern League	2003
14.	1,138	Florida State League	2005
15.	1,104	Midwest League	1982
16.	1,100	Midwest League	1983
17.	1,086	Midwest League	1987
18.	1,073	Florida State League	2006
19.	1,066	Florida State League	2007
20.	1,035	Pacific Coast League	1967

Ten Club Leagues

Rank	HR	League	Year
1.	1,549	Southwestern League	1956
2.	1,468	Pacific Coast League	1997
3.	1,423	California League	2005
4.	1,409	Eastern League	1997
5.	1,369	Pacific Coast League	1983
6.	1,365	Pacific Coast League	1994
7.	1,340	International League	1996
8.	1,318	California League	2007
9.	1,312	International League	1997
10.	1,296	International League	1963
11.	1,287	Southern League	1997
12.	1,244	Pacific Coast League	1963
13.	1,225	California League	1996
14.	1,215	California League	1997
15.	1,212	International League	1994
16.	1,204	Southern League	1986
17.	1,199	Southern League	1999
18.	1,197	Eastern League	1996
19.	1,187	International League	1993
20.	1,184	Eastern League	1998

Fourteen Club Leagues

Rank	HR	League	Year
1.	2,127	International League	1999
2.	2,028	International League	1998
3.	1,981	International League	2005
4.	1,940	International League	2004
5.	1,836	International League	2000
6.	1,759	International League	2001
7.	1,664	International League	2008
8.	1,630	International League	2002
9.	1,545	International League	2007
10.	1,501	International League	2003
11.	1,474	Mexican League	1987
12.	1,470	International League	2006
13.	1,431	South Atlantic League	1998
14.	1,395	South Atlantic League	1999
15.	1,370	Midwest League	2005
16.	1,357	Florida State League	1998
17.	1,314	Midwest League	1999
18.	1,313	Mexican League	1988
19.	1,312	Midwest League	2004
20.	1,271	Midwest League	2001
19.	1,246	South Atlantic League	1997
20.	1,228	Midwest League	1997

Top Home Run Seasons by League (cont.)

Sixteen Club Leagues

Rank	HR	League	Year
1.	2,529	Pacific Coast League	2004
2.	2,492	Pacific Coast League	2008
3.	2,435	Pacific Coast League	1999
4.	2,402	Pacific Coast League	2005
5.	2,373	Pacific Coast League	1998
6.	2,360	Pacific Coast League	2001
7.	2,270	Pacific Coast League	2007
8.	2,228	Pacific Coast League	2000
9.	2,156	Pacific Coast League	2002
10.	2,068	Mexican League	2000
11.	2,047	Pacific Coast League	2006
12.	2,032	Mexican League	2005
13.	2,004	Mexican League	1991
14.	1,951	Mexican League	1986
15.	1,888	Pacific Coast League	2003
16.	1,782	South Atlantic League	2004
17.	1,656	South Atlantic League	2005
18.	1,635	Mexican League	1985
19.	1,534	Mexican League	1992
20.	1,523	Mexican League	2001

Twenty Club Leagues

Rank	HR	League	Year
1.	1,016	Mexican League	1979
2.	852	Mexican League	1980

The 1980 Mexican League season ended on July 3rd due to a players strike.

There have been no other twenty club leagues.

The number of eight club leagues is dwindling. There were only four during the 2008 season. They were the Texas, Carolina, Northwest and Pioneer Leagues.

The sixteen club leagues were the domain of the Mexican League ten years ago. Since then, the Pacific Coast League, with some help from the South Atlantic League, is pushing the Mexican League down the list.

Top Season Home Run Rates by League

Home runs per game for both clubs. **Minimum of 1,000 league home runs**. *Rate carried out to decimal places to break ties where applicable.*

Rank	Rate	HR	League	Year
1.	2.53	1,220	Arizona-Mexico League	1956
2.	2.35	2,032	Mexican League	2005
3.	2.29	1,410	Big State League	1947
4.	2.20	2,529	Pacific Coast League	2004
5.	2.18	1,217	West Texas-New Mexico League	1948
6.	2.18	2,492	Pacific Coast League	2008
7.	2.17	1,549	Southwestern League	1956
8.	2.17	2,435	Pacific Coast League	1999
9.	2.16	1,210	West Texas-New Mexico League	1955
10.	2.16	1,205	Western League	1956
11.	2.15	1,200	West Texas-New Mexico League	1947
12.	2.15	2,068	Mexican League	2000
13.	2.12	2,127	International League	1999
14.	2.10	2,402	Pacific Coast League	2005
15.	2.10	1,033	Northern League	1936
16.	2.08	2,004	Mexican League	1991
17.	2.07	1,468	Pacific Coast League	1997
18.	2.07	2,373	Pacific Coast League	1998
19.	2.07	2,360	Pacific Coast League	1999
20.	2.04	1,423	California League	2005
21.	2.03	2,028	International League	1998
22.	2.02	1,158	American Association	1997
23.	2.01	1,136	West Texas-New Mexico League	1953
24.	1.99	1,409	Eastern League	1997
25.	1.97	1,981	International League	2005
26.	1.95	2,228	Pacific Coast League	2000
27.	1.94	1,113	American Association	1996
28.	1.94	1,107	Pacific Coast League	1974
29.	1.93	1,940	International League	2004
30.	1.93	1,369	Pacific Coast League	1983
31.	1.92	1,073	American Association	1987
32.	1.92	1,365	Pacific Coast League	1994
33.	1.91	1,036	American Association	1982
34.	1.90	1,066	Texas League	1998
35.	1.90	1,951	Mexican League	1986
36.	1.89	1,340	International League	1996
37.	1.89	2,156	Pacific Coast League	2002
38.	1.89	1,037	Carolina League	1994
39.	1.89	1,836	International League	2000
40.	1.86	1,287	Southern League	1997
41.	1.86	1,312	International League	1997
42.	1.84	1,025	Arizona-Mexico League	1955
43.	1.84	1,056	American Association	1993
44.	1.83	1,022	California League	1962
45.	1.83	1,028	Arizona-Texas League	1954
46.	1.82	1,011	Texas League	2006
47.	1.81	1,001	Longhorn League	1955
48.	1.81	1,147	Western Association	1924
49.	1.79	1,110	American Association	1955
50.	1.79	1,026	West Texas-New Mexico League	1950

The Pacific Coast League appears on the list thirteen times. It has made the list in eight out of the past ten seasons. The International League and the American Association are distant runner-ups with seven and six appearances on the list, respectively.

32 percent of the occurrences on the list have been during the past ten seasons (1999–2008).

Only two leagues on the list, the 1924 Western League and the 1936 Northern League, played prior to World War II.

Home Runs in One Inning

Buffalo hit five home runs in the second inning of an International League game against Albany on May 15, 1934. Butch Meyers hit the first one with a man on base. Then, with two outs, Greg Mulleavy, Les Mallon, Jack Smith and Bill Regan hit consecutive homers. It is interesting to note that these five batters accounted for only 36 home runs the entire season.

Ellis Burton clubbed switch-hit home runs in the eighth inning of the opening game, on May 3rd of the 1961 International League season. Playing for Toronto, Burton hit a two-run homer while batting left handed against visiting Jersey City. He came up for a second time in the inning with the bases loaded and connected from the right side for a grand slam. This was the first known time that a batter ever hit homers from both sides of the plate in an inning during a minor league game.

Gary Pellant of Alexandria in the Carolina League hit switch-hit home runs in the seventh inning of a game on April 30, 1979, against visiting Salem. Batting right-handed, Pellant hit a leadoff homer. He then came up later in the inning with a man on and clubbed one from the left side of the plate.

Dwayne Hosey, playing for Pawtucket of the International League, hit home runs from each side of the plate in the third inning of a game against Ottawa on August 10, 1996. This was the first game of a double header. One of the homers was a grand slam and the other was a two-run homer, giving Hosey six runs batted in for the inning. He also connected for another home run later in the game.

Omaha of the American Association hit four consecutive home runs against Oklahoma City on May 7, 1993. With two outs in the bottom of the eighth, Karl Rhodes, Terry Shumpert, Russ McGinnis and Bob Hamelin rocked Gerald Alexander.

Oscar Vitt and Paul Strand of Salt Lake City each hit two home runs in the third inning of a home game against the Vernon Tigers on May 13, 1923. This was the first game of a Pacific Coast League double header. Salt Lake City scored twelve runs in the inning.

Roy Peeler and Len Cross of Knoxville in the Tri-State League each hit two home runs in the fifth inning of a game on August 14, 1947. Knoxville scored ten runs in the game against Reidsville. Interestingly, Peeler was a pitcher.

For only the third time in minor league history, teammates each hit two home runs in the same inning. Alex Ochoa and Brent Miller of the Bowie club in the Eastern League each connected in the fourth inning as Bowie rolled up fourteen runs against Harrisburg on the way to a 28–10 win. The game was played at Shipley Field at the University of Maryland on June 5, 1994. This field, with its short fences, was being used temporarily by the Bowie Baysox.

Three players have hit two grand slam home runs in an inning. Ken Myers was the first, hitting his pair in the third inning of a game on May 2, 1947, while playing for Las Vegas of the Sunset League. Armando Flores, of Laredo in the Gulf Coast League, did it in the eighth inning of a June 25, 1952, game. Lance Junker of Redwood in the California League hit two in the ninth inning, on June 30, 1983, his first two home runs of the season.

Frank Shofner and Jerry Witte of Houston hit back-to-back home runs in the fifth inning and then repeated the feat in the sixth inning of a May 12, 1951, game. This was a Texas League game played at Tulsa.

Brothers Kitty and Roy Brashear of the Vernon Tigers hit back-to-back home runs in the first inning of a Pacific Coast League game on August 3, 1910, at Chutes Park in Los Angeles. What makes this feat even more unusual is that neither brother was much of a home run hitter. While both had long minor league careers, Kitty only hit 36 career home runs and Roy hit 69.

In the first game of a doubleheader at Tulsa on July 1, 1923, the first four batters of the game for Wichita (Western League) hit home runs. The batters were Lyman Smith, Jocko Conlon, Wes Griffin and Jim Blakesley. Wichita did not score any additional runs in the inning, but those four home runs were the margin of victory in their 11–7 win. Karl Black was the starting pitcher for Tulsa, and the manager yanked him after the fourth homer. Black really wasn't as bad a pitcher as that game indicated. He wound up the season with 29 wins, enough to lead the league in the category. Black's real name was Lautenschlager.

On May 28, 1921, Frank Schulte, Arthur Smith and Jewel Ens of Syracuse (International League) hit three consecutive pitches from Reading's Dean Barnhardt for home runs. This is the first known time that this feat has been accomplished. Since then, however, it has been duplicated several times. In a Pacific Coast League game on August 8th, 1952, three successive batters hit home runs off three successive pitches by Fred Sanford of Portland. The batters were Tookie Gilbert, Sam Chapman and Piper Davis. All connected in the first inning. The feat was performed twice in 1946. In the fifth inning of a game at Sulphur Dell in Nashville on July 8th, Pete Thomassie, Cy Block and Bill Manning hit three consecutive pitches off Bob Raney of Little Rock for home runs. The first three pitches thrown by Stan Kmet of Eau Claire (Northern League) in the sixth inning of an August 23, 1946, game were hit over the leftfield fence. Hal Schadt, Ed Gittens and Tony Jaros of St. Cloud did the damage. On the fourth pitch of the inning, Bruts Welsch singled.

Will Clark, playing for Fresno in the California League, hit a home run on June 21, 1985, in his first at bat in the minor leagues. Clark also hit a home run on his first at bat in the majors. That occurred on April 8, 1986, and came off Hall of Fame pitcher Nolan Ryan.

Pitcher Touchstone of Greenville (Carolina Association) hit a home run in the sixteenth inning of an August 4, 1908, game, defeating Greensboro, 1–0.

Pitcher Bunny Hearn of Springfield (Three I League) hit two solo home runs in the seventh inning of a game against Danville on August 28, 1912. Hearn also hit a home run in the first inning.

In the seventh inning of a home game against Omaha on August 9, 1952, Bill Pinckard of Denver (Western League) hit a long drive to left field. Dick Cordell made a frantic grab for the ball as he crashed into the fence. The ball bounced out of his glove, hit the wall, rebounded, and caromed off his head and over the fence. After a lengthy dispute, the umpires ruled that it was a home run. This gave Denver a 1–0 win.

In 1962, Jackie Warner, a nineteen-year-old youngster playing for San Jose of the California League, hit home runs in his first two at bats in organized baseball.

Bernard Lake of Sanford (Florida State League) pitched a nineteen-inning shutout against the DeLand club on July 19, 1947. He hit a home run in the last inning to win his own game.

Roger Haines of Richmond (Blue Grass League) was reported to have hit two grand slam home runs in the seventh inning of a game against Mt. Sterling, on July 1, 1912. This feat was reported in *Sporting Life* and in the *Louisville Courier Journal*. However, Richmond scored only ten runs in the inning. A minimum of eleven runs must be scored in an inning in order for one batter to hit two grand slams. Scratch him from the list!

Las Vegas of the Sunset League hit three grand slam homers in the third inning of a game on May 2, 1947, on the way to rolling up sixteen runs. As mentioned above, Ken Myers hit two of them. Pitcher Ned Klingensmith hit the third.

Steve Prihoda of Wichita (Texas League) may have set a minor league record by giving up five home runs in one inning of a home game against San Antonio on August 19, 1998. While a number of teams have hit five home runs in one inning, none are known to have hit them all off of one pitcher. Prihoda entered a scoreless game in the 11th inning. He quickly loaded the bases to set up a grand slam by Angel Pena. Pena later hit a solo home run as San Antonio pushed across twelve runs in the inning.

Indianapolis his four home runs during a ten run fifth inning in an International League game at Pawtucket on May 20, 1998. That, in itself, is not rare in the minor leagues. However, the ten runs were the result of a one-run homer, a two-run homer, a three-run homer and a grand slam. This is probably a first. The sequence was as follows: Pete Rose, Jr. hit a solo homer, Jason Williams hit a three-run shot, Glenn Murray hit a grand slam and Guillermo Garcia hit a two-run homer. The big inning gave Indianapolis a 10–4 lead.

Joe Pignatano of Fort Worth (Texas League) had an unusual experience in a game at Shreveport on May 29, 1955. Batting in the seventh spot of the batting order, he hit a homer in the second inning. Unfortunately, the lineup card had him hitting eighth. Shreveport appealed and the proper batter, Maury Wills, was called out. Pignatano then batted in his proper slot and hit another ball over the fence at about the same spot.

Albany of the Georgia-Florida League scored six runs on three consecutive pitches in a game at Moultrie on July 23, 1952. Denver Rikard belted a grand slam. On the next two pitches, Bob Murphy and Ron Plaza connected for homers.

Joe Carolan, a 21-year old youngster from Detroit, bought a ticket to a ballgame at Columbus, Georgia (Sally League), on April 24, 1954. He then obtained a scorecard to learn the name of the general manager of the club whom Carolan then asked for a tryout. When field manager George Kissell saw the 230 pounder send drives out of the park, he offered him a contract and put him in the starting lineup. Carolan came to bat for the first time in the second inning with the bases loaded and hit a grand slam off Calvin Howe of Macon to put Albany in the lead, 4–3. Carolan would go on to hit .231 in 33 games with four home runs.

Modesto hit five home runs in the second inning of a California League game against Visalia on June 26, 1954. Gus Suhr, Jr. son of the former major league first baseman, hit two of them. Ed Fairman, Frank Kerr and Herman Reich hit consecutive homers. Jerry Crosby had already hit a home run in the first inning to give Modesto a total of six through the first two innings of the game. Modesto won the game 13–0 as Al Ibanez threw a one-hitter.

Elmo Plaskett of Las Vegas knocked the ball out of the park in the second inning of a California League game at Fresno on August 10, 1958. After circling the bases, he realized he had not touched first base. He then made another trip around the bases. A new ball was put in play and pitcher Tom Fitzgerald took his stance on the mound and then threw to first base. Fresno appealed to the umpire and Plaskett was called out. Umpire Joe Fluery pointed out that the batter was required to circle the bases in reverse order in this situation.

Denver hit four home runs in an American Association game versus Louisville on June 27, 1960. After the first two batters were retired in the first inning, Steve Boros, Jim McDaniel, Larry Osborne and Ozzie Virgil blasted home runs. Later in the game, Denver batters collected three more home runs. Lousville knocked out three of their own to make a total of ten home runs in the game.

Joe Abernethy, Newton-Conover's playing manager, hit a high fly to rightfield in a game against Belmont (Western Carolina League) on June 7, 1961. Young Eddie Montellanico camped under the ball then lost it in the park lights. The ball hit him on top of his head and bounced over the fence for a home run. Eddie was knocked unconscious briefly but stayed in the game.

Chad Moeller of Salt Lake City (Pacific Coast League) hit two home runs in the sixth inning of a game against Oklahoma on June 12, 2000. This was the second time that Moeller had accomplished the feat. He first turned the trick on May 23, 1998 while playing for Fort Myers against Daytona in a Florida State League game.

Twin brothers Oreste and Vilato Marrero of Helena (Pioneer League) each hit a homer in the second inning of a game against Billings on June 25, 1987. This is believed to be a first for twins.

Ernie Lombardi has been reported to have hit two grand slams in an inning while playing for Ogden of the Pioneer League in 1927. A check of the entire season determined that this never happened. Ernie hit only four home runs all season.

Ron Carlyle of Oakland in the Pacific Coast League hit a ball which was reported to have traveled 618 feet. It went over the clubhouse at Emeryville Park in Oakland. This was a July 4 game in 1929. The pitcher for Mission was Ernie Nevers, the great football player.

Three Shots of Rye

In the most explosive inning by any hitter in the history of Organized Baseball, Gene "Half-Pint" Rye, playing for Waco in the Texas League, hit three home runs in the eighth inning of a contest on August 6, 1930. Most players spend their entire careers without even getting to bat three times in an inning. The odds are staggeringly against any player getting three hits in an inning, let alone three homers. In fact, only four major leaguers have managed to get three hits in an inning, and none, of course, hit three home runs.

The big fireworks display occurred during a night game at Katy Park in Waco against rival Beaumont. Waco scored eighteen runs in the big inning to turn a close game into a rout, ending up with a winning margin of 22 to 4. With Jerry Mallett on the mound for Beaumont, Rye led off the eighth inning and gave an indication of things to come when he drove the ball over the right field fence, but the ball curved foul by a couple of feet. Rye then stepped back in and hit one over the left field fence. Half-Pint came up for the second time in the inning with two men on base. By that time, Walter Newman was on the mound, having relieved Mallett. Rye stepped into one of Newman's offerings and the ball sailed out over the right field fence. Poor Walt Newman was still in there when Rye came to bat for the third time that inning. This time the bases were full, so Newman was really under pressure to get something over the plate. One of the pitches was to the batter's liking, and Rye slammed another one over the rightfield fence. Rye was not the only Waco player to have hit a homer that inning. Tony Piet and Charley Stuvengen also connected in the eighth.

When the dust cleared, Rye had set four Organized Baseball records for one inning: Most total bases (12); most extra bases on long hits (9); most runs batted in (8); and most home runs (3). Only the 8-RBI mark has been equaled during the following seventy-eight years.

Rye had a single earlier in the game, which gave him four hits in six at bats for the evening. He had no hand in his team's scoring other than during that one big inning.

The left-hand hitting Rye, whose real name was Eugene Randolph Mercantelli, garnered 26 home runs and drove in 92 runs over the course of the 1930 season. If one looks at his amazing inning on a percentage basis, an incredible twelve percent of his home run output and nine percent of his RBI output was produced in one single inning!

Rye began his Organized Baseball career with Waterloo in the Mississippi Valley League in 1925. Prior to that, he played some semipro ball in and around Chicago. After breaking in with Waterloo, he had stops at Rock Island, Cedar Rapids and Winston-Salem before showing up in Waco in 1929. His 26 home runs for Waco in 1930 were the most he hit in any one year in his career. The Boston Red Sox purchased Rye from Waco for delivery in 1931. Rye got injured early in the spring, which limited his playing with the Red Sox to 17 games. In those 17 games, he had a lowly .179 batting average and failed to hit a home run.

The Red Sox shipped him back to the minors later that season, to Galveston of the Texas League, and he never made it back for another try in the majors.

From Galveston, Rye went on to Houston (Texas League), Elmira (New York-Penn) and Davenport in the Western League, where he finished his professional career with 101 career home runs. That was not the end of Half-Pint, though, as he continued playing semipro ball in the tough Chicago leagues for a number of years thereafter.

Home Runs in One Game

Phoenix set a Pacific Coast League record by hitting ten home runs in the second game of a doubleheader on July 6, 1974. The game was played at bandbox Hughes Stadium in Sacramento. Sacramento added three homers to tie the league record for most home runs in a game by both teams. The record had been set just a month earlier by Sacramento and Spokane in the same park. The record didn't last very long, however. Sacramento and Tacoma each hit seven on August 6th for a total of fourteen. This mark was tied on August 20th when Sacramento hit nine home runs and Spokane added five home runs. *See details of the Sacramento park in the section on season home runs.*

Oreste and Vilato Marrero, twin brothers, each hit a home run in the same game on two occasions. The first time was in 1988 while playing for Helena in the Pioneer League. The second time came when both were with Beloit of the Midwest League during the 1990 season. Both of the homers came in the same inning and gave Beloit a 2–1 victory over Cedar Rapids.

In a Sunset League game at Las Vegas on May 2, 1947, the home team scored thirty runs against the visiting Ontario club. Olin Kelly began things for Las Vegas with a leadoff homer in the first inning. The club scored sixteen runs in the third inning, with twelve of those runs coming on three grand slams, two by Ken Myers and one by Pitcher Ned Klingensmith. Myers added two more homers in the game, Klingensmith added one more, Cal Felix chipped in with two and Sy Gregory hit one to give Las Vegas a total of ten home runs for the game.

Kansas City set an American Association record by hitting ten home runs in one game on June 29, 1952. It was the first game of a doubleheader played in St. Paul. Six of the homers came in the third inning, including four in succession.

Phil Alotta and Vince Pascale each hit four home runs in a Sunset League game against Ontario on June 1, 1947. Tom Lloyd added three more homers and Jim Boulanger hit one to give Reno a grand total of twelve home runs for the game. Ontario chipped in with four homers to give the two clubs a total of sixteen home runs in the game.

Albuquerque of the West Texas-New Mexico League hit twelve home runs against Lamesa on June 30, 1948. Len Attyd hit four. Will Dixon, Ron Bowan and Les Mulcahy each had two and Frank Shone and Len Pill had one apiece.

Douglas of the Arizona-Mexico League hit nine home runs in a game against Chihuahua on August 19, 1958. This, of course, is not a record, but the club did set a record that may be equaled but never broken. Each of the nine players in the line up connected for a homer. The game was called due to darkness in the eighth.

The first player known to have hit two grand slam home runs in a game was Dan Gunshannon of the Bristol club in the old Connecticut State League. On May 26, 1897, he hit balls over the center field fence in the first and third innings. Pitcher Parson Clune of Bridgewater settled down after that but Bristol still held on to win the game 8 to 5.

John Cantley, the pitcher for Opelika of the Georgia-Alabama League, has been credited in several publications with hitting three grand slam home runs in a game. The game in question took place at Opelika on June 5, 1914, and the opponent was Talladega. The original source for the information was the *Talladega Daily Home*. Opelika won the game 19–1. The line score credits Opelika with seven runs in the first, seven in the second, one in the fourth, two in the seventh and two in the eighth. If the line score is to be believed, then Cantley could not have hit three grand slams.

Ed Kneuper and Les Witherspoon of Texas City (Big State League) hit back-to-back home runs in two consecutive innings, the 8th and 9th. The game was on May 31, 1955, at Corpus Christi.

Three Quincy (Three Eye League) players performed the rare feat of hitting back-to-back-to-back home runs twice in the same game. Jack Killoren, Wayne Cummings and Spike Wyatt belted consecutive homers during a seven-run first inning. They repeated in the fourth as Quincy scored eight more runs. To add to the fun in the fourth, pitcher Bill Banker followed Wyatt with a home run to give the team four consecutive homers. Needless to say, Quincy won the game, 20–1, over Peoria.

It is not rare for a player to hit two grand slams in a game. However, it is unusual for it to occur twice in one day. On August 1, 1955, Bill Dennis of Lawton (Sooner State League) did so against Ardmore while Bob Quinn of Pulaski (Appalachian League) hit his pair against Johnson City.

Kearney of the Nebraska State League produced three grand slams on July 30, 1956, against Holdrege. Jay Ward hit two of them and Deron Johnson slammed the third as Kearney won the game, 20–1. Pitcher Hal Reniff had a no-hitter going into the ninth inning but it was spoiled with a homer by Tom Plath.

Los Angeles broke one Pacific Coast League record and tied another when they blasted Sacramento, 22–5, in a home game on June 22, 1957. The team set a record with five home runs in one inning. Bert Hamric hit two of them and Bobby Dolan, Steve Bilko and Jim Baxes had one apiece. Hamric hit one earlier in the game as sis Jim Fridley, Sparky Anderson and Tom Saffell. The nine home runs in a game tied the mark set by Vernon in 1923. It is interesting that starting pitcher Roger Osenbaugh was not pulled from the game until all 22 runs had been scored.

The Mexico City Reds and the Poza Rica Oilers set a Mexican League record with twelve home runs in the first game of a doubleheader at Merino Park in Poza Rica on June 15, 1960. The Reds hit seven of the round-trippers while winning the slugfest, 16–11. Four of the Oilers homers came in one inning including two by Also Salvent.

Steve Manning of Holyoke (Eastern Association) hit home runs in three consecutive innings off three different Bridgeport pitchers on June 2, 1912. While this has been accomplished a number of times in more recent years, it is probably a first for the Deadball Era.

Eric Hinske and Marcel Longmire of Williamsport hit back-to-back home runs in the second inning and then repeated in the third inning of a game on June 28, 1998. This was a home game against Watertown (New York-Pennsylvania League).

Buzz Arlett was one of the great minor league sluggers. For many years he held the career home run record with 432. Yet, he started his career in 1918 with Oakland of the Pacific Coast League as a pitcher. On June 23, the Oakland club found itself short of pitchers, and Buzz was called on to pitch both games of a doubleheader at Los Angeles. He won the first game, 1–0, allowing only four hits. He lost the second game, 3–2, giving up nine hits. Both were nine inning games. A little over a week later, on July 3rd at San Francisco, he pitched a three-hitter and won, 2–0. The two Oakland runs were the result of a two-run homer in the ninth by Arlett.

On Opening Day (May 4th) of the 1952 Northern League season, Aberdeen blasted twelve home runs and Fargo-Moorhead added three. The twelve by Aberdeen tied the known record set by Reno of the Sunset League on June 1, 1947. The fifteen by both clubs is one short of the sixteen hit by Reno and Ontario in the above 1947 game. The game was played at Redfield, South Dakota because the Aberdeen field was not quite ready for play. Although the fences at Redfield were 300 feet down the foul lines, the batters were aided by a strong wind. Four Aberdeen players hit two homers each including Ed Cholakian, who hit two in the seventh inning. Ed did not hit any more home runs that season in a total of 102 at bats.

Bill Bottenus of Springfield hit two home runs in the fourth inning of an Eastern League game against Binghamton on July 25, 1893. Bottenus then proceeded to hit another one in the fifth inning. Just prior to his home run in the fifth, he started an argument with umpire Doescher over a called strike. After circling the bases on his homer, Bottenus renewed his argument with the umpire. Doescher first fined him ten dollars but this only enraged Bill even more and then the umpire then tacked on an additional twenty-five dollar fine. When the second fine didn't work, Doescher threw him out of the game. Bottenus wouldn't leave and was forcibly escorted off the field by a policeman.

The table listing players with four or more home runs in a game does not include the feat being accomplished in independent leagues. However, a feat worth mentioning is a five home run game by Vince Barton (Hickory-Carolina League), who connected in the third, fifth, sixth, seventh and eighth innings of a game on August 28, 1938, against Kannapolis at Hickory. He grounded out in the first inning but then there was no stopping him. He had nine runs batted in and his longest homer was estimated at 500 feet. Barton played in 102 games for the Chicago Cubs in 1931 and 1932 where he hit a respectable sixteen home runs. He led the International League in 1934 with 32 homers.

Carl Dunagan, a pitcher for Des Moines of the Western League, hit home runs from both sides of the plate in a game on May 6, 1930.

Jesse Ibarra, playing for Jacksonville of the Southern League, hit grand slam home runs from each side of the plate in a home game against Memphis on July 25, 1997. This is believed to be a first for a switch-hitter.

Lu Blue, a future major leaguer, reportedly accomplished the left-right grand slam feat in 1917 while playing for Martinsburg of the Blue Ridge League. A check of all Martinsburg games revealed that it never happened. Martinsburg was a low scoring club and scored as many as eight runs in only a few games.

Irving Young, pitching for Minneapolis of the American Association, hit a home run in the tenth inning to win the second game of a doubleheader against Milwaukee on July 13, 1909. That capped a day's work for Young as he pitched shutouts in both games.

Kansas City set an American Association record with ten home runs in a game at St. Paul. This was the first game of a doubleheader on June 29, 1952. Six of the homers came in the third inning for another record. The team added three doubles and seven singles for 53 total bases as they won, 17–4. Roy Partee hit three of the homers, including two in the big inning. Vic Power, Kal Segrist and Bill Renna had two each and Andy Carey had one.

Tom Kanapkey of Columbus (Alabama-Florida League) hit home runs in three consecutive innings (sixth, seventh and eighth) in a home game versus Graceville on June 13, 1958. He had collected two singles earlier in the game.

Thirteen home runs were hit in a Pacific Coast League game at Colorado Springs on May 7, 1987. A combination of the 6,000 feet altitude plus winds gusting to 41 MPH toward the outfield fences was a contributing factor. Luis Medina and Ron Tingley of Colorado Springs each hit two of the eight for their club. Charlie Hayes clubbed two of the five by visiting Phoenix.

Steve Souchock hit home runs in three consecutive innings in the first game of a doubleheader at Los Angeles on April 16, 1950. Steve, playing for Sacramento of the Pacific Coast League, hit his first homer in the seventh off Bob Muncrief and his second off Jim Atchley in the eighth inning. He then came up in the ninth with the bases loaded and connected off Dutch McCall. Souchock came to bat for the second time in the ninth with a chance for a four home run game but the best he could do was hit a measly single.

Two Houston players hit back-to-back home runs in two consecutive innings. Frank Shofner and Jerry Witte connected in the fifth and sixth innings of a May 12, 1951 Texas League game at Tulsa.

Three consecutive home runs plus a grand slam featured a big eighth inning for Topeka on July 23, 1951. Manager Butch Nieman, Don Annen and Dick McConnell started the fireworks. Solly Drake later unloaded a grand slam as Topeka routed Salina, 18–5, in the Western Association game.

Rafael Fernandez of Texas Ciry (Gulf Coast League) hit home runs in the sixth, seventh and eighth innings of a game on May 7, 1952. Fernandez drove in seven runs but that wasn't enough as Lake Charles won the game, 10–9.

Home Runs in a Series of Games

Bob Sanguinett of Midland (West Texas League) hit at least one home run in each of the ten games he played in from June 25 through July 7, 1928. He hit a total of twelve home runs during the home run spree.

Former Michigan gridiron star Allen Weygandt (Topeka-Western League) went on a home run spree in May 1956. He hit two homers in the first game of a doubleheader on May 13th at Albuquerque then connected for three in the nightcap. He hit three more the next day. Weygandt ended the Albuqerque series with two HR on May 15th. At Tingley Field, Weygandt hit ten home runs in four games. The club then moved on to Runyon Field in Pueblo where he clubbed four more homers in six games. In these ten road games, the Yankee farmhand connected for fourteen home runs. For the year, Weygandt hit 49 HR and had a .304 batting average.

Bert Ellison (San Francisco, Pacific Coast League) hit eight home runs in three games in 1924. Ellison socked three home runs on Saturday May 24th. The next day, he connected for two in the first game of a doubleheader. He then proceeded to hit three more in the second game. The series was played at hitters' paradise Bonneville Park in Salt Lake City. Both teams combined for 38 HR during the seven game series.

Slugging third baseman Gene Lillard (Los Angeles, Pacific Coast League) hit eight home runs in six games between April 18 and April 22, 1935. Lillard led the PCL in home runs that year with 56.

Outfielder Bill Renna (San Francisco Seals-Pacific Coast League) also had a week to remember. During the week of August 3 through 9, 1959, he hit eight home runs in seven games.

Bob Bauer (Auburn, New York-Pennsylvania League) hit eight home runs in eight games in 1959. His spree began on June 13th and lasted through June 20th. For the year, Bauer only hit 22 home runs.

For many years, Tony Lazzeri (Salt Lake City, Pacific Coast League) had been credited with slugging eight home runs in five games from September 11 through 15, 1925. Recent careful checking of newspaper accounts, however, has shown that he only hit seven home runs in those five games.

Tom Winsett (Columbus-American Association) hit 21 home runs during the month of June 1936. Winsett wound up the year with 50 home runs, and he added one more with Brooklyn of the National League.

Bob Crues of Amarillo (West Texas-New Mexico League) also had a great month on the way to tying Joe Hauser's season home run record of 69. In August, 1948, Crues hit 20 home runs.

Dick Stuart (Lincoln-Westernn League) hit 23 home runs in the month of June 1956. He added another 17 in the month of July, making an incredible forty home runs in a two month period. If you add the sixteen home runs he hit in May, Stuart had an even more mind-boggling 56 homers in three months.

Phoenix of the Pacific Coast League hit at least one home run in 42 consecutive home games in 1959. George Brunet of Portland held them to five singles on July 22nd to put an end to the streak. The club hit a total of 196 HR, led by Willie McCovey with 29. Others on the club: Bill Wilson (23 HR), Bobby Prescott (21 HR), Bob Speake (20 HR) Benny Valenzuela (20 HR) and Jose Pagan (19 HR).

John Reider (Springfield-Western Association) had a very merry month of May in 1926. In a game at Okmulgee on May 4, he hit three home runs. The following day at Ardmore, he slammed two triples and a pair of home runs. The scheduled game on the 6th was rained out. On the 7th, still at Ardmore, Reider hit three more homers. In three consecutive games, he had thirteen at bats, ten runs and ten hits, good for 38 total bases. On May 17th and 18th versus McAlester Reider hit safely nine consecutive times. Included were three doubles in each game. And in spite of missing a week due to injury, John Reider hit eight doubles, three triples and eleven home runs during the month.

Harry Nolan (Rayne-Evangeline League) hit three home runs in each game of a doubleheader on August 25, 1934. The opposing team was New Iberia. Nolan hit a total of 25 home runs that year. The two players who finished as runners-up had only twelve. Nolan led the league with 101 RBI and finished third in batting with a .338 average.

Mike Calise (Louisville-American Association) failed to hit a homer on June 25, 1982, after homering in his previous eight games.

Elmer Smith (Portland-Pacific Coast League) hit nine home runs in eight games during a six-day period from August 19 through August 24, 1926. During the streak, Smith had two three home run games.

Louis Munn (Richmond-Blue Grass League) hit home runs in seven consecutive games in 1912, with the last one coming on August 16th. This was an amazing feat, and even more so for the Deadball Era.

Dave Hall (Waterloo-Midwest League) hit thirteen home runs in the first twenty games of the 1961 season. Teammate Bob Lawrence hit ten, while the club as a whole hit 41 roundtrippers. Hall was leading the league when promoted to the Eastern League. He hit only four more home runs that season. Meanwhile, Bob Lawrence went on to hit a league leading thirty home runs.

Rance Pless (Denver-American Association) hit four grand slam home runs during a 34-day period, from July 3 through August 5, 1957. Pless wound up the year with only 15 home runs and 82 RBI. In 1958, he got a 49-game shot with the Kansas City A's.

Former Olympic star Ty Griffin (Arkansas-Texas League) hit leadoff home runs in four consecutive games from August 11 through August 14, 1995. Griffin, a switch hitter, clubbed his first batting right and the last three batting left.

Charlie Gilbert (Nashville-Southern Association) hit seven home runs in the first four games of the 1948 season. He just barely missed an eighth homer when a drive bounced off the top of the fence and dropped back onto the playing field.

Infielder Mickey Burnett (Oakland Oaks-Pacific Coast League) was pinch-hit for twice during a six-day period in 1947. Glenn Crawford hit for him on August 15th, socking a grand slam home run. On August 20th, Will Hafey was sent in to pinch-hit for Burnett and also hit a grand slam home run. One would think that Burnett was not much of a hitter, but he finished the season batting .295. His manager was none other than Casey Stengel.

Joe Gordon, manager of the Pacific Coast League Sacramento Solons, put himself in to pinch-hit in each game of a doubleheader on September 16, 1952. On both trips to the plate that day he hit home runs. The first one was a grand slam that gave Sacramento a 4–1 victory. The former Yankee standout second baseman hit 16 home runs that year, but had reached the end of his career.

Wes Westrum played in 51 games for Jersey City of the International League at the beginning of the 1949 season, before being called up to the parent New York Giants. During that span, Westrum hit five grand slam home runs, shattering the league record of three in a season. His grand slams were hit on April 21st, the first game of a May 15th doubleheader, May 16th, June 6th and June 8th.

In mid-May, 1951, Dick Greco was sent down to Montgomery of the Sally League by Birmingham (Southern Association). In his first sixteen games with Montgomery, Greco hit eleven home runs. Greco had been hitting .321 with three HR for Birmingham. He wound up with 33 HR and a .310 batting average with Montgomery.

Jack Parks (Natchez-Cotton States League) hit eight home runs in five consecutive games from June 4 through June 8, 1948. He batted in an amazing twenty runs during the streak.

Austin Kearns (Dayton-Midwest League) had a hitting streak in which he hit home runs in each of eight games. The streak was from July 17 through July 24, 2000, and he went 18 for 25 with ten home runs, twenty runs batted in and nineteen runs scored. In one three game stretch, he was nine for nine with two doubles and five homers.

Dan Collier of Tulsa hit home runs in seven consecutive games through June 19, 1997 to set a Texas League record. Russ Burns in 1949 and Daryle Ward earlier in 1997 held the old record with six.

Dan Rohrmeier (Tacoma-Pacific Coast League) hit seven home runs during an eight game period from August 21 through 28, 1997. He connected five times during a four-game series at Salt Lake City and twice during four games at Edmonton. For good measure, he added three doubles and a triple during the spree.

Bill Serena, Lubbock, hit thirteen home runs in seven West Texas-New Mexico League playoff games in 1947.

Al Rosen hit five consecutive homers on July 26 and July 27, 1948 while playing for Kansas City against St. Paul (American Association).

John Romano (Waterloo-Three Eye League) hit home runs on nine consecutive days. He failed to connect in one game of a doubleheader during the streak, which went from July 25 to August 2, 1955. On August 3rd, he hit a drive that appeared to be over the fence but the Peoria outfielder made a leaping catch at the top of the barrier.

Glenn Cox, a pitcher (Buffalo-International League), went on a batting spree in early 1957. He hit two homers, one a grand slam, on May 26th while pitching a shutout against Rochester. Five nights later, he hit two more home runs plus a double as he beat Rochester again. This time he allowed one run. One June 5th, he defeated Miami, 2–1. In this game, he hit a single and a game-winning home run. He knocked in ten runs during his three game spree.

Claude Westmoreland of Albuquerque (Pacific Coast League) hit home runs in seven consecutive games from June 27 through July 3, 1977. He hit two on June 30th and two on July 3rd to give him nine homers during the streak.

Brothers Mike and Frank Skaff each hit two home runs for Baltimore on May 8, 1945, in a game at Buffalo. Mike also chipped in with a single and a double and he batted in six runs. Frank added a single to his collection and had five runs batted in. In his two previous games (a doubleheader on May 6th), Frank had three homers; two in the first game and one in the second.

Perry Werden (Minneapolis-Western League), hit eleven home runs during an eight game period from July 19 through July 27, 1895. He hit two on the 19th, two on the 22nd and four on the 23rd. He did not hit any on the 21st and 24th. During the streak he had 41 at bats and 23 hits with one double.

John Rodriguez, playing for Memphis of the Pacific Coast League, hit four grand slam home runs within a span of 22 games between June 15 and July 9, 2005.

A story has appeared in several publications, including the first edition of this book, about a rare home run feat by Roy Ostergard of Galveston in the 1923 Texas League. According to this story, Ostergard hit five home runs during a short period of time and they were all grand slams. Based on research over eighty years later by Tom Kayser, President of the Texas League, it never happened. Ostergard went on a home run spree during a seven day, nine-game period late in the season where he connected for eight homers. However, only two were grand slams. With two earlier in the season, he finished the season with four grand slams.

Odell Hale hit seven home runs on six consecutive days while playing for Alexandria of the 1929 Cotton States League. The last one came on June 10th versus Meridian.

Four or More Home Runs in a Game

Ninety-three players have had games in which they hit four or more home runs. One player performed the feat twice. One player hit eight home runs in a game, and four others hit five in a single contest. Forty-two of the players on the list made the majors, but only twenty-five of them played in as many as 100 major league games, and only six played in 1,000 or more big league games. George Kelly, a Hall of Famer, is probably the best known player on the list. However, Tom Brunansky and Matt Williams are more recognizable to contemporary fans. Williams is the top major league career home run hitter on the list with 378. He is followed by Brunansky with 271, Jim Lemon with 164, and Kelly with 148.

Buzz Arlett is the player with two four-homer games. They came within 33 days of each other and they both came against Reading, one at home and one on the road. Jay Clarke hit eight home runs in a single game. Pete Schneider, Lou Frierson, Cecil Dunn and Dick Lane had the five-homer games.

Fifteen major league players have hit four home runs in a game. All of them, with the exception of Bobby Lowe, can be considered as genuine home run hitters. Lowe hit his in bandbox Congress Street Grounds in Boston. Lou Gehrig, Willie Mays and Mike Schmidt are among the greats. This is not the case with the minor league hitters with four home runs in a game. Only fifteen, or seventeen percent, reached the 200 home run career level in the minors. Another twenty-seven reached the 100 level. Arlett is the top man on the list with 432 career home runs in the minors. He is followed by Joe Bauman with 337, Ab Wright with 323, Pud Miller with 268 and Keith Little with 265.

At the other end of the spectrum are players such as John Gillespie, Earl Waltz, Don DiChiara, Dick Lane, Frank Askland, Dan Cronin and Tommie Harris. Gillespie had only six career home runs, but he was a pitcher and, therefore, can be excused. Waltz had nine home runs in a four-year career and seven of them came during a three-game spree. DiChiara was in the minors for only two years and he hit a total of thirteen. Lane is an interesting case. He is the last player to hit five homers in a game. He hit only eighteen in a four-year minor league career and none during a twelve game stretch with the Chicago White Sox in 1949. Incidentally, three of Lane's five home runs on his big day were hit off former major leaguer Walter "Boom-Boom" Beck. Askland hit just eight home runs during a six-year career.

Dan Cronin and Tommie Harris are the mystery men on the list. SABR member Bob Richardson, an expert on baseball in New England during the 19th Century, found that Cronin played semi-pro ball in several New England states from 1888 through 1890 and then went on to play in the New England League in 1891 and 1892. That is all we know about his playing career. He died in Manchester, New Hampshire on May 5, 1896. Cronin did not hit any home runs during his two years in the New England League other than on his big day. There is no explanation as to why he caught fire that day. The ballpark was certainly not a home run haven. We know even less about Tommie Harris, even though he is a player of more recent vintage. Harris played in 29 games for Terrell in the Texas Association in 1926 without connecting for a homer. There is no record of him playing anywhere in 1927.

Then in 1928 he hit fourteen home runs for Midland of the West Texas League. That is the extent of our knowledge of Mr. Harris. Even our Texas baseball expert, Davis Barker, has been stumped on this one.

The most dramatic four home run game was played on August 31, 1954 at Roswell, New Mexico. Joe Bauman was shooting for the single season home run record of 69. Going into this Longhorn League game, Bauman's chances looked bleak. He needed six home runs in seven games to break the record. After the fireworks had concluded in the game, Joe's chances appeared much brighter. He then needed only two in the remaining six games to set a new mark. As minor league followers know, Bauman went on to hit four more home runs, pushing his season total to 72, a minor league record that still stands.

An amazing performance was turned in by Jay Clarke of the Corsicana club of the Texas League. Clarke hit eight home runs in a game on Sunday, June 15, 1902. Sunday ball was not allowed in Corsicana during those times, so the game was played in nearby Ennis. Very little is known about the Ennis ballpark. In an interview many years later, Clarke said that the right field fence was only about 210 feet down the foul line. There have been several versions of the box score of the game and none of them "prove out." They do, however, all agree that Corsicana clobbered Texarkana, 51 to 3.

Junior DeWitt pitched the entire game for Texarkana. There is an interesting story—whether it is true or not—that states that Junior was the son of C. B. DeWitt, a part owner of the Texarkana club. As the story goes, C.B. arranged to have his boy join the club and instructed the manager to let his son pitch. The somewhat perturbed manager put Junior into this particular gam and let him pitch and pitch and pitch. After the game, the manager was asked why he didn't change pitchers. He gave the simple reply, "The club owner told me to let the boy pitch, so I let him pitch".

Another story about the game is that the copy editor for the *Dallas Morning News* thought that the 8 home runs credited to Clarke must have been an error, and changed it to a "3." The copy editor reasoned that an 8 looks similar to a 3 and that it would be impossible for anyone to hit 8 home runs in a single game. A brief game story that accompanied the box score in the News indeed credited Clarke with three home runs. This is probably the source of the note that ran shortly thereafter in Sporting Life that gave an account of the game and credited Clarke with three home runs.

George Moreland, a noted historian, devoted two pages in his 1927 book, Balldom, to explaining why Jay Clarke should be credited with only three home runs. However, the official scorer of the game attested to the eight home runs under oath and this was published in the Dallas Morning News in 1916. In addition, William Ruggles, author of The History of the Texas League, stated that J. Doak Roberts and J. Walter Morris verified the eight home runs. Roberts was the managing director of the Corsicana club at the time of the game and he went on to serve as president of the Texas League for twelve years. Morris was the shortstop for Corsicana in the game, and he, also, served as president of the Texas League. Of course, Jay Clarke certainly agreed with the eight homers during numerous interviews in later years.

Another point of dispute is the number of runs batted in that Clarke had in the game. Figures of sixteen, twenty and twenty-two have been published at various times. Clarke thinks that he had about twenty. RBI were not an official statistic in those days and, thus, were not in box scores. Since there was no play-by-play of the game, we will never know.

Clarke's teammates chipped in with another thirteen home runs in the game. On the other side, Texarkana batters did not even hit one.

Jay Clarke was a full-blooded Indian from Ontario, Canada. 1902 was his rookie season, and he managed to hit only three more homers that season. His career in pro ball lasted through the 1925 season, with some time out during World War I to serve in the U. S. Marines. He spent six seasons in the majors, hitting only six home runs. His minor league total numbered only twenty-two. Clarke died of a heart attack at his home in River Rouge, Michigan, on June 15, 1949. Ironically, this was the anniversary of his big game.

The Vernon Tigers of the Pacific Coast League played a game at Salt Lake City's Bonneville Park on May 11, 1923 and "squeezed" out a 35 to 11 victory. Pete Schneider of the visiting team hit five home runs in the game. Pete could have asked the question, "What if?", about his performance in the game. Below are his at bats for the game:

Hit a home run in the first inning with one man on base.
Flied out in the second inning.
Hit grand slam home run in the third inning.
Hit three-run homer in the fourth inning.

Hit a ball in the sixth inning that struck two feet from the top of center field fence with Schneider winding up on second with a double. "What if I had the ball a little harder"? "What if I had hit the ball a little more to the left"?

In his second at bat in the sixth inning, hit a solo home run.

Hit a grand slam home run in the seventh inning.

Came up for the last time in the ninth and hit a terrific liner to the centerfielder. "What if I would have gotten under the ball a little more"?

Oh, well, sometimes you never get the breaks!

At first glance, Ab Wright's four home run feat might not seem so extraordinary. After all, his home runs were hit at bandbox Nicollet Park in Minneapolis. The only problem with that scenario is that Wright batted from the right side and Nicollet was friendly only to left-handed batters. Down the leftfield line it was a normal 324 feet and it jutted out to a deep 432 feet in center. The following is a rundown on Wright's four homers:

A 400-foot drive over the wall in deep right-center in the third inning.

Hit one an estimated 450 feet over the center field fence in the fourth inning.

Hit one over the left-center field wall which hit a building across the street in the fifth inning.

In the seventh inning, hit one even further than the previous one with the ball landing on the roof of the same building.

Bob Seeds, playing for Newark of the International League, had one of the greatest two-game batting sprees in the history of the game. On May 6, 1938, at Buffalo, Seeds hit four home runs and two singles, knocking in twelve runs. His homers, including a grand slam, came in four consecutive innings. The next day he added three more home runs to his collection.

Seeds tore up the International League during the first part of the 1938 season. After 59 games he was batting .335 with 28 home runs, 73 runs and 95 runs batted in. However, the New York Yankees owned the Newark club and they decided that Seeds did not fit into their future plans. They sold him to the New York Giants in June. Projecting Seeds' performance over a 154 game schedule, he would have hit 73 HR, scored 191 runs, and driven in a mind-boggling 248 runs.

Of the four players with five home run games, three chipped in with an additional hit. Schneider, as mentioned previously, had a double. Dunn and Lane each had a single. Surprisingly, in almost half of the four home run games, the player had at least one additional hit. Len Cross collected three singles and Bob Seeds added two singles. Twenty-one players had an additional single and one player had a double. Four players (Henry Bateman, Tommie Harris, Ab Wright and Derek Bryant) each added a triple to their collection.

Babe Paul, Lew Ford, Al Mallonee, and Micah Hoffpauir got minimum mileage out of their four homers. They all were solo home runs. Paul had an excuse— he was the leadoff batter and one of his shots came in the first inning.

Reno (Sunset League) teammates Phil Alotta and Vince Pascale each hit four home runs in the first game of a doubleheader on June 1, 1947. Another teammate, Tom Lloyd, chipped in with three homers. The Reno Silver Sox had a total of twelve home runs in the game and their opponent, Ontario, hit four. Six more home runs were hit in the second game of the doubleheader, giving the two teams a total of 22 home runs for the day. Both foul lines at the Reno Park, Moana Field, measured 320 feet. The catch is that every point on the outfield fences was equidistant from home plate. In other words, centerfield also measured 320 feet.

John Gillespie is the only pitcher in Organized Baseball to have hit four home runs in a game. Gillespie had an eight-year career in pro ball, including a one-year stint with the Cincinnati Reds in 1922. On August 9, 1923, he hooked up with Gary Fortune of Springfield in a seesaw battle at Bridgeport. The score after nine innings was knotted at nine. Bob Tecarr relieved Fortune to start the tenth. Gillespie was the first batter in the inning. In his first four appearances, he had singled once and homered in the third, sixth and eight innings, batting in four runs. Against Tecarr, Gillespie hit the ball over the short rightfield fence for his fourth homer of the day. Tecarr got out of the inning without any more damage. Then George Abrams came in to pitch for Bridgeport, relieving Gillespie. He preserved Gillespie's hard-earned victory.

GOING FOR THE FENCES

Three of the games on the list were not regular season games. Jim Lemon hit four home runs in an All-Star game. This, like many minor league All-Star games, was played between a group of all-stars from around the league and the club leading the league at the time of the game. Lemon was one of the all-stars playing against host Birmingham at Rickwood Field. Rickwood was one of the game's more spacious parks with a distance of 407 feet down the leftfield line and 470 feet to dead center. Lemon, a right-hander, hit two to left-center and two to right-center.

Dixie Upright hit four home runs for Waco in a Big State League semi-final playoff game in 1949. Waco won the game, the series, and the finals. More recently, in 1999, Eric Battersby hit four for Burlington in a semi-final playoff game in the Midwest League.

Quentin Martin, playing for Rocky Mount of the Coastal Plain League, almost made the four home run game list. In a game at Goldsboro on July 3, 1949, Martin hit his fourth home run of the game in the ninth inning. Shortly after hitting his home run, it began to rain. The rain kept coming and the game had to be called. Rocky Mount was ahead at the time, so all ninth inning stats were wiped out, including Martin's fourth home run.

Bubba Trammell of the Toledo (International League) club hit four homers against Richmond on August 9, 1997. They resulted in only five runs, but he really made them count. He hit one in the ninth with a man on to tie the score at ten and force the game into extra innings. He connected again in the thirteenth inning to win the game, 11–10.

Tyrone Horne of Arkansas in the Texas League hit for the cycle on July 27, 1998. No, not that kind of cycle. He hit a solo home run, a two-run homer, a three-run homer and a grand slam – not in that order.

Henry Bateman of Paris (Texas League) pitched a no-hitter against Fort Worth on July 11, 1903. This was less than two months after his four home run game. Bateman was normally an outfielder and first baseman.

Jerry Crosby hit home runs in four consecutive innings (4, 5, 6 and 7) in his four home run game in 1953.

A number of publications over the years have carried lists of four home run games. Many lists were incomplete and they all contained errors, particularly erroneous dates. In addition, a number of players have been incorrectly credited with four home run games. They are as follows:

Perry Werden – May 28, 1894. As per an article in Sporting Life, Werden did play in the game for Minneapolis, but the box score in Sporting Life credited him with only three home runs. The game story and box score in the Minneapolis Tribune also gave him three home runs.

John Crooks - 1898. The December 3, 1898 edition of The Sporting News reported that Crooks had hit five home runs for St. Paul in a game at Minneapolis during the past season. A check of all box scores for the season failed to come up with anything close to five.

Henry Beckendorf - 1904. A note in the September 24, 1904 edition of Sporting Life stated that Beckendorf of Kingston in the Hudson River League had recently hit four home runs in a game. A check of the two daily newspapers in Kingston revealed that Beckendorf had 4 hits in a game on August 17, but never had four home runs in a game that season.

— McElvey – April 10, 1912. The 1914 edition of Balldom credited McElvey with a four home run game on April 10, 1911 while playing for Minneapolis. The second edition of Balldom in 1927 changed the year to 1912 and specified that the club was Minneapolis of the American Association. Minneapolis opened the 1911 season on April 12. No player named McElvey appeared in the line up for Minneapolis and no home runs were hit in the game. The 1912 season opened on April 10 and, again, there was no McElvey in the line up. The name McElvey did not appear in the final American Association averages for either 1911 or 1912. The 1912 Central Kansas League had a club in Minneapolis, Kansas. The club transferred to Newton on July 12. Again, a McElvey did not appear in the league's final averages.

Pete Kilduff—1916. From an unknown source: Kilduff played for Omaha of the Western League in 1916 and hit only three home runs the whole year.

Daubert—July 16, 1921. As per the 1927 edition of Balldom, Daubert played for Eveleth of the Mesabi Range League. This was a semi-pro or independent league and not a member of the National Association. Incidentally, Jake Daubert, the well-known major leaguer, was with Cincinnati that season.

Fred Merkle—April 12, 1923. As per the 1927 edition of Balldom, Merkle played for Rochester of the International League on April 12 and hit four home runs. This was an exhibition game against the Philadelphia Athletics. There have been many four home run games by players in exhibition games.

Richard Bazinet—1962. As per an article in the May 11, 1963, edition of *The Sporting News*. Bazinet, playing for Auburn of the New York–Pennsylvania League, hit four homers in a game in 1962. This did not happen according to Leo Pickney, sports editor of the Auburn Citizen.

Miscellaneous Facts

- Sixty-one players were right-handed batters, twenty-nine were left-handed and three were switch-hitters.

- Of the switch-hitters, Walter Holke hit all of his homers batting left. Buzz Arlett hit his first three batting left and his last one batting right in his first four home run game. In his second four home run game, his first and last home runs were hit from the right side and the middle two from the port side. Jerry Crosby hit his first home run while batting right and the last three while batting left.

- Most home runs in a season (season in which player had his four home run game): Joe Bauman, 72; Pud Miller, 55; Buzz Arlett, 54; Cecil Dunn, 47; Keith Little, 47.

- Fewest home runs in a season (season in which player had his four home run game): Dan Cronin, 4; John Gillespie, 4; Frank Askland, 5; Waldo Jackley, 7; Pat Garman, 8; Curtis Roberts, 8.

- Most consecutive years with at least one four home run game: 6 (1997–2002).

- Most consecutive years without a four home run game, Deadball Era: 9 (1904–1912).

- Most consecutive years without a four home run game, lively ball era: 8 (1989–1996). After almost a nine year stretch (May 25, 1988, to May 21, 1997) without a four home run game, four players connected during a two year period.

- Number of four home run games in seven inning contests: 4.

- Number of four home run games in highest classification (at the time) leagues: 21 (International League, 7; Pacific Coast League, 7; American Association, 5; Mexican League, 2).

- Fifty-four four home run games were played at home (including Clarke's game at Ennis) and forty were road games.

- There were twelve four-home run games in leagues located in the Southwest during the ten-year period following World War II.

Players with Four or More Home Runs in a Game

A dash (—) in any column indicates that the information is not known. A plus sign (+) after the number in the RBI column indicates that the player may have had additional RBI in the game. The YR column is the player's home run total for the year. Under Notes are other batting statistics for the game, including single (S), double (D), triple (T), base on balls (BB), hit by pitch (HP), sacrifice hit (SH), grand slam home run (GS), and inside the park home runs (IPHR). Also noted is if a player's home runs came in four or five consecutive plate appearances (4C or 5C).

Eight Home Run Game

Date	Player	Club, League	Opponent	H/A	AB	R	H	RBI	YR	B	Notes
6/15/1902	Jay Clarke	Corsicana, Texas League	Texarkana	H	8	8	—	11	L		G played at Ennis, TX

Five Home Run Games

Date	Player	Club, League	Opponent	H/A	AB	R	H	RBI	YR	B	Notes
5/11/1923	Pete Schneider	Vernon, Pacific Coast League	Salt Lake City	A	8	6	6	14	19	R	D, 2 GS, 2 HR 7th inn.
5/30/1934	Lou Frierson	Paris, West Dixie League	Jacksonville	H	6	5	5	8	40	L	5 C
4/29/1936	Cecil Dunn	Alexandria, Evangeline League	Lake Charles	A	7	5	6	12	47	R	4 C in 1st 4 AB, S
7/3/1948	Dick Lane	Muskegon, Central League	Fort Wayne	A	7	6	6	10	12	R	S

Four Home Run Games

Date	Player	Club, League	Opponent	H/A	AB	R	H	RBI	YR	B	Notes
6/8/1889	John Crooks	Omaha, Western Association	St. Paul	A	5	5	5	13	16	R	S
5/31/1892	Dan Cronin	Pawtucket, New England League	Salem	A	4	5	4	13	4	R	4 C in 1st 4 AB, 1 GS
7/30/1894	Buck Freeman	Haverhill, New England League	Pawtucket	H	5	6	5	13	34	L	D, HP, 1 IPHR, 2 HR in next game
5/12/1895	Bill Bottenus	Buffalo, Eastern League	Wilkes-Barre	H	5	4	5	9	9	L	7 inning G, D, Leadoff batter
5/28/1895	Hercules Burnett	Evansville, Southern League	Memphis	H	5	4	4	—	26	R	BB
6/11/1895	Bill Kuehne	Minneapolis, Western League	Indianapolis	H	6	4	5	6	22	R	S
7/23/1895	Perry Werden	Minneapolis, Western League	Detroit	H	5	5	5	9+	45	R	S, BB, 2 HR in previous G
5/14/1903	Henry Bateman	Paris, Texas League	Corsicana	A	5	4	5	—	13	R	T
9/9/1913	Waldo Jackley	Ironton, Ohio State League	Hamilton	A	5	5	5	9	7	L	S, 4 C
6/24/1919	George Kelly	Rochester, International League	Reading	A	6	5	5	9	15	R	D, 4 C
8/31/1920	Frank Askland	Mitchell, South Dakota State Lg	Wessington Sp	H	4	4	4	6	5	L	BB, 4 C
5/28/1922	Denver Grigsby	Sapulpa, Southwestern League	Muskogee	A	5	4	5	6	17	L	S, HP, HR in next G
8/9/1923	John Gillespie	Bridgeport, Eastern League	Springfield	A	5	4	5	5	4	R	S, HR in 10th inning won G
7/19/1924	Wilbur Davis	Okmulgee, Western Association	Springfield	H	5	5	5	9	51	L	S, BB
7/15/1925	Earl Waltz	Waynesboro, Blue Ridge League	Martinsburg	A	5	4	5	5	9	R	S, 4 C, HR in 2 previous G
5/17/1926	Al Mallonee	Richmond, Virginia League	Portsmouth	A	6	5	5	4	24	L	D, HR in 2 previous G, HR in next G
7/14/1926	Al Maderas	Springfield, Three I League	Quincy	A	5	4	4	8	30	R	4 C

Players with Four or More Home Runs in a Game (cont.)

Date	Player	Club, League	Opponent	H/A	AB	R	H	RBI	YR	B	Notes
7/17/1927	Clay Hopper	Danville, Three I League	Quincy	A	6	5	4	8	13	R	1st G of DH
6/11/1928	Tommie Harris	Midland, West Texas League	Hamlin	H	5	5	5	—	14	L	T, BB
5/13/1930	Walter Holke	Hazleton, NY–Penn League	Scranton	H	5	4	4	5	20	S	All HR batting left-handed
6/8/1930	Ken Strong	Hazleton, NY–Penn League	Wilkes-Barre	H	5	4	4	8	41	R	4 C, 3 HR in DH of previous day
6/1/1932	Buzz Arlett	Baltimore, International League	Reading	A	4		4	7	54	S	BB, 1st 3 HR batting right-handed
7/4/1932	Buzz Arlett	Baltimore, International League	Reading	H	6	4	4	9	54	S	1 G of DH, 1st and 4th Batting R, 1 GS, HR in 2nd G of DH
6/14/1935	Dale Alexander	Kansas City, American Assn.	Minneapolis	A	6	4	4	5	16	R	4 C
6/15/1936	John Tobin	Marshall, East Texas League	Jacksonville	H	5	4	4	8	19	R	4 C
8/24/1936	Taylor Sanford	Danville, Bi-State League	Mayodan	H	5	5	5	6	27	R	D
5/6/1938	Bob Seeds	Newark, International League	Buffalo	A	6	4	6	12	28	R	2S, 4 C in 4th, 5th, 6th, 7th inn, 3 HR in next G
8/13/1938	Mel Wasley	Duluth, Northern League	Fargo-Moorhead	H	4	5	5	7	31	L	1st G of DH, BB, 4 C
7/4/1940	Ab Wright	Minneapolis, American Assn.	St. Paul	H	5	5	5	7	21	R	2nd G of DH, T, 4 C, HR in 1st G of DH
7/8/1940	Babe Paul	Muskogee, Western Association	Joplin	H	5	5	5	4	19	R	D, Leadoff batter
9/3/1945	Bill Hart	St. Paul, American Association	Minneapolis	A	6	4	4	9	17	R	1st G of DH, 4 C
5/3/1946	Ken Rhyne	Moultrie, Georgia-Florida Lg	Thomasville	H	—	5	5	9	22	L	S
5/2/1947	Ken Myers	Las Vegas, Sunset League	Ontario	H	6	5	5	12	33	L	BB, S, 2GS in 3rd inning, HR in next G
5/9/1947	Ross Morrow	Mooresville, N.C. State League	Concord	H	5	5	5	8	21	R	S, HR in next G
6/1/1947	Phil Alotta	Reno, Sunset League	Ontario	H	6	4	5	9	43	R	1st G of DH, D, 4 C
6/1/1947	Vince Pascale	Reno, Sunset League	Ontario	H	6	5	5	6	23	L	1st G of DH, S, Same G as Alotta
9/5/1947	Frank Carswell	Paris, Big State League	Austin	H	6	4	4	9	36	R	D, 2 HR in 2nd inning
5/18/1948	Floyd Yount	Newton-Conover, W. Car. Lg.	Lincolnton	H	—	5	5	—	43	R	4 C, HR in previous G
6/30/1948	Len Attyd	Albuquerque, West TX–NM Lg	Lamesa	A	6	5	4	6	18	R	BB
8/28/1948	Joe Fortin	Pampa, West TX–NM League	Lamesa	A	—	—	5	11	34	R	S
9/3/1948	Len Cross	Spartanburg, Tri-State League	Asheville	H	7	6	7	12	29	R	3 S, 4 C in 1st 4 innings
7/27/1949	Silvio DiMenna	Petersburg, Virginia League	Hopewell	H	5	4	4	9	19	L	4 C
8/15/1949	Jack Littrell	Hornell, Pony League	Olean	H	6	4	4	8	12	R	Last HR was GS
8/29/1949	Pud Miller	Lamesa, West TX–NM League	Borger	H	5	4	4	7	55	R	4 C, 1 GS
8/31/1949	Jim Warner	Wenatchee, Western Int. Lg.	Salem	H	7	5	5	9	43	R	BB, Leadoff batter, HR in previous G
9/10/1949	Dixie Upright	Waco, Big State League	Wichita Falls	H	5	4	5	6	17	L	S, League Playoff G, HR in next G
4/13/1951	Pilo Gaspar	Laredo, Gulf Coast League	Texas City	H	5	5	5	9	15	R	D, 4 C
4/4/1953	Ted Beard	Hollywood, Pacific Coast Lg	San Diego	A	5	4	4	6	17	L	4 C, drove in all club's runs
4/20/1953	Jerry Crosby	Colorado Springs, Western Lg	Pueblo	H	5	5	5	7	25	S	S, BB, 4 C, 1st batting right then 3 left-handed
8/1/1953	Dolph Regelsky	Meridian, Cotton States League	Hot Springs	H	5	5	5	7	19	R	S, BB, 4 C, HR in next G
5/20/1954	Jim Moore	Crowley, Evangeline League	Lafayette	H	5	5	5	6	21	R	S
8/6/1954	Bill Miller	Hazlehurst-Baxley, GA St. Lg.	Statesboro	A	—	—	5	—	14	R	
8/31/1954	Joe Bauman	Roswell, Longhorn League	Sweetwater	H	6	4	5	9	72	L	D
5/22/1955	Keith Little	Corpus Christi, Big State League	Austin	H	7	4	4	8	47	R	4 C

GOING FOR THE FENCES

Date	Player	Club, League	Opponent	H/A	AB	R	H	RBI	YR	B	Notes
7/4/1955	Paul Mohr	Amarillo, West TX–NM League	Clovis	H	5	4	5	11	27	L	2nd G of DH, D, 4 C, GS in 4th inning
7/19/1955	Jim Lemon	League All-Stars, Southern Assn.	Birmingham	A	5	4	4	7	24	R	League All-Star Game
8/11/1955	Sonny Tims	Pampa, West TX–NM League	Lubbock	A	5	4	5	7	22	R	S, 4 C
8/21/1955	Jodie Beeler	Plainview, West TX–NM League	Amarillo	A	4	4	4	6	24	R	2nd G of DH, BB, 4 C, 2 HR in first G of DH, 7 inning G
7/14/1956	Danny Ozark	Wichita Falls, Big State League	Beaumont	H	4	4	4	6	32	R	4 C, Club manager
8/27/1956	Curt Roberts	Columbus, International League	Havana	H	4	4	4	6	8	R	1st G of DH, 4 C, 7 inning G
6/13/1957	Guillermo Nuñez	Fresnillo, Central Mexican Lg.	Durango-Laguna	H	–	–	5	10	17	R	D, 4 C
6/13/1959	Bobby Lee Smith	Clinton, Midwest League	Dubuque	A	5	4	4	11	19	R	2 BB
5/29/1961	Al Nagel	Ardmore, Texas League	Amarillo	A	5	4	5	9	20	R	2nd G of DH, HR in 1st G of DH
6/25/1961	Don DiChiara	Batavia, NY–Penn League	Jamestown	H	4	4	4	5	12	L	1st G of DH, 4 C
8/20/1962	Charlie Dees	El Paso, Texas League	Amarillo	H	4	4	4	7	23	L	BB
7/1/1969	George Kalafatis	Montgomery, Southern League	Birmingham	H	5	5	5	8	21	L	S, No other HR hit in G
6/9/1977	Randy Bass	Tacoma, Pacific Coast League	Phoenix	A	5	4	4	8	25	L	BB, 10 inning G
7/14/1977	Gene Locklear	Syracuse, International League	Columbus	A	5	4	4	6	20	L	
6/24/1978	Mike Bishop	Quad Cities, Midwest League	Wausau	A	5	6	5	10	19	R	S, 2 BB, 4 C
6/18/1980	Tom Brunansky	El Paso, Texas League	Midland	A	7	4	4	9	24	R	4 C, All HR over 400 feet
7/6/1982	Dave Clements	Erie, NY–Penn League	Batavia	H	5	4	4	9	17	R	SH
6/2/1983	Franklin Stubbs	Albuquerque, Pacific Coast Lg.	Phoenix	H	5	4	4	7	16	L	2 HR in 2nd inning
5/14/1985	Derek Bryant	Tampico, Mexican League	Aguascalientes	A	6	5	5	7	38	R	T
6/9/1987	Wade Rowdon	Iowa, American Association	Louisville	H	5	5	4	6	18	R	BB
5/20/1988	Pat Garman	Gastonia, South Atlantic League	Myrtle Beach	H	4	5	4	7	8	R	BB
5/25/1988	Matt Williams	Phoenix, Pacific Coast League	Albuquerque	H	5	4	4	6	12	R	4 C
5/21/1997	Charles Phillips	New Orleans, American Assn.	Omaha	A	4	4	4	7	21	L	2nd G of DH, 7 inning G, 4 C
8/9/1997	Bubba Trammell	Toledo, International League	Richmond	H	7	4	4	5	28	R	13 inning G
4/22/1998	Eddie Williams	Las Vegas, Pacific Coast League	Calgary	A	5	4	5	10	20	R	S, 2 BB, HR in next G
7/27/1998	Tyrone Horne	Arkansas, Texas League	San Antonio	A	5	4	4	10	37	L	4 C, 1–3–0–2 men on base
9/13/1999	Eric Battersby	Burlington, Midwest League	Kane County	A	4	4	4	6	18	R	League playoff game, BB
5/19/2000	Miguel Ojeda	Mexico City Reds, Mexican Lg.	Monclova	H	4	5	4	8	25	R	BB
8/19/2001	Lew Ford	New Britain, Eastern League	Binghamton	A	5	4	4	4	7	R	BB
4/20/2002	Tony Mongeluzzo	Savannah, South Atlantic League	Asheville	A	4	4	4	5	9	R	BB, HR in previous G
7/14/2002	Garrett Jones	Quad City, Midwest League	Kane County	H	5	4	4	8	10	L	4 C
6/28/2004	Brandon Cashman	Spokane, Northwest League	Everett	A	6	4	4	9	7	R	4 C, HR in previous G
5/19/2007	Aaron Bates	Lancaster, California League	Lake Elsinore	H	5	4	5	6	28	R	S
6/23/2007	Brad Correll	Lancaster, California League	High Desert	H	5	4	4	8	23	R	
8/9/2008	Micah Hoffpauir	Iowa, Pacific Coast League	Round Rock	A	5	4	4	4	25	L	4 C

Three Home Runs in a Game—Nineteenth Century

Date	Player	Club, Opponent	League	Notes
7/4/1887	Joe Knight	Hamilton at Buffalo	International League	1st G of DH, also hit HR in 2nd G
9/1/1887	Hugh Duffy	Lowell vs Manchester	New England League	Also hit triple
5/9/1889	Bill Murphy	Hartford at New Haven	Atlantic Association	
5/17/1889	Duke Jantzen	Minneapolis vs Milwaukee	Western Association	
9/2/1889	Jim McGuire	Toronto vs Hamilton	International Association	
7/11/1890	Elmer Smith	Kansas City at St. Paul	Western Association	
8/28/1890	Tom Turner	Spokane vs Portland	Pacific Northwest League	
6/2/1891	Dell Darling	Minneapolis vs St. Paul	Western Association	
6/13/1892	Milt West	Columbus at Minneapolis	Western League	
6/7/1893	Frank Bonner	Wilkes-Barre vs Springfield	Eastern League	
7/25/1893	Bill Bottenus	Springfield at Binghamton	Eastern League	2 HR in 4th inning, ejected from game shortly after hitting HR in 5th inning
8/5/1893	Ed Flanagan	Dover vs Lewiston	New England League	
5/10/1894	Charles Nyce	Pottsville vs Harrisburg	Pennsylvania State League	
5/28/1894	Perry Werden	Minneapolis vs Grand Rapids	Western League	Hit grand slam in 10th inning to put club in lead 20–16 (Minneapolis batted 1st)
7/29/1894	Jake Drauby	Buffalo vs Binghamton	Eastern League	
8/12/1894	Ed Lewee	Buffalo vs Scranton	Eastern League	
6/9/1895	Tom Power	Syracuse at Buffalo	Eastern League	
6/29/1895	Perry Werden	Minneapolis vs St. Paul	Western League	
4/18/1898	Bill Kemmer	Houston vs Fort Worth	Texas League	All were 3R-HRs, 12 RBI

Home runs were not as common in the nineteenth century as later, especially with the advent of the lively-ball era. Three home run games are not at all unusual in the modern era.

There are undoubtedly some three home run games that can be added to this list. Many game stories in the nineteenth century were brief and home runs were not always considered important enough to mention.

Players with the Highest Balance of Home Runs and Stolen Bases—Season

HR	SB	Year	Player	Club, League
35	64	1961	Jose Cardenal	El Paso, Sophomore League
36	35	1963	Jose Cardenal	El Paso, Texas League
37	24	2008	Nelson Cruz	Oklahoma, Pacific Coast League
45	41	1934	Frank Demaree	Los Angeles, Pacific Coast League
36	44	1895	Dan Lally	Minneapolis, Western League
36	37	2001	Jacques Landry	Midland, Texas League
60	39	1925	Tony Lazzeri	Salt Lake City, Pacific Coast League
42	34	1951	Remy LeBlanc	New Iberia, Evangeline League
35	36	1949	Alex Monchak	Odessa, Longhorn League
34	41	1925	Leo Najo	Okmulgee, Western Association
36	39	1928	Paul Richards	Muskogee, Western Association
44	34	1924	Walt Simpson	Springfield, Eastern League
34	45	1982	Darryl Strawberry	Jackson, Texas League
51	47	1956	Len Tucker	Pampa, Southwestern League
43	36	1949	Jim Warner	Wenatchee, Western International League
42	41	1948	Dick Wilson	Mexicali, Sunset League
52	42	1930	Pat Wright	Fort Wayne, Central League
34	35	1956	Luis Zayas	Nogales, Arizona-Mexico League

Tony Lazzeri led the list in home runs with 60. Jose Cardenal had the top stolen base mark with 64. Cardenal also made the list twice. Five players had a spread of one between their home runs and stolen bases.

Players with the Highest Balance of Home Runs and Stolen Bases—Career

HR	SB	Player	Playing Span
212	594	Carlos Bernier	1948–1965
342	247	Bunny Brief	1910–1928
370	332	Matias Carrillo	1982–2008
346	244	Moose Clabaugh	1923–1940
257	265	Paul Easterling	1926–1951
275	263	Woody Fair	1934–1952
258	241	Spencer Harris	1921–1948
214	230	Brad Komminsk	1979–1993
256	283	Big Boy Kraft	1910–1924
238	239	Ed Levy	1936–1955
311	240	Jim Poole	1914–1946
222	235	Ken Richardson	1934–1951
212	284	Earl Smith	1911–1935
236	257	Len Tucker	1953–1963

Matias Carrillo led the list in home runs with 370. Carlos Bernier topped the list in stolen bases with 594, far outdistancing runner-up Earl Smith by 310. Ed Levy had the best balance with 238 home runs and 239 stolen bases.

Best Home Run to Strikeout Ratios
Minimum of 20 Home Runs

Best Ratio for a Season

Rank	HR/SO	HR	SO	Year	Player	Club, League
1	3.333	20	6	1949	Vern Washington	Gladewater, East Texas League
2	2.857	20	7	1925	Joe Bratcher	Peoria, Three I League
3	2.846	37	13	1947	Vern Washington	Texarkana, Big State League
4	2.818	31	11	1947	Al Lawrence	Waco, Big State League
5	2.636	29	11	1948	Vern Washington	Texarkana, Big State League
6	2.545	28	11	1925	Del Pratt	Waco, Texas League
7	2.333	21	9	1926	Cliff Crawford	Greenville, South Atlantic Association
8	2.235	38	17	1928	Danny Boone	High Point, Piedmont League
9	2.188	35	16	1954	Ed Barbarito	Quincy, Three I League
10	2.182	24	11	1927	Cliff Crawford	Greenville, South Atlantic Association
11	2.167	26	12	1925	Davie Miner	Okmulgee, Western Association
12	2.000	20	10	1930	Joe Hutcheson	Memphis, Southern Association
	2.000	20	10	1959	Tom Hamilton	St. Petersburg, Florida State League
14	1.941	33	17	1929	Molly Cox	Greensboro, Piedmont League
15	1.933	29	15	1953	Ed Barbarito	Quincy, Three I League
16	1.923	25	13	1926	Del Pratt	Waco, Texas League

Best Ratio for Two Consecutive Seasons

Rank	HR/SO	HR	SO	Years	Player
1	2.882	49	17	1948–1949	Vern Washington
2	2.250	45	20	1926–1927	Cliff Crawford

Best Ratio for Three Consecutive Seasons

Rank	HR/SO	HR	SO	Years	Player
1	2.867	86	30	1947–1949	Vern Washington
2	1.771	85	48	1925–1927	Del Pratt

Best Ratio for Four Consecutive Seasons

Rank	HR/SO	HR	SO	Years	Player
1	2.098	107	51	1946–1949	Vern Washington
2	1.076	142	132	1951–1954	Dean Stafford

The latest year for any player on the above list is 1959 (Tom Hamilton). Today's players like to swing for the fences and it doesn't bother them to strike out. During the recent 2008 season, the best ratio for a 20 home run hitter was 0.634. Half of the 20 home run hitters struck out over one hundred times. One player, who shall remain nameless, struck out 200 times.

Homerless Streaks

John Griffiths

Hit a home run on June 25, 1930, and did not hit another one until June 19, 1940. That amounted to homerless streaks of 1,337 games, and 4,936 at bats. John "Bunny" Griffiths was a 5 foot 6, 155 pound shortstop. He began his organized baseball career in 1925 for Martinsburg (Blue Ridge League) in 1925 and finished up with Hagerstown in the Inter-State League in 1947. Griffiths never made it to the majors, but did play two years for San Diego in the Pacific Coast League. He batted .282 in twenty-three seasons, and he managed to hit nineteen home runs.

Albert E. Wright

Hit a home run on September 1, 1935 (first game of a doubleheader for the Pacific Coast League San Francisco Mission), and did not hit another through the end of his career in 1946. Wright's homerless streak lasted for 1,321 games, and 4,611 at bats. This player is not to be confused with Albert O. "Ab" Wright, who hit 323 minor league home runs. Both played during the same time period.

San Francisco native Albert E. Wright began his career at home with the Pacific Coast League Missions in 1930 and played almost exclusively with Bay Area teams until he joined Portland in 1941, hitting between .250 and .288. Throughout his career, Wright played at second base. He ended his career with Bremerton in the Western International League in 1946. In his career, Wright only socked four home runs.

John O'Neil

Hit a home run on June 12, 1942, and did not hit another one through the end of his career in 1953. The homerless streak was 1,330 games, and 4,541 homerless at bats. It has recently been discovered that O'Neil played in 84 games for Salina of the California League in 1954 and hit two home runs. It will require some research to determine when he hit his first home run that season. In any event, we will be able to add to his homerless streak.

John O'Neil played in 46 major league games, racking up 94 at bats during his minor league streak. He did not hit a homer in the majors either, so that would give O'Neil an Organized Baseball homerless streak of 1,376 games, 4,635 at bats.

O'Neil began in 1939 in the Georgia-Florida League with Tallahassee, quickly moving on that season to Greenville in the Appalachian League, where he hit two of his five career home runs. A shortstop, O'Neil spent most of his career in the Pacific Coast League. It has recently been discovered that O'Neil played in 84 games for Selina of the California League in 1954 and hit 2 home runs. It will require some research to determine when he hit his first homer. In any event, he will be able to add to his homerless streak.

Lee Stebbens

Stebbens hit a home run on September 5, 1932, during the first game of a doubleheader, and never hit another one in his career, which concluded after the 1941 season. Added up, that gave Stebbens 1,123 straight homerless games and 4,263 homerless at bats.

In contrast to the other homerless streak players, Stebbins was a first baseman who hit seventeen home runs in his first year in pro baseball with Blackwell of the Southwestern League. Stebbins hit over .300 four times in the Texas League in the early to mid-thirties. After hitting .245 for Forth Worth in 1940, he finished up his career with Rayne (Evangeline League) in 1942. In all, he hit 36 home runs in his career.

Gene Hassell

Hassell never hit a home run in Organized Baseball. His career lasted from 1951 through 1961. He played 1,058 games, and racked up 3,323 at bats.

Gene Hassell began as a second baseman-third baseman with Wilson of the Coastal Plain League. Between 1952 and 1954, he never stole less than forty bases in a season. In his eleven-year career, Hassell hit over .300 on six occasions, including twice for Denver in the American Association. His career came to an end in Des Moines (Three I League) when he hit .198 in 25 games.

Luis Suárez

Luis Suárez also never hit a home run during his whole career, a career that began in 1944 and ended after the 1952 season. He appeared in 896 homerless games, and had 3,304 at bats in the minors.

Luís Abelardo Suárez was born on August 24, 1916 in Alto Songo, Cuba, and died in Havana on June 5, 1991. Suárez began his career at the top. He got into one game for Washington in 1944 before being shipped out to Chattanooga in the Southern Association, where he played 86 games at short with a .251 batting average. After being out of Organized Baseball for the 1945 season, he began a four-year stint as a third baseman-shortstop in the Florida International League, primarily with the Havana franchise. After getting off to a slow start in 1949 (.194 batting average), he joined the Big State League. He also played in the West Texas-New Mexico and Longhorn Leagues.

Ernie Sierra

Ernie Sierra played in 987 games through 1942 through 1954 with three years off for military service. He did not hit a home run in 3,507 at-bats during his entire minor league career. He also played in 53 games with 158 at bats in the pre-National Association Mexican League without a homer.

It Might Be OK to Quit While You're Ahead, but This Is Overdoing It!

Big Boy Kraft

Clarence "Big Boy" Kraft led the Texas League in home runs from 1922 through 1924, with totals of 32, 32 and 55, respectively. In 1924, he scored 150 runs, batted in another 196, and had a batting average of .349 to go along with his gaudy 55 homers.

Then he retired.

Kraft was 37 years old at the time of his retirement. He had started his pro career in 1910 and managed a three-game cup of coffee with the Boston Braves in 1914, but that was the extent of his major league career.

Big Boy Kraft was one of many pre-World War II players who tore up minor league pitching, yet could not make it in the big leagues. He quit to become an automobile dealer in Fort Worth, Texas.

Bud Heslet

Harry "Bud" Heslet came up through the Yankee farm system during a period when the system was loaded with promising players. After playing two years at Newark, the Yanks' top farm club, Heslet was cut loose, and caught on with Toronto for the 1950 season. He played in the International, Texas and Pacific Coast Leagues through 1955 without ever having played in a major league game.

In 1956, at the age of 36, he went to Visalia in the California League. Heslet had a "pretty good" season there, with 147 runs scored, 172 runs batted in, a .334 batting average and 51 home runs.

And with that, Bud Heslet decided to hang them up and pursue a career outside of baseball as a firefighter.

Butch Nieman

Elmer "Butch" Nieman played for Topeka of the Western Association from 1947 through 1951 and he led the league in home runs every one of those years!

Nieman quit baseball before the 1952 season, though he was still relatively young at age 33.

During World War II, he played for the Boston Braves for three years and posted fairly good numbers. Nieman returned to the minors in 1946— never to go back up to the big leagues despite some great numbers in the bush leagues.

Pedro Hernández

Pedro Hernández del Angel was a catcher and sometimes outfielder whose career only lasted two years in Organized Baseball. He played both seasons for Guanajuato in the Mexican Center League. The circuit was a feeder league for the Mexican League and was also a member of the National Association.

Hernandez' first year was good but not great: 21 home runs and a .275 batting average. It was his second and final year, 1966, that turned out to be an incredible one. Hernandez banged out fifty home runs to go along with 173 RBI and a batting average of .425 as a full-time catcher.

But that's where the story ends. A number of inquiries over the years have drawn nothing but blanks. The people at the Mexican Hall of Fame do not have any information on him. In fact, they were surprised as the rest of us that Hernandez never got a shot in the Mexican League.

This will probably remain the mystery of mysteries.

Frank Gravino

Like Stan Musial two years before, Gravino broke in as a pitcher with Williamson of the Mountain States League in 1940. Returning from World War II, he, like Musial, switched to the outfield, but unlike Musial, he never made it to the majors, topping out at Rochester in 1948.

Gravino never hit more than 21 HR until he led the Provincial League with 42 at St. Jean in 1951. After hitting 37 HR in 1952, including a Northern League leading 32 in 94 games at Fargo-Moorhead, Gravino may have had the most dominant home run season in history: 52 HR for Fargo-Moorhead in 1953. This figure was 34 home runs more than the runner up and 43 more than teammate Roger Maris collected. The following season he raised his home run total to 56, but his lead shrunk to "just 23" over runner up Dave Roberts.

Perhaps Gravino felt that he was slipping, since he retired at the end of the 1954 season. He was just 31 years old.

The Evolution of the Season Home Run Record

The National League began play in 1876, and is recognized as a major league by all baseball historians. Several other leagues formed in the next few years, starting with the 1877 season. While they were not exactly major leagues, they were never viewed as minor leagues, either. In a way, they were merely competitors of the National League.

Statistics are somewhat sketchy for those leagues. Three players are known to have hit one home run each in the 1877 International Association. George Derby of Hornell, in the 1878 International Association, hit two homers. Six players in the 1879 Northwestern League are known to have hit two home runs each. No other players are known to have hit two homers in a season through 1882.

Our story will begin with the 1883 season, when the Inter-State League and the Northwestern League were fairly stable leagues, and are recognized as legitimate minor leagues. The Inter-State League was the first of a number of leagues around the country using that name. This 1883 league had teams in New York, New Jersey, Pennsylvania and Delaware. Frank Fennelly, playing for Camden and Brooklyn, finished the season with a league leading six home runs. Since there have not been any home run stats compiled for the 1883 Northwestern League, we will consider Fennelly as the first season home run record holder. Fennelly went up to the majors the following year and remained there for the next seven years. In all, he collected 34 major league home runs, a very respectable number for the era. After his career in baseball ended, he went on to become a noted New England politician.

Tom "Oyster" Burns (another Tom Burns played in the National League for thirteen years during this same period) hit eleven home runs for Wilmington of the Eastern League in 1884 to set the new mark. The Wilmington team dropped out of the Eastern League in mid-August and joined the Union Association, replacing the Philadelphia club. Oyster Burns had an eleven year major league career and he led the National League in homers in 1890.

The record was again broken after one year. Dick Johnston of Richmond (Eastern League) hit sixteen home runs in 1885. Johnston had started his pro career with Richmond in 1884. Late in the 1884 season he went up to the majors for 39 games. Again in 1885 he started out with Richmond and then went up to the majors late in the season after having set a new minor league record. Johnston played in the majors for a total of eight years.

Walt Andrews, playing for Memphis in the Southern League, slugged 28 homers in 1887. This not only set a new minor league standard, but also bettered the major league record of 27 set by Ned Williamson in 1884. Williamson's major league mark stood until Babe Ruth came along. Andrews played in the minor leagues from 1884 through 1895 with only one 26-game stint in the majors in 1888.

Andrews' mark held until 1894 when Perry Werden, one of the top minor league players of the 19th Century, hit 43 home runs for Minneapolis of the Western League. This was an unheard of total for that era. No other player in the majors or minors reached the 40 mark until 1917. A short fence in Minneapolis undoubtedly helped Werden. His career lasted from 1884 through 1908, which included all or parts of seven seasons in the major leagues. He ended his minor league career with 171 home runs.

In 1895, Werden, still playing for Minneapolis of the Western League, upped the record to 45. Moreover, his team hit an amazing 220 home runs, a total exceeded by only a dozen minor league teams in the 20th Century.

Werden's record stood for twenty-eight years. Then, in 1923, Moses Solomon of Hutchinson in the Southwestern League hit 49 home runs. This was Solomon's third year in pro ball and he went up to the Giants for two games at the end of the season. But that turned out to be the extent of his major league career. He played in the minors through the 1929 season, but managed to add only another 29 home runs to his career totals.

Clarence "Big Boy" Kraft hit 55 home runs for Fort Worth (Texas League) in 1924. To say that he had a great year would be an understatement. Kraft scored 150 runs and drove in 196 while compiling a solid .349 average. The 1924 season was Big Boy's last year in pro ball and his best. He turned 37 years old just before the season so he was near the end of his career. Kraft had begun his career in 1910 in the Central League with his hometown team, Evansville. All said, what a way to go out!

Tony Lazzeri reached the magic sixty home run mark in 1925, two years before Ruth. Tony played for Salt Lake City in the Pacific Coast League. The long PCL schedule helped Lazzeri set his record. He played in 197 games for the Bees that year. In midyear, he had been sold to the Yankees for delivery the following Spring (1926), when he would join Ruth, Gehrig and company. When Babe Ruth hit his 60 home runs in 1927, Lazzeri finished third in the league in home runs with 18 (Gehrig was second with 47). Lazzeri hit 178 home runs in the majors and another 135 in the minors.

In 1926, Moose Clabaugh of the Tyler club in the East Texas League hit 62 home runs to eclipse Lazzeri's year-old record. Home runs were becoming a lot more common in the 1920s as evidenced by this being the fourth consecutive year to have a new home run record set. Clabaugh, who managed to play a few games in the majors in 1926, was one of the truly great minor league home run hitters, winding up with a career total of 346.

Joe Hauser upped the record to 63 in 1930 while playing for Baltimore of the International League. Hauser had been a very good hitter for the Philadelphia Athletics from 1922 through 1924. However, he broke his leg just prior to the start of the 1925 season and missed the whole campaign. Hauser did come back in time for the 1926 season and played three more years in the majors but he was not the same player he had been prior to the injury. Nevertheless, it did not appear that his hitting in the minors was affected at all.

In 1933, Joe Hauser, then playing for Minneapolis in the American Association, broke his own record by hitting 69 home runs. He is the only minor-league player to hit sixty or more home runs twice. Hauser finished his minor league career with 399 homers.

Bob Crues, playing for Amarillo in the West Texas-New Mexico League, matched Hauser's single season record by hitting 69 home runs in 1948. This is the only time the single season record has been held jointly by two players. The West Texas-New Mexico League was known as a home run league. However, to put Crues' record into perspective, the runner-up that year hit only 38 homers. Crues started out as a pitcher, and a good one at that. He had a 20–5 record in 1940, plus 3 wins in the playoffs (two of them shutouts). Then fate inter- vened. While at spring training with the Red Sox in 1941, he injured his arm. He gave up pitching, and turned to hitting home runs. During a three-year stretch, from 1946 through 1948, Bob Crues hit a total of 150 home runs.

Joe Bauman wrote the final chapter of this story. Bauman clubbed 72 home runs for Roswell of the Longhorn League in 1954. Seventy-two is a lot of home runs, but what is even more amazing is that he did it in only 138 games. Projecting that to a season with 600 at bats, he would have hit 87 home runs. Joe Bauman never played in the majors. In fact, he only got into one game at the Triple A level. Nevertheless, he sure tore up the leagues of the Southwest. He hit 221 home runs over one four-year period and led his league five times in his short nine-year career.

Bauman's record may stand forever. Of course, that statement has been made several times before and look what happened. Walter Johnson's strike out record went by the boards, as did Ty Cobb's career hit and stolen base records, Babe Ruth's career home run record and Lou Gehrig's consecutive game streak. The face of minor league ball has changed dramatically in the past 30 or 40 years. Today there are few "career" minor leaguers. There are virtually no independent teams today and co-op teams can't wait until they get real working agreements. In such an environment, the player who doesn't show promise of moving up is let go and replaced by another prospect, although this has changed somewhat in Triple A the last few years. When a player starts out fast during a season, he is moved up way before he has a chance to set any records.

The minors would have to revert back to what it once was for there to be a chance to top Joe Bauman's record.

Season Home Run Record Holders

Year	Player	Team	League	HR
1883	Frank Fennelly	Camden/Brooklyn	Inter-State League	6
1884	Oyster Burns	Wilmington	Eastern League	11
1885	Dick Johnston	Richmond	Eastern League	16
1887	Walt Andrews	Memphis	Southern League	28
1894	Perry Werden	Minneapolis	Western League	43
1895	Perry Werden	Minneapolis	Western League	45
1923	Moses Solomon	Hutchinson	Southwestern League	49
1924	Big Boy Kraft	Fort Worth	Texas League	55
1925	Tony Lazzeri	Salt Lake City	Pacific Coast League	60
1926	Moose Clabaugh	Tyler	East Texas League	62
1930	Joe Hauser	Baltimore	International League	63
1933	Joe Hauser	Minneapolis	American Association	69
1948	Bob Crues	Amarillo	West Texas-New Mexico League	69
1954	Joe Bauman	Roswell	Longhorn League	72

Tony Lazzeri's 1925 Home Run Log
Salt Lake City (Pacific Coast League)
Home Park—Bonneville Park

Tony Lazzeri was the first player in Organized Baseball to hit 60 home runs, two years before Babe Ruth. In fact, he broke Babe Ruth's record of 59 set in 1921 with the New York Yankees. The minor league record he beat belonged to Clarence "Big Boy" Kraft with 55 home runs, set the previous year with Fort Worth in the Texas League. Lazzeri played for the Salt Lake City Bees in the Pacific Coast League and the high altitude made Bonneville Park a noted offensive park throughout its history. Lazzeri's 60th home run has been a topic of controversy. In 1946, one of the players in the game stated that Sacramento "gave" Lazzeri his last home run of the season (an inside-the-park homer). The fielders ran the wrong way and didn't try very hard to get to the ball. In checking the Sacramento Bee for that game(the game was played in Sacramento), the beat reporter stated that the game was only unusual for its lack of any unusual plays. The following sentence blandly stated that Tony Lazzeri hit his 60th home run of the season.

HR	Date	Pitcher, Club	T	Ballpark
1	April 16	Jess Winters, Portland	R	Bonneville Park
2	April 16	Charlie Eckert, Portland	R	Bonneville Park
3	April 17	Bob Hasty, Portland	R	Bonneville Park
4	April 21	George Payne, Los Angeles	R	Washington Park
5	April 25	Charlie Root, Los Angeles	R	Washington Park
6	May 1	Doug McWeeney, San Francisco	R	Recreation Park
7	May 12	Charlie Root, Los Angeles	R	Bonneville Park
8	May 21	Nick Dumovich, Seattle	L	Bonneville Park
9	May 23	Johnny Miljus, Seattle	R	Bonneville Park
10	May 30 (1)	Charlie Eckert, Vernon	R	Washington Park
11	June 10	Billy Hughes, Sacramento	R	Bonneville Park
12	June 14 (1)	Laurie Vinci, Sacramento	L	Bonneville Park
13	June 14 (2)	Billy Hughes, Sacramento	R	Bonneville Park
14	June 14 (2)	Billy Hughes, Sacramento	R	Bonneville Park
15	June 16	Art Delaney, Oakland	R	Bonneville Park
16	June 16	Hub Pruett, Oakland	L	Bonneville Park
17	June 21 (2)	Hub Pruett, Oakland	L	Bonneville Park
18	June 26	Ollie Mitchell, San Francisco	L	Bonneville Park
19	June 27	Bob Geary, San Francisco	R	Bonneville Park
20	June 27	Bob Geary, San Francisco	R	Bonneville Park
21	June 27	Bob Geary, San Francisco	R	Bonneville Park
22	Jun 28 (1)	Marty Griffin, San Francisco	R	Bonneville Park
23	Jun 28 (1)	Jeff Pfeffer, San Francisco	R	Bonneville Park
24	June 30	Bob Hasty, Seattle	R	Dugdale Park
25	July 10	Rube Yarison, Portland	R	Vaughn Street Park
26	July 18	Willie Ludloph, Vernon	R	Bonneville Park
27	July 22	Charlie Root, Los Angeles	R	Bonneville Park
28	July 23 (2)	Whitey Glanzer, Los Angeles	R	Bonneville Park
29	July 24 (2)	Elmer Phillips, Los Angeles	R	Bonneville Park
30	July 29	Specs Shea, Sacramento	R	Bonneville Park
31	July 30	Frank Shellenback, Sacramento	R	Bonneville Park
32	July 31	Billy Hughes, Sacramento	R	Bonneville Park
33	July 31	Billy Hughes, Sacramento	R	Bonneville Park
34	August 2 (1)	Carroll Canfield, Sacramento	L	Bonneville Park
35	August 2 (1)	Ray Keating, Sacramento	R	Bonneville Park
36	August 19 (1)	Denny Burns, Portland	R	Bonneville Park
37	August 20	Lefty Ortman, Portland	L	Bonneville Park
38	August 28 (2)	Bob Hasty, Seattle	R	Bonneville Park

HR	Date	Pitcher, Club	T	Ballpark
39	August 30 (1)	Nick Dumovich, Seattle	L	Bonneville Park
40	September 2	Hub Pruett, Oakland	L	Oaks Park
41	September 5	Harry Krause, Oakland	L	Oaks Park
42	September 7 (1)	Earl Kunz, Oakland	R	Oaks Park
43	September 11	Willie Ludloph, Vernon	R	Washington Park
44	September 12	Clyde Barfoot, Vernon	R	Washington Park
45	September 13 (1)	Charlie Eckert, Vernon	R	Washington Park
46	September 13 (2)	Syl Johnson, Vernon	R	Washington Park
47	September 13 (2)	Syl Johnson, Vernon	R	Washington Park
48	September 15	Earl Kunz, Oakland	R	Bonneville Park
49	September 15	Earl Kunz, Oakland	R	Bonneville Park
50	September 19 (1)	Pete McKenry, Oakland	R	Bonneville Park
51	September 23	Bob Geary, San Francisco	R	Bonneville Park
52	September 23	Bob Geary, San Francisco	R	Bonneville Park
53	September 24	Guy Williams, San Francisco	L	Bonneville Park
54	September 30	Roy Meeker, Portland	L	Vaughn Street Park
55	October 1	Bonnie Hollingsworth, Portland	R	Vaughn Street Park
56	October 2	Lefty Ortman, Portland	L	Vaughn Street Park
57	October 11 (2)	Oscar Bowers, Seattle	R	Dugdale Park
58	October 11 (2)	Oscar Bowers, Seattle	R	Dugdale Park
59	October 17	Speed Martin, Sacramento	R	Moering Field
60	October 18 (2)	Frank Shellenback, Sacramento	R	Moering Field

Notes: T—Throws by Pitcher, Number in parentheses following date indicates game of doubleheader

Breakdowns

Home Runs by Park

Bonneville Park, Salt Lake City	39
Washington Park, Los Angeles	8
Vaughn Street Park, Portland	4
Dugdale Park, Seattle	3
Oaks Park, Oakland	3
Moering Field, Sacramento	2
Recreation Park, San Francisco	1
Oak Park, Stockton	0
Wrigley Field, Los Angeles	0

Home Runs by Month

April	5
May	5
June	14
July	9
August	6
September	15
October	6

Home Runs Against Club

Sacramento	12
San Francisco	10
Portland	9
Oakland	9
Vernon	7
Seattle	7
Los Angeles	6

Multiple Home Run Pitchers

Bob Geary	5
Billy Hughes	5
Charlie Eckert	3
Bob Hasty	3
Earl Kunz	3
Hub Pruett	3
Charlie Root	3
Oscar Bowers	2
Nick Dumovich	2
Sly Johnson	2
Willie Ludloph	2
Lefty Ortman	2
Frank Shellenback	2

Miscellaneous Statistics

Home Runs at Home	39
Home Runs on Road	21
One Home Run Games	37
Two Home Run Games	10
Three Home Run Games	1
Home Runs off Lefties	13
Home Runs off Righties	47

— *Compiled by Carlos Bauer and Larry Gerlach*

Moose Clabaugh's 1926 Home Run Log
Tyler (East Texas League)
Home Park—Trojan Park

Tony Lazzeri's minor league home run record lasted but a year. Clabaugh's record was the fourth straight year that minor league home run records were set: 1923 Moses Solomon with 49; 1924 Big Boy Kraft with 55; and Lazzeri's 60 home runs the year before. One of the most striking things about his record is that Clabaugh hit his 62 home runs in a league where his team only played 122 games, Moose appearing in all but one. Clabaugh's record would stand for four years.

HR	Date	Pitcher, Club	T	Ballpark	I	R	Score
1	April 22	Stanley Anderson, Texarkana	-	Trojan Park	3	1	11–8
2	April 22	Stanley Anderson, Texarkana	-	Trojan Park	4	2	11–8
3	April 23	J. P. Ogden, Texarkana	R	Trojan Park	1	1	9–2
4	April 25	Gus Burleson, Greenville	R	Urguhart Park	3	1	10–17
5	May 2	Red Hill, Greenvile	R	Trojan Park	4	0	9–2
6	May 2	Red Hill, Greenvile	R	Trojan Park	5	0	9–2
7	May 4 (1)	J. P. Ogden, Texarkana	R	American Legion Park	6	1	10–4
8	May 4 (1)	J. P. Ogden, Texarcana	R	American Legion Park	8	2	10–4
9	May 9	Gus Foreman, Marshall	L	Trojan Park	1	1	3–4
10	May 11	Ed Hopkins, Marshall	R	Trojan Park	3	2	13–6
11	May 13	Verne Roberts, Paris	R	Trojan Park	2	0	11–10
12	May 13	Verne Roberts, Paris	R	Trojan Park	6	1	11–10
13	May 19	Bennie Bendyke, Paris	-	Bearcat Field	3	1	7–4
14	May 22	Murray Richbourg, Texarkana	-	Trojan Park	3	2	10–3
15	May 22	Murray Richbourg, Texarkana	-	Trojan Park	5	0	10–3
16	May 22	Henry Wilkens, Texarkana	-	Trojan Park	7	2	10–3
17	May 27	Oral Craig, Longview	L	Trojan Park	4	1	3–4
18	May 28	Roy Appleton, Lonview	R	Trojan Park	8	1	5–4
19	May 29	Kitty Kittenbiel, Longview	-	Trojan Park	2	2	19–4
20	May 29	R. H. Laird, Lonview	-	Trojan Park	6	2	19–4
21	June 3	Oral Craig, Lonview	R	Cannibals Park	4	1	2–5
22	June 6 (1)	E. King Gill, Paris	-	Bearcat Field	2	1	6–7
23	June 8 (1)	Ed Hopkins, Marshall	R	Trojan Park	2	0	8–5
24	June 8 (1)	Ed Hopkins, Marshall	R	Trojan Park	3	1	8–5
25	June 18	Rufe Wafer, Greenvile	L	Trojan Park	5	0	4–1
26	June 20	— Denson, Longview	-	Cannibals Park	10	0	4–3
27	June 21	H. Ferguson, Longview	-	Cannibals Park	4	2	5–5
28	June 27	Vince Devaney, Paris	R	Trojan Park	3	2	6–2
29	June 28	Noel Haynes, Paris	R	Trojan Park	1	1	4–1
30	June 30	— Davis, Texarkana	-	American Legion Park	1	2	15–5
31	July 1	Cactus Keck, Texarkana	R	American Legion Park	4	1	4–13
32	July 6	John Cox, Longview	-	Trojan Park	2	1	10–11
33	July 7	H. Ferguson, Longview	-	Trojan Park	3	0	13–6
34	July 8	Lupe Rodriguez, Greenville	L	Urguhart Park	9	1	2–1
35	July 12	Cactus Keck, Texarkana	R	Trojan Park	3	0	8–7
36	July 13	Bill Cason, Texarkana	-	Trojan Park	4	1	14–4
37	July 13	Bill Cason, Texarkana	-	Trojan Park	4	1	14–4
38	July 17	Elon Hogsett, Marshall	L	Turney Park	7	1	4–3
39	July 18	Tom Farrell, Marshall	-	Turney Park	5	1	9–4
40	July 24	Oral Craig, Longview	L	Cannibals Park	7	0	5–6
41	July 26	John Cox, Longview	-	Cannibals park	7	3	11–6
42	July 28	Fred Gernandt, Greenville	L	Trojan Park	2	1	14–9
43	July 28	Fred Gernandt, Greenville	L	Trojan Park	4	1	14–9
44	July 31	Bennie Bendyck, Longview	-	Trojan Park	9	0	3–13
45	August 1	Oral Craig, Longview	L	Trojan Park	2	0	12–13

HR	Date	Pitcher, Club	T	Ballpark	I	R	Score
46	August 1	John Cox, Longview	-	Trojan Park	6	2	12–13
47	August 2	H. Ferguson, Longview	-	Trojan Park	6	0	5–11
48	August 2	H. Ferguson, Longview	-	Trojan Park	8	1	5–11
49	August 3	Charlie Sullivan, Marshall	R	Trojan Park	7	1	5–1
50	August 6	Cactus Keck, Texarkana	R	American Legion Park	6	3	5–6
51	August 7	Henry Wilkins, Texarkana	-	American Legion Park	1	2	6–2
52	August 8	J. P. Ogden, Texarkana	R	American Legion Park	10	0	4–6
53	August 10	— Emmons, Paris	-	Bearcat Field	2	2	11–7
54	August 11	— Emmons, Paris	-	Bearcat Field	8	1	11–15
55	August 12	Roy Appleton, Paris	R	Bearcat Field	1	2	10–8
56	August 12	Roy Appleton, Paris	R	Bearcat Field	8	0	10–8
57	August 13	Fred Gernandt, Greenville	L	Trojan Park	7	1	4–5
58	August 15	Rufe Wafer, Greenville	L	Trojan Park	6	1	12–9
59	August 18	Charlie Sullivan, Marshall	R	Turney Park	9	1	3–4
60	August 20	Tige Stone, Paris	R	Trojan Park	8	0	3–13
61	August 21	— Emmons, Paris	-	Trojan Park	2	0	3–1
62	August 22	Noel Haynes, Paris	R	Trojan Park	3	2	6–7

Notes: T—Throws by Pitcher, I—Inning, R—Runners on base, Score lists Tyler first, Number in parentheses following date indicates game of doubleheader

Breakdowns

Home Runs by Park
Trojan Park, Tyler	39
American Legion Park, Texarkana	7
Bearcat Field, Paris	6
Cannibals Park, Longview	5
Turney Park, Marshall	3
Urquhart Park, Greenville	2

Home Runs by Month
April	4
May	16
June	10
July	14
August	18

Home Runs Against Club
Texarkana	16
Longview	16
Paris	13
Greenville	9
Marshall	8

Multiple Home Run Pitchers
Oral Craig	4
J. P. Ogden	4
H. Ferguson	4
Five tied with 3	

Home Runs by Innings
1st Inning	6
2nd Inning	9
3rd Inning	10
4th Inning	8
5th Inning	4
6th Inning	8
7th Inning	6
8th Inning	6
9th Inning	3
10th Inning	2

Miscellaneous Statistics
Home Runs at Home	39
Home Runs on Road	23
One Home Run Games	37
Two Home Run Games	11
Three Home Run Games	1
Home Runs off Lefties	11
Home Runs off Righties	25
Unknown	26
Solo Home Runs	17
Two-Run Home Runs	28
Three-Run Home Runs	15
Grand Slams	2

— Compiled by Davis Barker

Joe Hauser's 1930 Home Run Log
Baltimore (International League)
Home Park—Oriole Park

Joe Hauser broke Moose Clabaugh's four-year old record by one. Oriole Park in Baltimore was a great park for left-handed batters. The dimensions seemed at first glance to be about normal with 310 feet down the right field line. However, the right field power alley was only slightly longer than down the foul line. It is surprising that the left-hand hitting Hauser hit only 34 of his homers in friendly Oriole Park against 29 on the road.

HR	Date	Pitcher, Club	T	Ballpark	I	R	Score
1	April 20	Harry Holsclaw, Montreal	R	Oriole Park	9	1	9–7
2	April 21	Martin Griffin, Montreal	R	Oriole Park	3	2	9–1
3	April 22	Gowell Claset, Montreal	L	Oriole Park	3	0	6–5
4	April 24	Herb Thormahlen, Montreal	L	Oriole Park	2	1	4–12
5	May 3	Clarence Fisher, Toronto	R	Oriole Park	6	2	19–6
6	May 7	Paul Derringer, Rochester	R	Red Wing Stadium	2	0	5–7
7	May 12	Harry Holsclaw, Montreal	R	Montreal Stadium	2	1	5–2
8	May 13	Gowell Claset, Montreal	L	Montreal Stadium	3	1	11–4
9	May 18	Leon Williams, Buffalo	L	Bison Stadium	2	0	7–4
10	May 30 (2)	Don Hankins, Reading	L	Lauer Park	1	0	10–7
11	May 31	Gordon Rhodes, Jersey City	R	West Side Park	7	1	6–9
12	June 1 (1)	Maurice Bream, Jersey City	R	West Side Park	2	0	5–4
13	June 3	George Bell, Reading	R	Oriole Park	6	2	18–2
14	June 3	George Bell, Reading	R	Oriole Park	7	1	18–2
15	June 4	Ernie Woolfolk, Reading	L	Oriole Park	1	1	10–9
16	June 5	Lon Warneke, Reading	R	Oriole Park	4	2	22–5
17	June 11 (1)	Fred Fussell, Buffalo	L	Oriole Park	7	2	11–6
18	June 13	Leo Mangum, Buffalo	R	Oriole Park	7	0	6–3
19	June 15 (2)	Tex Carleton, Rochester	R	Oriole Park	5	1	6–7
20	June 18 (1)	Fred Ostermueller, Rochester	L	Oriole Park	5	1	9–6
21	June 18 (1)	Fred Ostermueller, Rochester	L	Oriole Park	6	2	9–6
22	June 19	Gowell Claset, Montreal	L	Oriole Park	12	0	4–6
23	June 21	Martin Griffin, Montreal	R	Oriole Park	1	1	4–5
24	June 29 (1)	Andy Chambers, Newark	R	Bears Stadium	5	2	15–5
25	June 29 (1)	Jess Petty, Newark	L	Bears Stadium	7	0	15–5
26	July 4 (1)	George Bell, Reading	R	Oriole Park	7	0	13–10
27	July 5	Nelson Greene, Reading	L	Oriole Park	6	2	5–3
28	July 11	Leo Mangum, Buffalo	R	Bison Stadium	3	1	10–5
29	July 13 (1)	John Wilson, Buffalo	R	Bison Stadium	3	2	5–7
30	July 13 (2)	Leo Mangum, Buffalo	R	Bison Stadium	3	1	12–2
31	July 13 (2)	Leon Williams, Buffalo	L	Bison Stadium	6	1	12–2
32	July 16	Paul Derringer, Rochester	R	Red Wing Stadium	1	1	4–5
33	July 17	Bob McGraw, Rochester	R	Red Wing Stadium	7	1	5–8
34	July 20 (1)	Gowell Claset, Montreal	L	Montreal Stadium	8	1	6–14
35	July 21	Herb Thormahlen, Montreal	L	Montreal Stadium	8	2	5–0
36	July 23 (1)	Nelson Greene, Reading	L	Lauer Park	1	0	4–2
37	July 23 (2)	Leroy Herrmann, Reading	R	Lauer Park	7	1	9–0
38	July 27 (1)	George Grant, Jersey City	R	Oriole Park	1	0	10–5
39	July 27 (2)	Maurice Bream, Jersey City	R	Oriole Park	1	1	5–2
40	July 30 (2)	Myles Thomas, Newark	R	Oriole Park	7	0	5–8
41	August 1	Jim Faulkner, Newark	L	Oriole Park	1	1	3–2
42	August 2	John Pitts, Jersey City	L	West Side Park	3	0	9–0
43	August 5	Maurice Bream, Jersey City	R	West Side Park	4	0	11–6
44	August 5	Maurice Bream, Jersey City	R	West Side Park	5	0	11–6

GOING FOR THE FENCES

HR	Date	Pitcher, Club	T	Ballpark	I	R	Score
45	August 5	John Pitts, Jersey City	L	West Side Park	8	1	11–6
46	August 9 (1)	Paul Derringer, Rochester	R	Oriole Park	7	1	5–13
47	August 9 (2)	Larry Irvin, Rochester	L	Oriole Park	6	1	10–2
48	August 10 (2)	Tex Carleton, Rochester	R	Oriole Park	1	1	11–4
49	August 11	Paul Derringer, Rochester	R	Oriole Park	9	1	8–6
50	August 12	Leon Williams, Buffalo	L	Oriole Park	2	0	22–4
51	August 13	Gorham Leverette, Buffalo	R	Oriole Park	3	1	10–5
52	August 13	Henry Wertz, Buffalo	R	Oriole Park	6	2	10–5
53	August 14	Dave Danforth, Buffalo	L	Oriole Park	1	1	7–4
54	August 14	Dave Danforth, Buffalo	L	Oriole Park	9	2	7–4
55	August 17 (1)	Phil Page, Toronto	L	Oriole Park	9	0	2–1
56	August 29	Ira Smith, Rochester	R	Red Wing Stadium	1	1	3–7
57	September 1 (1)	Nelson Greene, Reading	L	Lauer Park	3	1	9–2
58	September 1 (1)	Nelson Greene, Reading	L	Lauer Park	6	0	9–2
59	September 2 (2)	George Bell, Reading	R	Lauer Park	9	1	8–14
60	September 7 (1)	George Miner, Jersey City	R	Oriole Park	5	0	12–4
61	September 11	Leo Mangum, Newark	R	Oriole Park	2	0	3–1
62	September 20	Myles Thomas, Newark	R	Bears Stadium	3	1	5–1
63	September 20	Myles Thomas, Newark	R	Bears Stadium	7	1	5–1

Notes: T—Throws by Pitcher, I—Inning, R—Runners on base, Score lists Minneapolis first, Number in parentheses following date indicates game of doubleheader

Breakdowns

Home Runs by Park
Oriole Park, Baltimore	34
Lauer Park, Reading	6
West Side Park, Jersey City	6
Bison Stadium, Buffalo	5
Bears Stadium, Newark	4
Montreal Stadium, Montreal	4
Red Wing Stadium, Rochester	4
Maple Leaf Stadium, Toronto	0

Home Runs by Month
April	4
May	7
June	14
July	15
August	16
September	7

Home Runs Against Club
Buffalo	12
Reading	12
Rochester	11
Montreal	10
Jersey City	9
Newark	7
Toronto	2

Multiple Home Run Pitchers
George Bell	4
Maurice Bream	4
Gowell Claset	4
Paul Derringer	4
Nelson Greene	4
Leo Mangum	3
Myles Thomas	3
Leon Williams	3
Seven tied with	2

Home Runs by Innings
1st Inning	11
2nd Inning	7
3rd Inning	10
4th Inning	2
5th Inning	5
6th Inning	8
7th Inning	11
8th Inning	3
9th Inning	5
12th Inning	1

Miscellaneous Statistics
Home Runs at Home	34
Home Runs on Road	29
One Home Run Games	44
Two Home Run Games	8
Three Home Run Games	1
Home Runs off Lefties	26
Home Runs off Righties	37
Solo Home Runs	20
Two-Run Home Runs	31
Three-Run Home Runs	12
Grand Slams	0

—Compiled by Carlos Bauer and Bob McConnell

Joe Hauser's 1933 Home Run Log
Minneapolis (American Association)
Home Park—Nicollet Park

In 1933 Joe Hauser became the only player ever in the mnor leagues to hit 60 home runs twice in a career. The Minneapolis park, Nicolett Park, had a notoriously short right-field fence, 279 feet down the foul line. Hauser took advantage of his home park to an extent he did not in Baltimore (an amazing 50 HR hit at home). One of the most amazing things about his record is his hitting 31 home runs off of left-handers, even more amazing when you consider that Hauser batted from the port side. During one stretch, he hit 23 of 31 home runs off lefthanders. His record would be tied fifteen years later and then beaten in 1954 by Joe Bauman.

HR	Date	Pitcher, Club	T	Ballpark	I	R	Score
1	April 27	Monte Pearson, Toledo	R	Nicollet Park	1	2	13–8
2	April 28	Roxie Lawson, Toledo	R	Nicollet Park	1	2	15–11
3	April 28	Roxie Lawson, Toledo	R	Nicollet Park	3	3	15–11
4	April 28	Ralph Winegarner, Toledo	R	Nicollet Park	8	0	15–11
5	May 3	Paul Dean, Columbus	R	Nicollet Park	3	2	7–8
6	May 3	Paul Dean, Columbus	R	Nicollet Park	5	1	7–8
7	May 6	Bill Thomas, Indianapolis	R	Nicollet Park	2	0	11–10
8	May 10	Archie McKain, Louisville	L	Nicollet Park	6	0	10–9
9	May 11 (1)	Johnny Marcum, Louisville	R	Nicollet Park	3	0	4–6
10	May 14	Floyd Newkirk, St. Paul	R	Lexington Park	6	0	15–5
11	May 23	Americo Polli, Milwaukee	R	Nicollet Park	1	2	19–5
12	May 23	Harold Hillon, Milwaukee	R	Nicollet Park	7	1	19–5
13	May 24	Garland Braxton, Milwaukee	L	Nicollet Park	8	1	5–8
14	May 26	Joe Blackwell, Kansas City	L	Nicollet Park	1	1	9–3
15	May 26	Joe Blackwell, Kansas City	L	Nicollet Park	3	0	9–3
16	May 30 (2)	Les Munns, St. Paul	R	Nicollet Park	9	0	7–6
17	May 31	Floyd Newkirk, St. Paul	R	Lexington Park	1	1	6–1
18	June 3	Bill Lee, Columbus	R	Cooper Stadium	9	0	1–5
19	June 4 (2)	Jim Lindsay, Columbus	R	Cooper Stadium	1	0	7–9
20	June 4 (2)	Jim Lindsay, Columbus	R	Cooper Stadium	4	1	7–9
21	June 8 (2)	Forrest Twogood, Toledo	L	Swane Field	4	0	7–10
22	June 9 (2)	Ralph Winegarner, Toledo	R	Swane Field	9	0	7–10
23	June 10	Bill Thomas, Indianapolis	R	Perry Stadium	1	0	4–3
24	June 13 (2)	Phil Weinert, Louisville	L	Parkway Field	1	1	9–13
25	June 14	Archie McKain, Louisville	L	Parkway Field	5	0	7–6
26	June 21 (1)	Garland Braxton, Milwaukee	L	Borchert Field	6	1	5–7
27	June 25 (1)	Emil Yde, St. Paul	L	Nicollet Park	5	0	3–5
28	June 25 (2)	Les Munns, St. Paul	R	Nicollet Park	3	0	10–1
29	June 25 (2)	Les Munns, St. Paul	R	Nicollet Park	4	1	10–1
30	June 26	Lou Fette, Kansas City	R	Nicollet Park	5	0	10–6
31	June 28	Duster Mails, Kansas City	L	Nicollet Park	6	0	4–3
32	June 29	Garland Braxton, Milwaukee	L	Nicollet Park	9	0	9–8
33	July 9 (1)	Roxie Lawson, Toledo	R	Nicollet Park	1	1	9–12
34	July 9 (1)	Forrest Twogood, Toledo	L	Nicollet Park	7	0	9–12
35	July 9 (2)	Thornton Lee, Toledo	L	Nicollet Park	3	0	8–3
36	July 10	Clarence Heise, Columbus	L	Nicollet Park	3	1	8–6
37	July 11	Bud Teachout, Columbus	L	Nicollet Park	3	0	14–6
38	July 11	Bud Teachout, Columbus	L	Nicollet Park	4	3	14–6
39	July 12	Bill Lee, Columbus	R	Nicollet Park	6	1	5–7
40	July 13	Clarence Heise, Columbus	L	Nicollet Park	8	0	10–9
41	July 14 (1)	Clyde Hatter, Louisville	L	Nicollet Park	7	1	8–2
42	July 16 (2)	Johnny Marcum, Louisville	R	Nicollet Park	1	1	8–6
43	July 17	Stew Bolen, Indianapolis	L	Nicollet Park	6	0	5–10
44	July 19 (1)	Stew Bolen, Indianapolis	L	Nicollet Park	9	3	7–5
45	July 20	Stew Bolen, Indianspolis	L	Nicollet Park	7	0	8–9

Joe Hauser's 1933 Home Run Log, (cont.)

HR	Date	Pitcher, Club	T	Ballpark	I	R	Score
46	July 21	Fred Stiely, Milwaukee	L	Nicollet Park	1	2	7–6
47	July 22	Harold Hillin, Milwaukee	R	Nicollet Park	4	1	13–9
48	July 23 (1)	Garland Braxton, Milwaukee	L	Nicollet Park	1	1	7–8
49	July 23 (1)	Garland Braxton, Milwaukee	L	Nicollet Park	3	0	7–8
50	July 27 (1)	Harold Hillin, Milwaukee	R	Borchert Field	9	0	11–8
51	July 28	Garland Braxton, Milwaukee	L	Borchert Field	8	0	6–5
52	July 30 (2)	Joe Blackwell, Kansas City	L	Muehlbach Field	3	0	15–2
53	August 5 (1)	Stew Bolen, Indianapolis	L	Perry Stadium	8	1	3–10
54	August 12	Forrest Twogood, Toledo	L	Swane Field	3	0	8–4
55	August 13 (1)	Ralph Winegarner, Toledo	R	Swane Field	5	0	3–0
56	August 15	Clyde Hatter, Louisville	L	Nicollet Park	4	2	13–6
57	August 16	Dick Bass, Louisville	R	Nicollet Park	4	1	16–1
58	August 17	Ken Penner, Louisville	R	Nicollet Park	3	0	5–8
59	August 18	Jim Turner, Indianapolis	R	Nicollet Park	6	0	11–6
60	August 20 (2)	Bill Thomas, Indianapolis	R	Nicollet Park	7	1	14–6
61	August 24	Ralph Winegarner, Toledo	R	Nicollet Park	5	0	15–8
62	August 26	Bill Lee, Columbus	R	Nicollet Park	3	1	8–6
63	September 4 (1)	Les Munns, St. Paul	R	Lexington Park	7	0	5–3
64	September 4 (1)	Les Manns, St. Paul	R	Lexington Park	9	0	5–3
65	September 4 (2)	Floyd Newkirk, St. Paul	R	Nicollet Park	2	1	5–11
66	September 7	Paul Gregory, Milwaukee	R	Nicollet Park	1	1	8–7
67	September 8	Forest Pressnell, Milwaukee	R	Nicollet Park	4	1	7–3
68	September 9	Duster Mails, Kansas City	L	Nicollet Park	4	1	6–8
69	September 9	Duster Mails, Kansas City	L	Nicollet Park	9	2	6–8

Notes: T—Throws by Pitcher, I—Inning, R—Runners on base, Score lists Minneapolis first

Breakdowns

Home Runs by Park

Nicollet Park, Minneapolis	50
Lexington Park, St. Paul	4
Swane Field, Toledo	4
Cooper Stadium, Columbus	3
Borchert Field, Milwaukee	3
Parkway Field, Louisville	2
Perry Stadium, Indianapolis	2
Muehlbach Field, Kansas City	1

Home Runs by Month

April	4
May	13
June	15
July	20
August	10
September	7

Home Runs Against Club

Milwaukee	13
Toledo	12
Columbus	11
Louisville	9
St. Paul	9
Indianapolis	8
Kansas City	7

Multiple Home Run Pitchers

Garland Braxton	6
Les Munns	5
Stew Bolen	4
Ralph Winegarner	4
Eight tied with 3	
Eight tied with 2	

Miscellaneous Statistics

Home Runs at Home	50
Home Runs on Road	19
One Home Run Games	44
Two Home Run-Games	11
Three Home Run-Games	1
Home Runs off Lefties	31
Home Runs off Righties	38
Solo Home Runs	36
Two-Run Home Runs	24
Three-Run Home Runs	6
Grand Slams	3

—Compiled by Stew Thornley

Bob Crues' 1948 Home Run Log
Amarillo (West Texas–New Mexico League)
Home Park—Gold Sox Field

The West Texas-New Mexico League was one of the greatest home run leagues ever in 1948 and Bob Crues' home run record led to the National Association deadening the ball for all the minor leagues for the 1949 season. But too much can be made of "rabbit" baseballs in the 1948 West Texas–New Mexico League and of Bob Crues' record in particular. The runner up to Crues, Virgil Richardson, only had 38 home runs, some thirty-one fewer. Bob Crues also set a record which has a chance of remaining on the books for a good long time, if not forever. He drove in an incredible 254 runs in 1948.

HR	Date	Pitcher, Club	T	Ballpark	R
1	April 21	Dick Davidson, Abilene	R	Blue Sox Stadium	0
2	April 23	Chester Zara, Lamesa	L	Lobo Field	3
3	April 25	Howard Bass, Pampa	R	Oiler Park	2
4	April 25	Hal Kunkle, Pampa	L	Oiler Park	2
5	April 30	J. B. Garland, Lamesa	R	Gold Sox Field	1
6	May 2	Sid Jamison, Borger	L	Gold Sox Field	1
7	May 3	Bob Glass, Borger	L	Huber Park	1
8	May 6	Joe Behl, Albuquerque	R	Gold Sox Field	0
9	May 8	Mel Kramer, Clovis	R	Gold Sox Field	1
10	May 8	Mel Kramer, Clovis	R	Gold Sox Field	0
11	May 9	Marv Alexander, Lubbock	R	Sam Rosenthal Field	0
12	May 16	Royce Mills, Lubbock	R	Gold Sox Field	0
13	May 16	Royce Mills, Lubbock	R	Gold Sox Field	3
14	May 17	Foster White, Pampa	R	Gold Sox Field	1
15	May 17	Foster White, Pampa	R	Gold Sox Field	1
16	May 18	Hal Kunkle, Pampa	L	Gold Sox Field	1
17	May 20	Dick Davidson, Abilene	R	Blue Sox Stadium	3
18	May 21	Bill Meier, Abilene	R	Blue Sox Stadium	1
19	May 22	Leon Hayes, Lamesa	L	Lobo Field	1
20	May 29	Bernie Coapland, Abilene	R	Gold Sox Field	0
21	May 30	Wade Hazel, Abilene	L	Gold Sox Field	3
22	May 30	Bill Morris, Abilene	L	Gold Sox Field	1
23	June 1	Stan Grzywacz, Lamesa	R	Gold Sox Field	2
24	June 2	Leon Hayes, Lamesa	L	Gold Sox Field	0
25	June 3	Hugh King, Borger	R	Gold Sox Field	2
26	June 3	Ed Carnett, Borger	L	Gold Sox Field	0
27	June 3	Ed Carnett, Borger	L	Gold Sox Field	0
28	June 4	Clay Fries, Borger	L	Gold Sox Field	2
29	June 8	Clay Fries, Borger	L	Huber Park	2
30	June 12	Mel Kramer, Clovis	R	Gold Sox Field	1
31	June 13	Darwin Dobbs, Clovis	R	Gold Sox Field	1
32	June 17	Billy Russell, Lubbock	R	Sam Rosenthal Field	2
33	June 18	Mel Kramer, Clovis	R	Bell Park	0
34	June 27	Howard Bass, Pampa	R	Gold Sox Field	0
35	July 5	Stan Grywacz, Lamesa	R	Lobo Field	0
36	July 5	Stan Grywacz, Lamesa	R	Lobo Field	0
37	July 8	Merlin Hubbard, Pampa	R	Oiler Park	1
38	July 9	Art Bowland, Abilene	R	Gold Sox Field	2
39	July 11	Ray Miller, Abilene	R	Gold Sox Field	2
40	July 12	Lee Ellyson, Lamesa	R	Gold Sox Field	0
41	July 14	Leon Hayes, Lamesa	L	Gold Sox Field	3
42	July 17	Bob Glass, Borger	L	Gold Sox Field	0
43	July 17	Bob Glass, Borger	L	Gold Sox Field	1

Bob Crues' 1948 Home Run Log, (cont.)

HR	Date	Pitcher, Club	T	Ballpark	R
44	July 18	Jim Cain, Borger	R	Huber Park	1
45	July 19	Clay Fries, Borger	L	Huber Park	1
46	July 19	Clay Fries, Borger	L	Huber Park	1
47	July 20	Ray Edwards, Borger	R	Huber Park	1
48	July 23	Frank Shone, Albuquerque	R	Gold Sox Field	1
49	July 23	Frank Shone, Albuquerque	R	Gold Sox Field	1
50	July 24	Al Kavanagh, Clovis	R	Gold Sox Field	0
51	July 25	Darwin Dobbs, Clovis	R	Gold Sox Field	1
52	July 27	Billy Russell, Lubbock	R	Sam Rosenthal Field	2
53	July 27	Billy Russell, Lubbock	R	Sam Rosenthal Field	0
54	July 31	Darwin Dobbs, Clovis	R	Bell Park	0
55	August 10	Howard Bass, Pampa	R	Gold Sox Field	2
56	August 12	Bernie Coapland, Abilene	R	Blue Sox Stadium	1
57	August 13	Lee Ellyson, Lamesa	R	Lobo Field	3
58	August 17	Joe Clardy, Abilene	L	Gold Sox Field	1
59	August 17	Joe Clardy, Abilene	L	Gold Sox Field	0
60	August 23	Ed Carnett, Borger	L	Huber Park	0
61	August 27	Darwin Dobbs, Clovis	R	Gold Sox Field	1
62	August 28	Mel Kramer, Clovis	R	Gold Sox Field	2
63	September 1	Charles O'Neill	L	Bell Park	3
64	September 1	Mel Kramer, Clovis	R	Bell Park	0
65	September 2	Vigil Butler, Albuquerque	L	Tingley Field	2
66	September 4	Roy Parker, Pampa	L	Gold Sox Field	3
67	September 4	Roy Parker, Pampa	L	Gold Sox Field	0
68	September 5	George Payte, Pampa	R	Gold Sox Field	0
69	September 5	George Payte, Pampa	R	Gold Sox Field	1

Notes: T—Throws by Pitcher, R—Runners on base

Breakdowns

Home Runs by Park
Gold Sox Field, Amarillo	41
Huber Park, Borger	7
Lobo Field, Lamesa	5
Blue Sox Stadium, Abilene	4
Bell Park, Clovis	4
Sam Rosenthal Field, Lubbock	4
Oiler Park, Pampa	3
Tingley Field, Albuquerque	1

Home Runs by Month
April	5
May	17
June	12
July	20
August	8
September	7

Home Runs Against Team
Borger	14
Clovis	12
Pampa	12
Abilene	11
Lamesa	10
Lubbock	6
Albuquerque	4

Multiple Home Run Pitchers
Mel Kramer	6
Clay Fries	4
Five tied with 3	
Eleven tied with 2	

Miscellaneous Statistics
Home Runs at Home	41
Home Runs on Road	28
One Home Run Games 38	
Two Home Run-Games 14	
Three Home Run-Games	1
Home Runs off Lefties 43	
Home Runs off Righties 26	
Solo Home Runs	23
Two-Run Home Runs	25
Three-Run Home Runs 13	
Grand Slams	8

—Source 1954 West Texas-New Mexico League Record Book

Joe Bauman's 1954 Home Run Log
Roswell (Longhorn League)
Home Park—Fair Park Stadium

Joe Bauman did what many thought would be impossible just a week before the season closed: Beat or even tie Joe Hauser and Bob Crues' all-time minor league home run record. On August 30, with only 63 home runs, Sweetwater rolled into town for a two-game series. Bauman hit his 64th home run in the first game. On the 31st, Bauman went from an also ran to a contender. He hit four home runs and a double bringing his season home run total to 68, within one of the record. He tied the record on September 2, but went homerless at Big Spring on the 3rd and the 4th of September, managing a lone single in 7 at bats. The club traveled to Artesia, with its large dimensions, for a season-ending doubleheader. Bauman broke the record in the first game, becoming the first and only player ever to hit seventy home runs in a season. In the final game of the season, he added two more for good measure.

HR	Date	Club	Ballpark
1	April 22	Carlsbad	Fair Park Stadium
2	April 22	Carlsbad	Fair Park Stadium
3	April 23	Carlsbad	Montgomery Field
4	April 25	San Angelo	Guinn Field
5	April 27	Odessa	Fair Park Stadium
6	April 27	Odessa	Fair Park Stadium
7	April 28	San Angelo	Fair Park Stadium
8	April 29	San Angelo	Fair Park Stadium
9	April 29	San Angelo	Fair Park Stadium
10	April 30	Odessa	Oiler Park
11	May 12	Artesia	Fair Park Stadium
12	May 15	Midland	Indian Park
13	May 20	Carlsbad	Fair Park Stadium
14	May 20	Carlsbad	Fair Park Stadium
15	May 21	Carlsbad	Fair Park Stadium
16	May 21	Carlsbad	Fair Park Stadium
17	May 22 (1)	Odessa	Fair Park Stadium
18	May 22 (2)	Odessa	Fair Park Stadium
19	May 27	Odessa	Oiler Park
20	May 30	Big Spring	Steer Park
21	June 3	Midland	Fair Park Stadium
22	June 6	Sweetwater	Fair Park Stadium
23	June 6	Sweetwater	Fair Park Stadium
24	June 9	Midland	Indian Park
25	June 11	Big Spring	Fair Park Stadium
26	June 13	Atresia	Fair Park Stadium
27	June 14	Artesia	Fair Park Stadium
28	June 14	Artesia	Fair Park Stadium
29	June 19	Odessa	Oiler Park
30	June 22	San Angelo	Fair Park Stadium
31	June 23	Odessa	Fair Park Stadium
32	June 24	Odessa	Fair Park Stadium
33	June 24	Odessa	Fair Park Stadium
34	June 25	San Angelo	Guinn Field
35	July 1	Artesia	Municipal Stadium
36	July 4	Big Spring	Steer Park
37	July 6	Artesia	Fair Park Stadium
38	July 7	Big Spring	Fair Park Stadium
39	July 7	Big Spring	Fair Park Stadium
40	July 8	Big Spring	Fair Park Stadium
41	July 10	Sweetwater	Sportsman's Park
42	July 12	Midland	Indian Park
43	July 13	Carlsbad	Montgomery Field

GOING FOR THE FENCES

Joe Bauman's 1954 Home Run Log, (cont.)

HR	Date	Club	Ballpark
44	July 14	Carlsbad	Montgomery Field
45	July 17	San Angelo	Fair Park Stadium
46	July 20	San Angelo	Guinn Field
47	July 20	San Angelo	Guinn Field
48	July 21	San Angelo	Guinn Field
49	July 24	Odessa	Fair Park Stadium
50	August 1	Midland	Fair Park Stadium
51	August 2	Sweetwater	Sportsman's Park
52	August 4	Midland	Indian Park
53	August 5	Midland	Indian Park
54	August 10	Carlsbad	Montgomery Field
55	August 14	Odessa	Oiler Park
56	August 16	Odessa	Oiler Park
57	August 19	Odessa	Fair Park Stadium
58	August 22 (1)	San Angelo	Fair Park Stadium
59	August 22 (1)	San Angelo	Fair Park Stadium
60	August 22 (2)	San Angelo	Fair Park Stadium
61	August 26	Midland	Indian Park
62	August 27	Sweetwater	Sportsman's Park
63	August 29	Artesia	Fair Park Stadium
64	August 30	Sweetwater	Fair Park Stadium
65	August 31	Sweetwater	Fair Park Stadium
66	August 31	Sweetwater	Fair Park Stadium
67	August 31	Sweetwater	Fair Park Stadium
68	August 31	Sweetwater	Fair Park Stadium
69	September 2	Midland	Fair Park Stadium
70	September 5 (1)	Artesia	Municipal Stadium
71	September 5 (2)	Artesia	Municipal Stadium
72	September 5 (2)	Artesia	Municipal Stadium

Notes: Number in parentheses following date indicates game of doubleheader

Breakdowns

Home Runs by Park
Fair Park Stadium, Roswell	43
Indian Park, Midland	6
Guinn Field, San Angelo	5
Oiler Park, Odessa	5
Montgomery Field, Carlsbad	4
Municipal Stadium, Artesia	4
Sportsman's Park, Sweetwater	3
Steer Park, Big Spring	2
Spudder Park, Wichita Falls	0

Home Runs by Month
April	10
May	10
June	14
July	15
August	19
September	4

Home Runs Against Club
Odessa	14
San Angelo	13
Artesia	10
Carlsbad	10
Sweetwater	10
Midland	9
Big Spring	6
Wichita Falls	0

Miscellaneous Statistics
Home Runs at Home	43
Home Runs on Road	29
One Home Run Games	44
Two Home Run Games	12
Three Home Run Games	0
Four Home Run Games	1

—Compiled by Bill Weiss

Dick Stuart's 1956 Home Run Log
Lincoln (Western League)
Home Park—Gold Sox Park

Dick Stuart had the finest home run month ever in Organized Baseball: 23 home runs in the month of June, 1956. He followed that up with 17 home runs in July. A total of forty home runs in two months has to be a record and he hit an even more incredible 56 in just three months. In August, the press started speculating on Stuart hitting eighty home runs for the year. Always streaky (he had four 3-HR games and six 2-HR games), Stuart went cold at the end of the season and didn't even threaten Joe Bauman's minor league record. One of the notable things about Stuart's totals is that he hit a great many more home runs on the road than at home (38 homers on the road, 28 at home). Stuart hit an additional two home runs in the playoffs against Hugh Blanton and Jim Turgerson of Amarillo.

HR	Date	Pitcher, Club	T	Ballpark
1	April 22	Joe Waters, Topeka	R	Sherman Field
2	May 9	Audie Malone, Amarillo	R	Sherman Field
3	May 10	Mike Coen, Amarillo	R	Sherman Field
4	May 10	Ron Berdrow, Amarillo	R	Sherman Field
5	May 14	Bud Bauhoffer, Albuquerque	R	Tingley Field
6	May 15	Andy Bush, Amarillo	R	Gold Sox Field
7	May 16	Ron Mahrt, Amarillo	R	Gold Sox Field
8	May 17	Ron Bedrow, Amarillo	R	Gold Sox Field
9	May 17	Ron Mahrt, Amarillo	R	Gold Sox Field
10	May 17	Fred Zirella, Amarillo	R	Gold Sox Field
11	May 18	Russ Heman, Colorado Springs	R	Memorial Park
12	May 20 (2)	Dick Ramos, Colorado Springs	R	Memorial Park
13	May 22	Marshall Bridges, Topeka	L	Community Park
14	May 25 (1)	George Storti, Sioux City	R	Soos Park
15	May 27 (1)	Dick Atkinson, Sioux City	R	Soos Park
16	May 29 (1)	Ted Thiem, Sioux City	R	Soos Park
17	May 30 (1)	Stew Alton, Topeka	R	Sherman Field
18	June 1	Fred Burdette, Des Moines	R	Sherman Field
19	June 1	Carl Johnson, Des Moines	R	Sherman Field
20	June 5 (1)	Russ Wingo, Des Moines	R	Pioneer Stadium
21	June 6	Tom Guderian, Des Moines	R	Pioneer Stadium
22	June 8	Dick Drilling, Albuquerque	R	Sherman Field
23	June 10	Joe Baliga, Pueblo	R	Sherman Field
24	June 10	Joe Baliga, Pueblo	R	Sherman Field
25	June 11	Jim Mertlik, Pueblo	R	Sherman Field
26	June 13	Larry Sherry, Pueblo	R	Sherman Field
27	June 16	Rudy Arias, Colorado Springs	R	Sherman Field
28	June 17 (1)	Chuck Rabung, Colorado Springs	R	Sherman Field
29	June 17 (2)	Dick Ramos, Colorado Springs	R	Sherman Field
30	June 19	Jim Mertlik, Pueblo	R	Runyon Field
31	June 20	Armando Suarez, Pueblo	L	Runyon Field
32	June 22	Jim Turgerson, Amarillo	R	Gold Sox Park
33	June 23	Hugh Blanton, Amarillo	R	Gold Sox Park
34	June 23	Hugh Blanton, Amarillo	R	Gold Sox Park
35	June 24	Ernie Funk, Amarillo	R	Gold Sox Park
36	June 24	Jim Turgerson Amarillo	R	Gold Sox Park
37	June 24	Jim Turgerson Amarillo	R	Gold Sox Park
38	June 25	Reggie Lee, Albuquerque	L	Tingley Field
39	June 25	Tommy Puehl, Albuquerque	R	Tingley Field
40	June 26	Al Osorio, Albuquerque	R	Tingely Field
41	July 2	John Rieder, Des Moines	R	Pioneer Park
42	July 2	Tom Guderian, Des Moines	R	Pioneer Park
43	July 2	Tom Guderian, Des Moines	R	Pioneer Park
44	July 3	Jack O"Donnell, Topeka	L	Community Park

Dick Stuart's 1956 Home Run Log, (cont.)

HR	Date	Pitcher, Club	T	Ballpark
45	July 4 (2)	Marshall Bridges, Topeka	L	Community Park
46	July 8 (2)	Bob Clear, Sioux City	R	Soos Park
47	July 12	John Andre, Des Moines	R	Sherman Field
48	July 14	Mike Coen, Amarillo	R	Sherman Field
49	July 17	Dick Drilling, Albuquerque	R	Sherman Field
50	July 17	Loren Myers, Albuquerque	R	Sherman Field
51	July 19 (1)	Ted Shandor, Albuquerque	R	Sherman Field
52	July 20	Gene Hines, Pueblo	R	Sherman Field
53	July 20	Chuck Ready, Pueblo	R	Sherman Field
54	July 20	Chuck Ready, Pueblo	R	Sherman Field
55	July 24	Mike Coen, Amarillo	R	Gold Sox Park
56	July 25 (2)	Maury Fisher, Amarillo	R	Gold Sox Park
57	July 28	Ron Wells, Pueblo	R	Runyon Field
58	August 1	Rudy Arias, Colorado Springs	R	Memorial Park
59	August 3	Ernie Funk, Albuquerque	R	Sherman Field
60	August 4	Ted Shandor, Albuquerque	R	Sherman Field
61	August 6	Jimmy Peete, Albuquerque	L	Sherman Field
62	August 17	Bob Faust, Pueblo	R	Runyon Field
63	August 24	John Andre, Des Moines	R	Sherman Field
64	August 29	Tom Le Gros, Des Moines	R	Pioneer Park
65	September 1	Dick Atkinson, Sioux City	R	Soos Park
66	September 3	Bob Willis, Topeka	R	Sherman Field

Notes: T—Throws by Pitcher. Number in parentheses following date indicates game of doubleheader.

Breakdowns

Home Runs by Park

Sherman Field, Lincoln	28
Gold Sox Field, Amarillo	13
Pioneer Stadium, Des Moines	6
Soos Park, Sioux City	5
Runyon Field, Pueblo	4
Tingley Field, Albuquerque	4
Community Baseball Park, Topeka	3
Memorial Field, Colorado Springs	3

Home Runs by Month

April	1
May	16
June	23
July	17
August	7
September	2

Home Runs Against Club

Amarillo	17
Albuquerque	11
Pueblo	11
Des Moines	10
Colorado Springs	6
Topeka	6
Sioux City	5

Multiple Home Run Pitchers

Mike Coen	3
Tom Guderian	3
Jim Turgerson	3
John Andre	2
Dick Atkinson	2
Rudy Arias	2
Joe Baliga	2
Hugh Blanton	2
Marshall Bridges	2
Dick Drilling	2
Ernie Funk	2
Ron Mahrt	2
Jim Mertlik	2
Dick Ramos	2
Ted Shandor	2

Miscellaneous Statistics

Home Runs at Home	28
Home Runs on Road	38
One Home Run Games	42
Two Home Run Games	6
Three Home Run Games	4
Home Runs off Lefties	6
Home Runs off Righties	60

—*Compiled by Larry Gerlach and Bill Weiss*

Frosty Kennedy's 1956 Home Run Log
Plainview (Southwestern League)
Home Park—Jaycee Park

One wag once said that he doubted that Kennedy had hit sixty home runs. After all, he explained, how could Frosty have ever seen the ball through all of his cigar smoke! 1956, nevertheless, was Frosty Kennedy's last hurrah in Organized Baseball, as he only played one more year. He split 1957 between Savannah in the Sally League (6 HR, .227 Avg.) and Boise in the Pioneer League, where he hit one last round tripper before returning to his native Southern California to pursue a career in scouting…and never without a cigar in his mouth!

HR	Date	Club	Ballpark
1	April 19	Midland	Jaycee Park
2	April 22	Ballinger	Runnels Field
3	April 22	Ballinger	Runnels Field
4	April 23	Midland	Municipal Park
5	April 26	Ballinger	Jaycee Park
6	April 28	Ballinger	Jaycee Park
7	April 29	Carlsbad	Montgomery Field
8	May 7	Roswell	Fair Park Stadium
9	May 9	Roswell	Fair Park Stadium
10	May 10	Pampa	Jaycee Park
11	May 10	Pampa	Jaycee Park
12	May 11	Pampa	Jaycee Park
13	May 13	Hobbs	Bender Park
14	May 14	Roswell	Jaycee Park
15	May 14	Roswell	Jaycee Park
16	May 15	Roswell	Jaycee Park
17	May 18	Pampa	Oiler Field
18	May 24	San Angelo	Jaycee Park
19	May 26	San Angelo	Jaycee Park
20	June 5	Ballinger	Runnels Field
21	June 7	Ballinger	Runnels Field
22	June 9	Midland	Jaycee Park
23	June 9	Midland	Jaycee Park
24	June 13	Carlsbad	Montgomery Field
25	June 14	Carlsbad	Montgomery Field
26	June 15	Carlsbad	Jaycee Park
27	June 15	Carlsbad	Jaycee Park
28	June 24	Pampa	Jaycee Park
29	June 25	Hobbs	Bender Park
30	June 25	Hobbs	Bender Park
31	June 26	Hobbs	Bender Park
32	June 27	Hobbs	Bender Park
33	June 30	Roswell	Jaycee Park
34	July 1	Pampa	Oiler Park
35	July 3	El Paso	Dudley Field
36	July 6	Clovis	Bell Park
37	July 9	San Angelo	Jaycee Park
38	July 10	San Angelo	Jaycee Park
39	July 10	San Angelo	Jaycee Park
40	July 15	Clovis	Jaycee Park
41	July 16	San Angelo	Guinn Field
42	July 20	Midland	Municipal Park
43	July 21	Midland	Municipal Park
44	July 22	Midland	Municipal Park
45	August 5	Hobbs	Bender Park
46	August 8	Roswell	Fair Park Stadium

Frosty Kennedy's 1956 Home Run Log, (cont.)

HR	Date	Club	Ballpark
47	August 8	Roswell	Fair Park Stadium
48	August 13	Pampa	Jaycee Park
49	August 18	Roswell	Jaycee Park
50	August 23	El Paso	Dudley Field
51	August 25 (1)	Clovis	Bell Park
52	August 25 (2)	Clovis	Bell Park
53	August 26	Clovis	Bell Park
54	August 27	Clovis	Bell Park
55	August 27	Clovis	Bell Park
56	August 29	San Angelo	Jaycee Park
57	August 30	Clovis	Jaycee Park
58	August 30	Clovis	Jaycee Park
59	August 31	Clovis	Jaycee Park
60	September 6	San Angelo	Guinn Field

Notes: Number in parentheses following date indicates game of doubleheader

Breakdowns

Home Runs by Park

Jaycee Park, Plainview	27
Bell Park, Clovis	6
Bender Park, Hobbs	6
Runnels Field, Ballinger	4
Municipal Park, Midland	4
Fair Park Stadium, Roswell	4
Montgomery Field, Carlsbad	3
Dudley Field, El Paso	2
Oiler Park, Pampa	2
Guinn Field, San Angelo	2

Home Runs by Month

April	7
May	12
June	14
July	11
August	15
September	1

Home Runs Against Club

Clovis	10
Roswell	9
San Angelo	8
Midland	7
Pampa	7
Ballinger	6
Hobbs	6
Carlsbad	5
El Paso	2

Miscellaneous Statistics

Home Runs at Home	27
Home Runs on Road	33
One Home Run Games	40
Two Home Run Games	10
Three Home Run Games	0

—*Compiled by Bill Weiss, Lefty Blasco, and Bob Hoie*

Minor League Players with Five or More Home Run Titles

Titles	Player	Year	Club, League	Home Runs
8	Bunny Brief	1911	Traverse City, Michigan State League	10
		1912	Traverse City, Michigan State League	13
		1916	Salt Lake City, Pacific Coast League	33
		1920	Kansas City, American Association	23
		1921	Kansas City, American Association	42
		1922	Kansas City, American Association	40
		1925	Milwaukee, American Association	37
		1926	Milwaukee, American Association	26

Titles	Player	Year	Club, League	Home Runs
8	Ken Guettler	1945	Kingsport, Appalachian League	13
		1947	Griffin, Georgia-Alabama League	25
		1948	Montgomery/Gadsden, Southeastern League	24
		1951	Portsmouth, Piedmont League	30
		1952	Portsmouth, Piedmont League	28
		1953	Portsmouth, Piedmont League	30
		1955	Portsmouth, Piedmont League	41
		1956	Shreveport, Texas League	62

Titles	Player	Year	Club, League	Home Runs
7	Ray Perry	1948	Redding, Far West League	36
		1949	Redding, Far West League	45
		1950	Redding, Far West League	44
		1951	Redding, Far West League	18
		1952	El Dorado, Cotton States League	15
		1953	Bakersfield, California League	36
		1954	Bakersfield, California League	37

Titles	Player	Year	Club, League	Home Runs
7	Muscle Shoals	1939	Johnson City, Appalachian League	16
		1946	Kingsport, Appalachian League	21
		1947	Kingsport, Appalachian League	32
		1949	Reidsville, Carolina League	55
		1951	Kingsport, Appalachian League	30
		1954	Kingsport, Mountain States League	18
		1955	Kingsport, Appalachian League	33

Titles	Player	Year	Club, League	Home Runs
7	Norm Small	1940	Mooresville, North Carolina State League	25
		1942	Mooresville, North Carolina State League	32
		1946	Mooresville, North Carolina State League	18
		1947	Mooresville, North Carolina State League	31
		1948	Mooresville, North Carolina State League	33
		1949	Mooresville, North Carolina State League	41
		1950	Mooresville, North Carolina State League	32

Minor League Players with Five or More Home Run Titles (cont.)

Titles	Player	Year	Club, League	Home Runs
6	Steve Balboni	1979	Fort Lauderdale, Florida State League	26
		1980	Nashville, Southern League	34
		1981	Columbus, International League	33
		1982	Columbus, International League	32
		1992	Oklahoma City, American Association	30
		1993	Oklahoma City, American Association	36

Titles	Player	Year	Club, League	Home Runs
6	Bernardo Brito	1984	Batavia, New York-Pennsylvania League	19
		1985	Waterloo, Midwest League	29
		1986	Waterbury, Eastern League	18
		1987	Williamsport, Eastern League	24
		1990	Portland, Pacific Coast League	25
		1991	Portland, Pacific Coast League	27 tied

Titles	Player	Year	Club, League	Home Runs
6	Ernie Calbert	1911	Harrisburg/Jackson, Kitty League	10
		1914	Huntington/Charleston, Ohio State League	17
		1915	Ironton, Ohio State League	13
		1917	Muskogee, Western Association	43
		1922	Hamilton, Michigan-Ontario League	28
		1923	Decatur, Three I League	18 tied

Titles	Player	Year	Club, League	Home Runs
6	Merv Connors	1935	Palestine, West Dixie League	29
		1936	Longview, East Texas League	24
		1941	Texarkana, Cotton States League	29
		1942	Dallas/Fort Worth, Texas League	27
		1950	Kilgore, East Texas League	26 tied
		1952	Amarillo, West Texas-New Mexico League	47

Titles	Player	Year	Club, League	Home Runs
6	Frank Huelsman	1900	Peoria/Danville, Central League	5
		1909	New Orleans, Southern Association	5
		1911	Great Falls, Union Association	17
		1913	Salt Lake City, Union Association	22
		1914	Salt Lake City, Union Association	23
		1915	Albuquerque, Rio Grande Valley Association	10

Titles	Player	Year	Club, League	Home Runs
6	Big Boy Kraft	1910	McLeansboro, Kitty League	4 tied
		1911	Flint, Southern Michigan Association	19
		1917	Wilkes-Barre, New York State League	7 tied
		1922	Fort Worth, Texas League	32
		1923	Fort Worth, Texas League	32
		1924	Fort Worth, Texas League	55

Titles	Player	Year	Club, League	Home Runs
6	Andy Lotshaw	1906	Jacksonville, Kitty League	11
		1907	Charleston, Eastern Illinois League	10
		1911	Canton, Illinois-Missouri League	29
		1912	Canton, Illinois-Missouri League	11
		1914	Champaign, Illinois-Missouri League	10
		1919	Flint/Brantford, Michigan-Ontario League	13

Titles	Player	Year	Club, League	Home Runs
6	Ted Norbert	1930	Chambersburg, Blue Ridge League	27
		1938	San Francisco, Pacific Coast League	30
		1941	Portland, Pacific Coast League	20
		1942	Portland, Pacific Coast League	28
		1943	Milwaukee, American Association	25
		1945	Seattle, Pacific Coast League	23

Titles	Player	Year	Club, League	Home Runs
6	Perry Werden	1886	Lincoln, Western League	11
		1888	New Orleans, Southern League	5
		1894	Minneapolis, Western League	43
		1895	Minneapolis, Western League	45
		1896	Minneapolis, Western League	18 tied
		1900	Minneapolis, Western League	9 tied

Players with Five Home Run Titles

Joe Bauman
Bull Durham
Buck Freeman
Joe Hauser
Pancho Herrera
Bud Heslet
Moe Hill
Stan Keyes
Al Neil
Gordon Nell
Butch Nieman
Tony Robello
Lew Whistler
Yam Yaryan

Players with Fourteen or More Seasons Between First and Last Home Run Titles

Years	Player	First Title	Last Title
18	Yam Yaryan	1919 Western League	1937 Alabama-Florida League
17	Merv Connors	1935 West Dixie League	1952 West Texas-New Mexico League
16	Vince DiMaggio	1932 Arizona-Texas League	1948 California League
16	Leo "Muscle" Shoals	1939 Appalachian League	1955 Appalachian League
16	Joe Stanley	1901 Virginia-North Carolina League	1917 Virginia League
16	Rudy York	1935 Texas League	1951 Middle Atlantic League
15	Zeke Bonura	1933 Texas League	1948 Colonial League
15	Bunny Brief	1911 Michigan State League	1926 American Association
15	Frank Huelsman	1900 Central League	1915 Rio Grande Valley Association
15	Chet Laabs	1935 Three I League	1950 International League
15	Ted Norbert	1930 Blue Ridge League	1945 Pacific Coast League
15	Harry Rice	1923 Three I League	1938 Florida State League
15	Lew Whistler	1888 Texas League	1903 Southern Association
14	Steve Balboni	1979 Florida State League	1993 American Association
14	Nick Cullop	1925 Southern Association	1939 Texas League
14	Buck Freeman	1894 New England League	1908 American Association
14	Joe Hauser	1919 Eastern League	1933 American Association
14	Clarence "Big Boy" Kraft	1910 Kitty League	1924 Texas League
14	Elmer Smith	1913 Northern League	1927 Pacific Coast League
14	Perry Werden	1886 Western League	1900 American League

Notes

- Yam Yaryan won five home run titles during a minor league career that stretched from the 1917 season all the way through the 1940 season. Yaryan won his first title in 1919 and his last one in 1937.

- Chet Laabs won a home run title in 1935, his first year in pro baseball, and his second title in 1950, his last year in pro ball. Laabs spent most of the years between in the majors. Clarence "Big Boy" Kraft also won a home run crown in his first and last years in pro ball, a stretch of fourteen years.

- Rick Lancellotti led three leagues in home runs, each in a different decade. He led the Eastern League in 1979, the Pacific Coast League in 1986 and the International League in 1991.

- Rudy York holds the record for most years between first and second home run titles. It took him sixteen years to win his second title. He won the Texas League title in 1935 and won the Middle Atlantic League title in 1951. Zeke Bonura went fifteen years (1933 to 1948) between his only two titles. As mentioned above, Laabs also went fifteen years between his only two titles. The only other player with thirteen or more years between his only two titles is Austin Knickerbocker, who won the Northern League crown in 1940 and later won the Kitty League title in 1953.

- Leo "Muscle" Shoals won his first of seven titles in the Appalachian League in 1939 and his last, also in the Appalachian League, in 1955. In between, he played in seven other leagues.

Top Minor League Home Run Hitter, Yearly Leader

Totals for hitters who played in two leagues in a season are used when applicable. There are 15 such cases.

Year	HR	Player	Club	League
1883	6	Frank Fennelly	Camden/Brooklyn	Inter-State Association
1884	11	Oyster Burns	Wilmington	Eastern League
1885	16	Dick Johnston	Richmond	Eastern League
1886	11	Ted Scheffler	Portland	New England League
	11	Perry Werden	Lincoln	Western League
	11	Gurdon Whiteley	Newburyport/Lynn	New England League
	11	George Wilson	Newburyport/Lynn	New England League
1887	28	Walt Andrews	Memphis	Southern League
1888	16	John Carroll	St. Paul	Western Association
1889	27	Charlie Reilly	St. Paul	Western Association
1890	21	John Carroll	Minneapolis	Western Association
1891	18	Ed Breckenridge	Grand Rapids (16)	Northwestern League
			Oshkosh (2)	Wisconsin State League
	18	Dell Darling	Minneapolis	Western Association
1892	20	Ed Breckinridge	Columbus (18)	Western League
			Troy (2)	Eastern League
1893	25	Abe Lizotte	Lewiston	New England League
1894	43	Perry Werden	Minneapolis	Western League
1895	45	Perry Werden	Minneapolis	Western League
1896	25	Ed Breckinridge	Brockton	New England League
	25	George Yeager	Pawtucket	New England League
1897	31	Jim Williams	St. Joseph	Western Association
1898	23	Buck Freeman	Toronto	Eastern League
1899	25	Erv Beck	Toledo	Inter-State Association
1900	22	Bert Schils	Anaconda (19)	Montana State League
			Toledo (3)	Inter-State Association
1901	27	Frank Roth	Evansville	Three I League
1902	16	Charles Buelow	Rockford	Three I League
1903	25	Joe Marshall	San Francisco	Pacific National League
1904	21	Truck Eagan	Tacoma	Pacific Coast League
1905	21	Truck Eagan	Tacoma	Pacific Coast League
1906	13	John Ganzel	Grand Rapids	Central League
1907	18	Buck Freeman	Minneapolis	American Association
1908	18	Pat Newnam	San Antonio	Texas League
1909	23	Ray Perkins	Holyoke	Connecticut State League
1910	30	Ping Bodie	San Francisco	Pacific Coast League
1911	29	Gavvy Cravath	Minneapolis	American Association
1912	30	Bull Durham	Bay City/Lansing (25)	Southern Michigan Association
			Oshkosh (5)	Wisconsin-Illinois League
1913	39	Charles Swain	Victoria (34)	Northwestern League
			Sacramento (5)	Pacific Coast League
1914	31	Bill Bankston	Cordele	Georgia State League
1915	34	Otto Besse	McAlester	Western Association
1916	33	Bunny Brief	Salt Lake City	Pacific Coast League
1917	43	Ernie Calbert	Muskogee	Western Association
1918	12	Art Griggs	San Francisco	Pacific Coast League
	12	Earl Sheely	Salt Lake City	Pacific Coast League
1919	28	Earl Sheely	Salt Lake City	Pacific Coast League
1920	41	Yam Yaryan	Wichita	Western League
1921	42	Bunny Brief	Kansas City	American Association
1922	40	Bunny Brief	Kansas City	American Association
1923	49	Moses Solomon	Hutchinson	Southwestern League
1924	55	Big Boy Kraft	Fort Worth	Texas League
1925	60	Tony Lazzeri	Salt Lake City	Pacific Coast League
1926	62	Moose Clabaugh	Tyler	East Texas League
1927	40	Elmer Smith	Portland	Pacific Coast League

Top Minor League Home Run Hitter, Yearly Leader (cont.)

Totals for hitters who played in two leagues in a season are used when applicable. There are 15 such cases.

Year	HR	Player	Club	League
1928	45	Smead Jolley	San Francisco	Pacific Coast League
1929	55	Ike Boone	San Francisco Mission	Pacific Coast League
1930	63	Joe Hauser	Baltimore	International League
1931	47	Dave Barbee	Hollywood	Pacific Coast League
1932	54	Buzz Arlett	Baltimore	International League
1933	69	Joe Hauser	Minneapolis	American Association
1934	48	Buzz Arlett	Minneapolis (41)	American Association
			Birmingham (7)	Southern Association
1935	56	Gene Lillard	Los Angeles	Pacific Coast League
1936	50	Tom Winsett	Columbus	American Association
1937	43	Maurice VanRobays	Ogdensburg	Canadian-American League
1938	45	Ollie Carnegie	Buffalo	International League
1939	58	Tony Robello	Pocatello	Pioneer League
1940	41	Lou Novikoff	Los Angeles	Pacific Coast League
1941	38	Les Burge	Atlanta	Southern Association
	38	Howard Muderski	Johnstown	Pennsylvania State Association
1942	34	Don Manno	Welch	Mountain State League
1943	25	Ted Norbert	Milwaukee	American Association
1944	30	John Cappa	Allentown	Inter-State League
1945	38	Frank Skaff	Baltimore	International League
1946	48	Joe Bauman	Amarillo	West Texas-New Mexico League
1947	58	Buck Frierson	Sherman-Denison	Big State League
1948	69	Bob Crues	Amarillo	West Texas-New Mexico League
1949	55	Pud Miller	Lamesa (52)	West Texas-New Mexico League
			Gladewater (3)	East Texas League
	55	Muscle Shoals	Reidsville	Carolina League
1950	53	Jesse McClain	Harlingen	Rio Grande Valley League
1951	47	Jack Harshman	Nashville	Southern Association
1952	50	Joe Bauman	Artesia	Longhorn League
1953	53	Joe Bauman	Artesia	Longhorn League
1954	72	Joe Bauman	Roswell	Longhorn League
1955	48	Keith Little	Corpus Christi (47)	Big State League
			Columbus (1)	International League
1956	66	Dick Stuart	Lincoln	Western League
1957	56	Steve Bilko	Los Angeles	Pacific Coast League
1958	43	Rocky Nelson	Toronto	International League
1959	43	Frank Howard	Victoria (27)	Texas League
			Spokane (16)	Pacific Coast League
1960	37	Ray Reed	Boise	Pioneer League
	37	R.C. Stevens	Salt Lake City	Pacific Coast League
1961	40	Bobby Sanders	Magic Valley	Pioneer League
1962	59	Ramiro Caballero	Guanajuato	Mexican Center League
1963	41	Arlo Engel	El Paso	Texas League
1964	49	Hector Espino	Monterrey (46)	Mexican League
			Jacksonville (3)	International League
1965	39	Bobby Prescott	Poza Rica	Mexican League
1966	55	Heriberto Vargas	Guanajuato	Mexican Center League
1967	43	Elrod Hendricks	Jalisco (41)	Mexican League
			Seattle (2)	Pacific Coast League
1968	49	Tony Solaita	High Point-Thomasville	Carolina League
1969	43	Pancho Herrera	Carmen (39)	Mexican Southeast League
			Miami (4)	Florida State League
1970	37	Hal Breeden	Richmond	International League
1971	43	Adrian Garrett	Tacoma	Pacific Coast League
1972	37	Hector Espino	Tampico	Mexican League
1973	39	Jim Fuller	Rochester	International League

Year	HR	Player	Club	League
1974	55	Bill McNulty	Sacramento	Pacific Coast League
1975	35	Andres Mora	Saltillo	Mexican League
1976	42	Roger Freed	Denver	American Association
1977	42	Danny Walton	Albuquerque	Pacific Coast League
1978	34	Bill Foley	Burlington	Midwest League
	34	Champ Summers	Indianapolis	American Association
1979	41	Rick Lancellotti	Buffalo	Eastern League
1980	37	Randy Bass	Denver	American Association
1981	42	Tim Laudner	Orlando	Southern League
1982	50	Ron Kittle	Edmonton	Pacific Coast League
1983	37	Stan Holmes	Visalia	California League
1984	40	Derek Bryant	Tampico	Mexican League
1985	43	Danny Tartabull	Calgary	Pacific Coast League
1986	54	Jack Pierce	Leon	Mexican League
1987	42	Nelson Barrera	Mexico City Reds	Mexican League
1988	36	Leo Hernandez	Union Laguna	Mexican League
1989	39	Leo Hernandez	Campeche	Mexican League
1990	33	Phil Plantier	Pawtucket	International League
1991	37	Roy Johnson	Campeche	Mexican League
1992	47	Ty Gainey	Mexico City Reds	Mexican League
1993	38	Matias Carrillo	Mexico City Tigers	Mexican League
	38	Sam Horn	Charlotte	International League
1994	37	Billy Ashley	Albuquerque	Pacific Coast League
1995	40	Todd Greene	Midland (26)	Texas League
			Vancouver (14)	Pacific Coast League
1996	42	Phil Hiatt	Toledo	International League
1997	37	Paul Konerko	Albuquerque	Pacific Coast League
	37	Matt Raleigh	Binghamton	Eastern League
1998	46	Chris Hatcher	Omaha	Pacific Coast League
1999	41	J.R. Phillips	Colorado Springs	Pacific Coast League
2000	45	Eduardo Jimenez	Saltillo	Mexican League
2001	44	Phil Hiatt	Las Vegas	Pacific Coast League
2002	35	Ivan Cruz	Memphis	Pacific Coast League
2003	34	Graham Koonce	Sacramento	Pacific Coast League
2004	46	Ryan Howard	Reading (37)	Eastern League
			Scranton-Wilkes-Barre (9)	International League
2005	43	Brandon Wood	Rancho Cucamonga (43)	California League
			Salt Lake City (0)	Pacific Coast League
2006	36	Kevin Witt	Durham	International League
2007	39	Craig Brazell	Omaha (32)	Pacific Coast League
			Wichita (7)	Texas League
2008	42	Dallas McPherson	Albuquerque	Pacific Coast League

Frank Roth is credited with 36 home runs in 1901 in several publications. However, a thorough check of all box scores for the season turned up only 27 home runs. This was still good enough to lead the minors.

Bob Unglaub, playing for Williamsport of the Tri-State League, hit fourteen home runs in 1906. This topped John Ganzel's total of thirteen. The Tri-State League, however, was not a member of the National Association.

Joe Bauman led the minors four times, including three consecutive years, 1952 through 1954. Ed Breckinridge, Perry Werden, and Bunny Brief each led the minors three times.

Leading the minors in home runs is not a ticket to stardom in the majors. Of the 118 players on the above list, 29 never played a game in the majors and another 29 played in fewer than 100 major league games. Joe Bauman, the four-time leader, is one of those players who never reached the majors. Only Oyster Burns, Gavvy Cravath, Buck Freeman, Frank Howard and Ryan Howard led a major league in home runs.

GOING FOR THE FENCES

Year-by-Year League Home Run Leaders

We have tried to make a logical listing of leagues to give continuity to the tabulations. See the Introduction for further explanation.

The years of operation, including incomplete years, are given for each league under the league's name. If no information is available for a given year, we do not list that year in the tabulation.

There have been several short-lived leagues for which no home run leaders are known. Thus, those leagues are not listed.

Alabama–Florida League
1936–1941, 1946–1962
Called Alabama State League, 1940–1941, 1946–1950

Year	HR	Player, Club
1936	20	Joe Gonzales, Ozark
1937	17	Yam Yaryan, Andalusia
1938	14	Gilbert Leatherwood, Troy
1939	20	Bruce Middlebrooks, Troy
1940	31	Gordon Goodell, Tallassee
1941	32	Forrest Austin, Tallassee
1946	17	Melvin Schwab, Ozark
	17	Harold Walther, Greenville/Geneva
1947	24	Andy Archipoli, Ozark
1948	17	John Powell, Andalusia
1949	15	Tom McBride, Geneva/Ozark
1950	15	Lamar Bowden, Dothan
1951	13	Charles Quimby, Tallahassee
1952	24	William Buchanan, Eufaula
1953	27	Charles Quimby, Fort Walton Beach/Graceville
1954	31	John Streza, Fort Walton Beach
1955	37	Charles Grant, Donaldsonville
1956	40	Neb Wilson, Donaldsonville
1957	30	Bob Wellman, Graceville
1958	24	Neb Wilson, Fort Walton Beach/Pensacola
1959	21	Jim Bethea, Montgomery
	21	Pete Walski, Montgomery
1960	23	Jose Villar, Selma
1961	20	Pedro Fernandez, Fort Walton Beach
1962	22	Nelson Gardner, Dothan

Alabama State League
1940–1941, 1946–1950
See Alabama–Florida League

American Association
1902–1962, 1969–1997
Not a member of the National Association in 1902

Year	HR	Player, Club
1902	18	Harry Lumley, St. Paul
1903	16	Mike Grady, Kansas City
1904	13	Jim Jackson, St. Paul
1905	13	Wyatt Lee, Toledo
1906	8	Danny Green, Milwaukee
1907	18	Buck Freeman, Minneapolis
1908	10	Buck Freeman, Minneapolis
	10	Tony James, Columbus
1909	7	Tony James, Columbus
1910	14	Gavvy Cravath, Minneapolis
1911	29	Gavvy Cravath, Minneapolis
1912	10	Tony James, Kansas City
1913	12	Joe Riggert, St. Paul
1914	19	Hap Felsch, Milwaukee
1915	9	Pete Compton, Kansas City
	9	Joe Riggert, St. Paul
1916	15	Beals Becker, Kansas City
1917	15	Beals Becker, Kansas City
1918	6	Joe Riggert, St. Paul
1919	15	Elmer Miller, St. Paul
1920	23	Bunny Brief, Kansas City
1921	42	Bunny Brief, Kansas City
1922	40	Bunny Brief, Kansas City
1923	31	Carl East, Minneapolis
1924	28	Elmer Smith, Louisville
1925	37	Bunny Brief, Milwaukee
1926	26	Bunny Brief, Milwaukee
1927	32	Frank Emmer, Minneapolis
1928	32	Spencer Harris, Minneapolis
1929	33	Dusty Cooke, St. Paul
1930	54	Nick Cullop, Minneapolis
1931	28	Cliff Crawford, Columbus
1932	49	Joe Hauser, Minneapolis
1933	69	Joe Hauser, Minneapolis
1934	41	Buzz Arlett, Minneapolis
1935	43	Johnny Gill, Minneapolis
1936	50	Tom Winsett, Columbus
1937	29	Roy Pfleger, Minneapolis
1938	43	Ted Williams, Minneapolis
1939	46	Vince DiMaggio, Kansas City
1940	39	Ab Wright, Minneapolis
1941	26	Ab Wright, Minneapolis
1942	24	Bill Norman, Milwaukee
1943	25	Ted Norbert, Milwaukee
1944	24	Babe Barna, Minneapolis
1945	25	Babe Barna, Minneapolis
1946	46	Jerry Witte, Toledo
1947	23	Carden Gillenwater, Milwaukee
1948	30	Mike Natisin, Columbus
1949	41	Chuck Workman, Minneapolis
1950	29	Lou Limmer, St. Paul
1951	29	Tookie Gilbert, Minneapolis
1952	31	Bill Skowron, Kansas City
1953	34	George Wilson, Minneapolis
1954	38	Rocky Colavito, Indianapolis
1955	36	Marv Throneberry, Denver
1956	42	Marv Throneberry, Denver
1957	40	Marv Throneberry, Denver
1958	29	Johnny Callison, Indianapolis
1959	30	Ron Jackson, Indianapolis
1960	34	Larry Osborne, Denver
1961	32	Cliff Cook, Indianapolis

American Association, continued

Year	HR	Player, Club
1962	27	Leo Burke, Dallas-Fort Worth
1969	25	Danny Walton, Oklahoma City
1970	33	Cotton Nash, Evansville
1971	27	Bill McNulty, Iowa
1972	25	Bob Hansen, Evansville
1973	33	Cliff Johnson, Denver
1974	26	Adrian Garrett, Wichita
1975	29	Hector Cruz, Tulsa
1976	42	Roger Freed, Denver
1977	40	Frank Ortenzio, Denver
1978	34	Champ Summers, Indianapolis
1979	39	Karl Pagel, Wichita
1980	37	Randy Bass, Denver
1981	28	George Bjorkman, Springfield
1982	46	Ken Phelps, Wichita
1983	31	Carmelo Martinez, Iowa
1984	37	Joe Hicks, Iowa
1985	29	Dave Hostetler, Indianapolis/Iowa
1986	24	Lloyd McClendon, Denver
1987	32	Brad Komminsk, Denver
1988	23	Van Snider, Nashville
1989	26	Greg Vaughn, Denver
1990	29	Juan Gonzalez, Oklahoma City
1991	22	Dean Palmer, Oklahoma City
1992	30	Steve Balboni, Oklahoma City
1993	36	Steve Balboni, Oklahoma City
1994	30	Drew Denson, Nashville
1995	23	Brooks Kreschnick, Iowa
1996	32	Lee Stevens, Oklahoma City
1997	31	Richie Sexson, Buffalo

American League
1900

See Western League II

Appalachian League I
1911–1914, 1921–1925, 1937–1955

Year	HR	Player, Club
1911	11	B. B. Woodward, Asheville
1912	9	E. J. Pope, Morristown
1913	20	John Cochran, Rome
1921	18	Joe Price, Johnson City
1923	15	Joe Price, Johnson City
1924	13	Elbert Slayback, Morristown
1937	5	Hal Lee, Elizabethton
1938	6	Erastus Grigg, Elizabethton
	6	John Hobson, Johnson City
	6	Clovis White, Elizabethton
1939	16	Muscle Shoals, Johnson City
1940	19	Bob Williams, Elizabethton
1941	19	Harold Martin, Greenville
1942	15	Andy Seminick, Elizabethton
1943	9	Beattie Feathers, Kingsport
1944	13	Gil Coan, Kingsport
1945	13	Ken Guettler, Kingsport
1946	21	Muscle Shoals, Kingsport
1947	32	Muscle Shoals, Kingsport
1948	22	Jim Dickey, Johnson City

Year	HR	Player, Club
1949	20	John Karpinski, Bluefield
1950	26	Don Boring, Elizabethton
1951	30	Muscle Shoals, Kingsport
1952	21	Harold Kolar, Kingsport
1953	27	Dick Stanton, Johnson City
1954	26	Bob Quinn, Pulaski
1955	33	Mike Coppola, Wytheville
	33	Muscle Shoals, Kingsport

Appalachian League II
1957–present

Year	HR	Player, Club
1957	11	Ken Clark, Wytheville
1958	14	Danny Cater, Johnson City
1959	18	Larry Daniels, Johnson City
1960	24	Joy Gritts, Wytheville
1961	14	Jim Winn, Harlan
1962	16	John Riddle, Bluefield
1963	11	Chuck Howard, Kingsport
	11	Matt Szykowny, Wytheville
1964	20	Ross Moschitto, Johnson City
1965	20	Dick Hense, Wytheville
1966	9	Earl Hash, Johnson City
1967	16	Richie Zisk, Salem
1968	18	Larry Mansfield, Covington
1969	13	Larry Fritz, Marion
1970	14	Tom Hallumo, Marion
1971	10	Terry Whitfield, Johnson City
1972	16	Dave Michalec, Wytheville
	16	Bob Wilson, Johnson City
1973	13	John Shupe, Johnson City
1974	19	Fay Thompson, Covington
1975	13	Marshall Brant, Marion
1976	17	Mark Corey, Bluefield
1977	14	Danny Logan, Bluefield
	14	Bruce Tonascia, Kingsport
1978	12	Ron Grout, Elizabethton
1979	16	Harold Williams, Kingsport
1980	14	Larry Sheets, Bluefield
1981	14	Orestes Destrade, Paintsville
1982	16	Dan Pasqua, Paintsville
1983	16	Chris Baird, Pulaski
	16	Glenn Braggs, Paintsville
1984	18	Tim Casey, Paintsville
1985	10	Brandon Bailey, Kingsport
	10	Dave Justice, Pulaski
	10	Rob Tomberlin, Pulaski
1986	14	Scott Johnson, Burlington
1987	14	Terry Brown, Bluefield
1988	16	Vince Zawaski, Kingsport
1989	13	Tom Hardgrove, Martinsville
1990	22	Paul Russo, Elizabethton
1991	19	Manuel Ramirez, Burlington
1992	15	Dan Frye, Princeton
1993	16	Preston Wilson, Kingsport
1994	18	Jake Patterson, Elizabethton

GOING FOR THE FENCES

Year	HR	Player, Club
1995	14	Darron Ingram, Princeton
1996	18	Calvin Pickering, Bluefield
1997	18	Matt Berger, Bristol
1998	17	Manuel Lutz, Bristol
1999	16	Kevin Mench, Pulaski
2000	13	Charlie Dees, Bluefield/Pulaski
	13	Alexis Gordon, Bluefield
2001	16	Jonny Gomes, Princeton
2002	18	Wes Bankston, Princeton
2003	15	Dusty Gomon, Elizabethton
2004	24	Mitch Einertson, Greenville
2005	18	Eric Campbell, Danville
2006	13	Mark Shorey, Johnson City
2007	17	Cody Johnson, Danville
2008	15	Angel Morales, Elizabethton

Arizona–Mexico League
1955–1958
See Arizona–Texas League

Arizona Rookie League
1988–present

Year	HR	Player, Club
1988	8	Leon Glenn, Peoria Brewers
	8	Ed Ricks, Scottsdale Athletics
1989	7	Leon Glenn, Brewers
1990	9	Jonas Hamlin, Cardinals
1991	9	Steve Cerio, Cardinals
1992	3	Greg Boyd, Rockies/Cubs
	3	Brian Guzik, Angels
	3	Jason Imperial, Brewers
	3	Mark Pooschke, Giants
	3	Hiram Ramirez, Giants
1993	5	Leon Hamburg, Athletics
	5	John Jones, Athletics
	5	Fred Soriano, Athletics
1994	5	Darren Tawwater, Cardinals
1995	5	Pete Paciorek, Padres
	5	Daryl Rutherford, Padres
1996	9	Shane Cronin, Padres
1997	11	Jesus Basabe, Athletics
1998	6	Javier Colina, Rockies
	6	Dave Kelton, Cubs
1999	13	Luis Garcia, Mexico
2000	9	Christian Presichi, Mexico
	9	Eric Storey, Rockies
2001	9	Chris Tritle, Athletics
2002	8	Matt Creighton, Cubs
2003	16	Wladimir Balentien, Mariners
2004	10	Miguel Vega, Royals
2005	7	Kyle Blanks, Padres
2006	7	Gerardo Avila, Mariners
	7	Wellington Dotel, Mariners
	7	Carlos Peguero, Mariners
2007	14	Andrew D'alessio, Giants
2008	9	John Contreras, Cubs
	9	Nelson Perez, Cubs

Arizona State League
1928–1930
See Arizona-Texas League

Arizona–Texas League
1928–1932, 1937–1941, 1947–1950, 1952–1958
Called Arizona State League, 1928–1930
Called Arizona-Mexico League, 1955–1958

Year	HR	Player, Club
1928	14	Larman Cox, Phoenix
1929	23	Leo Burns, Bisbee
1930	22	George Steward, Bisbee
1931	34	Walter Carson, Globe
1932	25	Vince DiMaggio, Tucson
1937	10	James Nicholson, El Paso
1938	20	Bill Creager, Bisbee
1939	17	Al Montgomery, Bisbee
1940	10	Joe Skeber, El Paso
1941	15	Douglas Smith, Tucson
1947	38	Pete Hughes, Phoenix
1948	27	Dan Baich, Globe-Miami
1949	37	Gene Clough, Bisbee-Douglas
1950	28	Hector Lara, El Paso
1952	45	Marv Williams, Chichuahua
1953	34	Charles Lundgren, Tuscon
1954	47	Claudio Solano, Cananea
1955	38	Humberto Barbon, Nogales/Yuma
1956	45	Claudio Solano, Cananea
1957	41	Claudio Solano, Cananea
1958	35	Jose Echeverria, Chichuahua

Arkansas–Missouri League
1934–1940
Called Arkansas State League, 1934–1935.

Year	HR	Player, Club
1934	12	William Beams, Bentonville
1935	21	Howard Roberts, Cassville
1936	28	Kermit Lewis, Siloam Springs
1937	20	Gene Gibson, Siloam Springs
1938	22	Butch Moran, Rogers
1939	24	Steve Greble, Neosho
1940	12	Adolph Arlitt, Carthage

Arkansas State League
1934–1935
See Arkansas-Missouri League.

Atlantic Association
1889–1890, 1908

Year	HR	Player, Club
1889	18	Bill Campion, Worcester
1890	12	Dan Lally, New Haven
1908	4	Pat Sullivan, Lewiston

Atlantic League
1896–1900, 1914

Year	HR	Player, Club
1896	13	John Rothfuss, Newark
1897	14	Socks Seybold, Lancaster
1898	17	Socks Seybold, Richmond
1899	11	Socks Seybold, Richmond
1900	4	John Burns, Wilkes-Barre
	4	Bill Clymer, Wilkes-Barre
	4	Fred Ketcham, Wilkes-Barre
1914	7	Jim Elcock, Newburgh

Bi-State League
1915, 1934–1942

Illinois and Wisconsin

Year	HR	Player, Club
1915	5	Art Mueller, Elgin
	5	Clay Schoonover, Racine
	5	Eddie Wise, Streator

North Carolina and Virginia

Year	HR	Player, Club
1934	26	Eddie Weston, Mayodan
1935	30	Blackie Carter, Leakesville
1936	34	Woody Traylor, Danville
1937	29	Herb Leary, Reidsville
1938	33	Ray Scantling, Reidsville
1939	27	Amerigo Scagliarini, Mayodan
1940	25	Orville Nesselrode, South Boston
1941	29	Tom Burnett, Martinsville
1942	29	Harry Soufas, Rocky Mount

Big State League
1947–1957

Year	HR	Player, Club
1947	58	Buck Frierson, Sherman-Denison
1948	32	Al McCarty, Wichita Falls
1949	27	Al Meriwether, Greenville
1950	39	Johnny Powers, Waco
1951	32	Dean Stafford, Sherman-Denison
1952	47	Dean Stafford, Paris/Tyler
1953	39	Albert Neil, Wichita Falls
1954	38	Dean Stafford, Galveston/ Corpus Christi
1955	47	Keith Little, Corpus Christi
1956	32	Rudy Mayling, Abilene
	32	Danny Ozark, Wichita Falls
1957	28	Don Miles, Victoria

Blue Grass League
1908–1912, 1922–1924

Year	HR	Player, Club
1910	6	Bob Bramlage, Richmond
	6	Hogan Yancy, Lexington
1911	13	Charles Ellis, Lexington
1912	22	Louis Munn, Richmond
1922	14	Ray Class, Maysville
1923	20	Rush Meadows, Lexington
1924	20	Don Hurst, Paris

Blue Ridge League
1915–1918, 1920–1930, 1946–1950

Maryland, Pennsylvania, and West Virginia

Year	HR	Player, Club
1915	6	Clyde Barnhart, Frederick
1916	9	Clyde Barnhart, Frederick
	9	Robert Orrison, Frederick
1917	15	John Bates, Martinsburg
1918	3	Eddie Hooper, Cumberland
1920	12	Harold Yordy, Waynesboro
1921	20	Walter Kimmick, Waynesboro
1922	30	Hack Wilson, Martinsburg
1923	25	Reg Rawlings, Martinsburg
1924	21	Reg Rawlings, Martinsburg
1925	19	George Thomas, Hagerstown
1926	19	Reg Rawlings, Martinsburg
1927	13	Joe Roetz, Hanover
	13	Frank Roscoe, Hanover
1928	13	George Thomas, Hagerstown
1929	17	Pat Shea, Chambersburg
1930	27	Ted Norbert, Chambersburg

North Carolina and Virginia

Year	HR	Player, Club
1946	16	Edwin Morgan, Mount Airy/Galax
1947	12	Noel Casbier, Lenoir
1948	13	Bill Akins, Mount Airy
1949	15	Lloyd Wilcox, Radford
1950	14	Bob Horan, Galax

Border League
1912–1913, 1946–1951

Sometimes called Eastern Michigan League, 1912–191.

Michigan and Ontario

Year	HR	Player, Club
1913	2	Ralph Bell, Ypsilanti
	2	Otto Gallant, Ypsilanti
	2	Frank Loranger, Wyandotte
	2	Jack Shafer, Ypsilanti

New York, Ontario, and Quebec

Year	HR	Player, Club
1946	20	Bob Dill, Ogdensburg/Auburn
1947	25	Tony Gridaitis, Ogdensburg
	25	Don Phelps, Geneva
1948	24	Bill Reardon, Kingston
1949	22	Pete Kousagan, Geneva
1950	31	Pete Kousagan, Geneva
1951	12	Olav Kollevoll, Ogdensburg
	10	John Sosh, Ogdensburg

GOING FOR THE FENCES

Buckeye League
1915

Year	HR	Player, Club
1915	4	Dan Costello, Findlay
	4	Ted Egan, Findlay

California League I
1879–1894, 1896

Year	HR	Player, Club
1880	5	John Smith, SF Knickerbockers
1881	3	John Smith, SF Knickerbockers
1882	1	Henry Moore, San Francisco Nationals
	1	Adolph Scher, San Francisco Nationals
1883	1	— Barnes, San Francisco Haverlys
	1	Mike Finn, San Francisco Niantic Woonsocket
	1	Lou Hardie, San Francisco Haverlys
	1	— Lemmer, San Francisco Redingtons
	1	Charles Sullivan, SF Niantic Woonsocket
1884	1	Tom Buckley, San Franciscos
	1	John Smith, San Francisco Haverlys/San Franciscos
1885	2	Jack Arnold, SF Occidentals/SF Haverlys
1886	2	Russ Flint, Sacramento
	2	Bill McLaughlin, Sacramento
1887	3	Billy Newbert, Sacramento
1888	3	Lew Hardie, Oakland
1889	10	Lew Hardie, Oakland
1890	12	Fred Roberts, Sacramento
1891	7	Ed Cartwright, San Francisco
	7	Bill Everett, San Jose
	7	Rube Levy, San Francisco
1892	10	Fred Carroll, Oakland
1893	8	Fred Carroll, San Francisco
1894	1	Dave Bodie. San Francisco
	1	— Carter, Petaluma
	1	— Green, Petaluma
	1	George Kelly, Petaluma
	1	Harry Walters, Stockton
1896	3	Russ Pace, Stockton

California League II
1898–1902

After playing for several weeks in 1898, the league merged with the Pacific States League to form the Pacific Coast League. The league reverted back to the California League in 1899.

Year	HR	Player, Club
1898	1	Willie Caverly, Sacramento
	1	— Goodwin, San Jose
	1	Lew Hardie, Oakland
	1	Bill Sykes, San Jose
1899	7	Truck Eagan, Sacramento
1900	11	Truck Eagan, Sacramento
1901	15	Henry Krug, San Francisco
1902	8	Bill Dunleavy, Oakland

California League III
1941–1942, 1946–present

Year	HR	Player, Club
1941	20	Mel Serafini, Fresno
1942	10	Ed Nulty, Santa Barbara
1946	24	Harry Goorabian, Stockton
1947	30	Bill Enos, Modesto
1948	30	Vince DiMaggio, Stockton
1949	37	Jess Pike, Bakersfield
1950	30	Dick Wilson, Modesto
1951	40	Dick Wilson, Modesto
1952	34	Ben Downs, Fresno
1953	36	Ray Perry, Bakersfield
1954	37	Ray Perry, Bakersfield
1955	33	Russ Rosburg, Modesto
1956	51	Bud Heslet, Visalia
1957	27	Dick Wilson, Bakersfield
1958	40	Bart Dupon, Bakersfield
1959	37	Rich Barry, Modesto
1960	22	Richard Edwards, Bakersfield
1961	32	Dick Nen, Reno
1962	44	Larry Daniels, Bakersfield
1963	40	Jose Vidal, Reno
1964	40	Ollie Brown, Fresno
1965	30	Mike Epstein, Stockton
1966	46	Dave Duncan, Modesto
1967	33	Joe Lis, Bakersfield
1968	35	Tom Robson, Visalia
1969	27	Ernie Davis, Modesto
1970	24	Larry Fritz, Visalia
1971	32	Frank Ortenzio, San Jose
1972	32	Skip James, Fresno
1973	28	John Balaz, Salinas
1974	27	Gary Alexander, Fresno
1975	20	Claude Westmoreland, Bakersfield
1976	29	Dan Graham, Reno
1977	36	Kelly Snider, Lodi
1978	29	Steve McManaman, Visalia
1979	31	Mark Funderburk, Visalia
1980	29	Greg Brock, Lodi
1981	33	Rob Deer, Fresno
1982	28	Kevin McReynolds, Reno
1983	37	Stan Holmes, Visalia
1984	20	Mark Bonner, Redwood
1985	24	Eric Hargrave, Reno
	24	Mark McGwire, Modesto
1986	35	Brad Pounders, Reno
1987	21	Bill Stevenson, Reno
1988	22	Warren Newsom, Riverside
1989	27	Ruben Gonzalez, San Bernardino
1990	24	Ken Whitfield, Reno
1991	32	Jay Gainer, High Desert
1992	28	Marty Cordova, Visalia
1993	28	John Toale, High Desert
1994	35	Todd Greene, Lake Elsinore
1995	30	Steve Cox, Modesto
1996	35	Chris Kirgan, High Desert

California League III, continued

Year	HR	Player, Club
1997	33	Stanton Cameron, High Desert
	33	Mike Glendening, Bakersfield
	33	Mike Stoner, High Desert
1998	24	Tim Flaherty, Bakersfield
	24	Anthony Johnson, Rancho Cucamonga
1999	32	Jack Cust, High Desert
2000	30	Juan Silvestre, Lancaster
2001	26	Tim Flaherty, San Jose
	26	Billy Martin, Lancaster
	26	Xavier Nady, Lake Elsinore
2002	31	Jorge Soto, Visalia
2003	31	Kyle Nichols, Lancaster
2004	29	Michael Napoli, Rancho Cucamonga
2005	43	Richard Wood, Rancho Cucamonga
2006	26	Brandon Burgess, Lancaster
2007	26	Tommy Everidge, Stockton
2008	39	Chris Carter, Stockton

California State League I
1883, 1885–1886, 1888

Year	HR	Player, Club
1883	1	John Egan, San Francisco
	1	Jack Lawton, San Francisco
	1	Chief Williams, Marysville
1885	1	Eddie Conn, SF Occidentals- Oak
1886	3	Silver Lewis, San Francisco Damianas
1888	1	Happy Cate, San Francisco Emersons
	1	— Herenghi, San Franciscos
	1	Eddie Moran, San Franciscos
	1	George Stultz, SF Clevelands
	1	Otto Young, Santa Cruz

California State League II
1903–1910, 1913–1915

Not a member of the National Association in 1903–1909, 1912

Year	HR	Player, Club
1907	3	Ben Henderson, Stockton
1909	9	Bill Carney, Fresno
	9	Monte Pfyl, Stockton
1910	9	Eddie Housholder, Fresno
1912	2	Joe Giannini, San Francisco/Stockton
	2	Walt Golvin, Modesto
	2	— Houghton, Oakland-Richmond
1913	7	Rino Williams, Watsonville
1914	2	Tom Pierce, Fresno

California State League III
1929

Year	HR	Player, Club
1929	15	Red Porter, Bakersfield

Canadian League
1885, 1896–1899, 1905, 1911–1915

Year	HR	Player, Club
1885	5	Ed Stapleton, Hamilton
1896	4	John Lyons, Galt
1898	6	Charles Jones, Chatham
1899	5	Buck Congalton, Hamilton
	5	Charles Conwell, Hamilton
	5	George Lohman, London
	5	Joe Schrall, Hamilton
1911	7	Ambrose Kane, Brantford
1913	10	Bill Wright, Guelph
1914	7	Harry Deneau, Brantford
1915	5	William Brown, Guelph
	5	John Cooper, Brantford
	5	Mike Mullen, Brantford
	5	Pete Powers, Ottawa
	5	Jack Schaefer, Guelph

Canadian–American League
1936–1942, 1946–1951

Year	HR	Player, Club
1936	15	Jim Stevenson, Ottawa
1937	43	Maurice VanRobays, Ogdensburg
1938	34	Tony Gridaitis, Ogdensburg
1939	22	John Lehman, Gloversville-Johnstown
1940	31	Paul Badgett, Amsterdam
1941	32	Lee Riley, Rome
1942	20	Joe Morjoseph, Gloversville-Johnstown
1946	15	Al Rosen, Pittsfield
1947	15	Ben Gregg, Schenectady
1948	27	Gene Hasson, Pittsfield
1949	27	Don Marshall, Schenectady
1950	19	Garland Lawing, Quebec
1951	18	John Jones, Amsterdam

Cape Breton Colliery League
1937–1939

Year	HR	Player, Club
1937	8	Chris Pickering, New Waterford
1938	6	Lester Crabb, Glace Bay
1939	9	Lester Crabb, Glace Bay

Carolina League
1945–present

Year	HR	Player, Club
1945	12	Maurice Abrams, Martinsville
	12	Gus Granzig, Leaksville
	12	Jerome Gutt, Martinsville
	12	Tommy Kirk, Martinsville
1946	41	Gus Zernial, Burlington
1947	31	Eugene Petty, Danville
1948	35	Russ Sullivan, Danville
1949	55	Muscle Shoals, Reidsville
1950	27	Fred Vaughan, Greensboro

GOING FOR THE FENCES

Year	HR	Player, Club
1951	28	Ray Jablonski, Winston-Salem
	28	Carl Miller, Reidsville
1952	25	Dale Powell, Danville
1953	29	Jack Hussey, Raleigh
1954	38	Jim Pokel, Fayetteville
1955	31	Harold Holland, Danville
1956	51	Leon Wagner, Danville
1957	30	Gene Oliver, Winston-Salem
	30	Bob Perry, Danville
1958	25	Bert Barth, Wilson
	25	Jackie Davis, High Point-Thomasville
1959	30	Don Lock, Greensboro
1960	35	Ed Olivares, Winston-Salem
1961	31	Chuck Weatherspoon, Wilson
1962	33	Bert Barth, Rocky Mount
1963	30	Walt Matthews, Durham
1964	28	Edwin Chasteen, Raleigh
1965	28	Mike Derrick, Kinston
1966	28	Barry Morgan, Kinston
1967	30	Hal King, Asheville
1968	49	Tony Solaita, High Point-Thomasville
1969	31	Greg Luzinski, Raleigh-Durham
1970	27	Cliff Johnson, Raleigh-Durham
1971	22	Charlie Spikes, Kinston
1972	23	Bob Gorinski, Lynchburg
1973	18	Jim Obradovich, Lynchburg
	18	Terry Whitfield, Kinston
1974	30	Randy Bass, Lynchburg
1975	20	Jim Morrison, Rocky Mount
1976	23	Marshall Brant, Lynchburg
1977	22	John Hughes, Peninsula
1978	29	Ozzie Virgil, Peninsula
1979	18	Gary Pellant, Alexandria
1980	24	Craig Brooks, Winston-Salem
1981	34	Gerald Davis, Salem
1982	29	David Malpeso, Winston-Salem
1983	31	Ken Gerhart, Hagerstown
1984	29	Randy Day, Peninsula
1985	28	Jim Dickerson, Winston-Salem
1986	26	Ron Gant, Durham
1987	28	Hensley Meulens, Prince William
1988	21	Mickey Pina, Lynchburg
1989	27	Phil Plantier, Lynchburg
1990	18	Greg Blosser, Lynchburg
1991	18	Tracy Sanders, Kinston
1992	32	Bubba Smith, Peninsula
1993	27	Bubba Smith, Winston-Salem
1994	29	Toby Rumfield, Winston-Salem
1995	26	Juan Thomas, Prince William
1996	21	Freddy Garcia, Lynchburg
	21	Jose Guillen, Lynchburg
1997	34	Dan Peoples, Kinston
1998	22	Mike Glavine, Kinston
1999	25	Andy Bevins, Potomac
2000	23	Troy Farnsworth, Potomac
2001	20	Doug Gredvig, Frederick
2002	26	Josh Bonifay, Lynchburg
2003	21	Chris Shelton, Lynchburg
2004	25	Darren Blakely, Winston-Salem
2005	29	Thomas Collaro, Winston-Salem
	29	Leo Daigle, Winston-Salem
2006	24	Jason Fransy, Frederick
2007	25	Micah Schnurstein, Winston-Salem
2008	21	Ernesto Mejia, Myrtle Beach
	21	Beau Mills, Kinston

Carolina Baseball Association
1908–1912

Year	HR	Player, Club
1908	9	Joe Jackson, Greenville
1909	11	Harvey Ritter, Spartanburg
1910	4	James Carlisle Smith, Anderson
1911	17	Richard Smith, Greenville
1912	16	Bill Schumaker, Winston-Salem

Central Association
1908–1917, 1947–1949

Year	HR	Player, Club
1908	10	Al Linderbeck, Quincy
1909	10	Homer Gray, Jacksonville
	10	Al Linderbeck, Quincy
1910	9	Bill Donahue, Quincy
	9	Tom Owens, Quincy
1911	14	Don Senno, Ottumwa
1912	21	John Sullivan, Ottumwa
1915	9	Cliff Lee, Muscatine
	9	Lyle Sours, Muscatine
1916	18	Bull Durham, Muscatine/Marshalltown
1917	9	John Mokan, Fort Dodge
1947	34	Roy Sievers, Hannibal
1948	23	Jack Tanner, Keokuk
1949	37	Jack Tanner, Cedar Rapids

Central League
1888, 1897, 1900, 1903–1917, 1920–1922,
1926, 1928–1930, 1932, 1934, 1948–1951

Year	HR	Player, Club
1888	4	Jim Knowles, Jersey City
1900	5	Frank Huelsman, Peoria/Danville
1904	9	Dick Knox, Evansville
	9	George McConnell, Wheeling
1905	10	Jimmy Ryan, Evansville
1906	13	John Ganzel, Grand Rapids
1908	12	Punch Knoll, Evansville
1909	11	Hank Butcher, Evansville
	11	Punch Knoll, Evansville
1910	18	Larry LeJeune, Evansville
1911	11	Bull Durham, Wheeling
	11	Emil Grefe, Evansville-South Bend
	11	Hubert Hadley, Evansville-South Bend
	11	Punch Knoll, Dayton
1912	25	Larry LeJeune, Grand Rapids

Central League, continued

Year	HR	Player, Club
1913	15	Bill Keene, Springfield
1914	15	Howard Baker, Evansville
1915	10	Fred Bratschi, Fort Wayne
1916	18	Earl Sykes, Dayton
1917	10	Frank Walker, Springfield
1920	11	Vincent Tydeman, Ludington
1921	21	Joe Hamel, Ludington
1922	12	Charles Miller, Lansing
1926	4	Eddie Radtke, Ludington
1928	27	Jim Jordan, Dayton
1929	41	Tripp Sigman, Canton
1930	52	Pat Wright, Fort Wayne
1932	26	Babe Phelps, Youngstown
1934	6	Ralph Rhein, Fort Wayne
1948	31	Joe Morjoseph, Dayton
1949	25	Ron Bowen, Saginaw
1950	24	Ron Bowen, Muskegon
1951	31	Ed Krage, Muskegon

Central California League
1910–1911

Year	HR	Player, Club
1911	3	Heine Schuerin, Alameda

Central Inter-State League
1888–1890

Year	HR	Player, Club
1888	6	A. W. Snyder, Crawfordsville/Terre Haute
1889	22	Lew Whistler, Evansville
1890	12	George McVey, Terre Haute

Central Mexican League
1955–1957
Not a member of the National Association in 1955

Year	HR	Player, Club
1955	19	Blas Guzman, Aguascalientes
1956	28	Blas Guzman, Fresnillo
	28	Lupe Pedroza, Fresnillo
1957	27	Juan Hernandez, Durango-Laguna

Central New York League
1888

Year	HR	Player, Club
1888	8	Jack Walsh, Auburn

Central Pennsylvania League
1887–1888

Year	HR	Player, Club
1887	6	Jake Drauby, Sunbury/Mahoney/Minersville/Ashland

Central Texas League
1914–1917
Sometimes called Texas Trolley League

Year	HR	Player, Club
1914	5	Ben Kyser, Corsicana
1915	7	Roy Leslie, Ennis
	7	Wilson White, Terrell
1916	10	Warren Comstock, Marlin
	10	A. Edens, Terrell

Coastal Plain League
1937–1941, 1946–1952

Year	HR	Player, Club
1937	24	Joe Bistroff, Snow Hill
	24	Al Joyner, Ayden
1938	25	Ben Roth, New Bern
1939	32	Joe Bistroff, Snow Hill
1940	18	Luis Olmo, Wilson
1941	26	Tom Kurst, Rocky Mount
1946	21	Charles Munday, Rocky Mount
1947	25	Harry Soufas, New Bern
1948	35	John Hanley, Rocky Mount
1949	27	Quentin Martin, Rocky Mount
1950	24	William Smith, Goldsboro
1951	20	James McComas, Wilson
1952	12	Felix Frazier, Wilson

Cocoa Rookie League
1964

Year	HR	Player, Club
1964	2	John Agnetti, Mets
	2	Gerald Lyscio, Twins
	2	Albert Yates, Mets

Colonial League
1914–1915, 1947–1950
Not a member of the National Association in 1915

Year	HR	Player, Club
1914	9	John Gilmore, Pawtucket
1915	4	Frank Kiley, Taunton/Brockton
1947	21	Frank Lamanna, Waterbury
1948	23	Zeke Bonura, Stamford
1949	26	Leo Eastham, Waterbury
1950	11	Carlos Santiago, Poughkeepsie

Connecticut Association
1910

Year	HR	Player, Club
1910	4	George Dunlap, Middletown

Connecticut State League
1884–1885, 1888, 1891, 1897–1912

Year	HR	Player, Club
1885	2	Bill Thomas, Meriden
1895	2	Dan Gunshannon, Hartford

GOING FOR THE FENCES

Year	HR	Player, Club
1896	5	Thomas Iver, Bridgeport
1897	12	Terry Rogers, Bridgeport
1898	5	Roger Conner, Waterbury
1899	11	Frank Woodruff, New London/Bridgeport
1900	14	Danny Murphy, Norwich
1901	12	Danny Murphy, Norwich
	12	Frank Woodruff, Norwich/New London
1902	7	Bob Drew, Meriden
1903	5	Jack Tighe, Norwich
1904	7	Emil Batch, Holyoke
1905	9	Walt Hartley, Holyoke
1906	5	Percy Rising, New London
1907	8	Lou Lapine, Holyoke
1908	10	George Simmons, New Haven
1909	23	Ray Perkins, Holyoke
1910	15	Pop Foster, Holyoke
1911	7	Fred Eley, Bridgeport
	7	Pop Foster, New Haven
1912	9	Pop Foster, New Haven

Cotton States League
1902–1908, 1910–1913, 1922–1932, 1936–1941, 1947–1955

Year	HR	Player, Club
1911	11	Guy Tutweiler, Hattiesburg
1922	4	Bill Waldron, Greenwood
1923	5	Fred Eichrodt, Meridian
1924	16	Sammy Vick, Brookhaven
1925	17	Hershell Bobo, Hattiesburg
1926	20	George Ferrell, Monroe
1927	12	Charles Gibson, Hattiesburg
1928	21	Horace Long, Jackson
1929	28	Stormy Davis, Lake Charles
1930	40	Ralph Winegarner, El Dorado
1931	17	Horace Long, Jackson
1932	12	James Long, El Dorado/Baton Rouge
1936	29	Milt Stroner, El Dorado
1937	26	Kermit Lewis, El Dorado
1938	18	Judson Kirke, Jr., Pine Bluff
1939	32	Al Gardella, Hot Springs
1940	25	Monte Duncan, Hot Springs
	25	Ed Zydowski, Hot Springs
1941	29	Merv Connors, Texarkana
1947	27	Floyd Fogg, Clarksdale
1948	22	Jack Parks, Natchez
1949	22	Dan Phalen, Hot Springs
1950	25	Richard Atkins, Natchez
1951	27	Pete Konyar, Pine Bluff
1952	15	Ray Perry, El Dorado
1953	41	Harold Martin, Hot Springs
1954	28	Pelham Austin, El Dorado
1955	19	Marshall Gilbert, Monroe

Cumberland Valley League
1896

Year	HR	Player, Club
1896	6	Harry Tate, Hagerstown

Dakota League
1921–1922
See South Dakota League

Dixie League
1916, 1933

Alabama and Georgia

Year	HR	Player, Club
1916	9	Fred Chambers, Dothan

Arkansas, Louisiana, Mississippi, and Texas

Year	HR	Player, Club
1933	17	Stormy Davis, Waco/Pine Bluff/Longview

Dominican Summer League
1985, 1987–1988, 1990–present

Year	HR	Player, Club
1985	8	Eliot Jose, Andulleros
	8	Ignacio Javier, Piratas
1987	6	Roberto Valdez, Piratas
1988	2	Joaquin de la Cruz, Tigres
	2	Facanel Medina, Piratas
	2	Clemente Jose, Plataneros
	2	Rudy Pemberton, Tigres
1990	13	Jose Diaz, Baltimore-Chicago AL
1991	13	Israel Alcantara, Expos
1992	14	Lorenzo de la Cruz, Blue Jays East
1993	15	Carlos Adolfo, Expos
1994	18	Jose Amado, Mariners
	18	Carlos Soriano, Mets
	18	Miguel Tejada, Athletics
1995	15	Ignacio Suero, Blue Jays
1996	19	Juan Silvestre, Mariners
1997	14	Emmanuel Mendez, Rockies
1998	19	Wilton Pena, White Sox
1999	19	Amaury Pena, White Sox
2000	15	Nelson Cruz, Mets East
2001	11	Rodolfo Guillen, Yankees
	11	Tiago Campos, Reds
2002	22	Wilson Reves, Red Sox
2003	10	Gilbert Alcantara, White Sox
2004	9	Alex Lachappelle, White Sox
2005	10	Norberto Ortiz, Angels
2006	9	Kelvin Diaz, Indians
2007	11	Luis Jimenez, Angels
2008	13	Darling Read, Indians

East Dixie League
1934–1935

Year	HR	Player, Club
1934	19	Cecil Bolton, Greenville
1935	28	Earl Nelson, Greenville

East Texas League
1916, 1923–1926, 1931, 1936–1940, 1946, 1949–1950

Year	HR	Player, Club
1916	3	Hank Utzman, Lufkin
1923	31	Lillard Belcher, Marshall/Paris
1924	35	Pete Daniels, Marshall
1925	41	Jack Holloway, Tyler
1926	62	Moose Clabaugh, Tyler
1931	4	Martin Hauser, Henderson
1936	24	Merv Connors, Longview
	24	Clary Hack, Gladewater
1937	28	Tony Robello, Jacksonville
1938	38	Tony Robello, Jacksonville
1939	26	Gil Turner, Marshall
1940	19	Tom Jordan, Marshall
1946	30	Frank Sacka, Paris
1949	23	Nick Gregory, Kilgore
1950	26	Merv Connors, Kilgore
	26	Jack Jones, Longview

Eastern Association
1881–1883, 1891, 1913–1914

Year	HR	Player, Club
1891	5	Dan Lally, New Haven
	5	Pete Sweeney, Rochester
1913	8	Tom Stankard, Meriden/Springfield
1914	7	Francis Shields, Waterbury

Eastern League
1884–1887, 1892–1911
See International League II.

Eastern League I
1916–1932

Year	HR	Player, Club
1916	8	Fletcher Low, Springfield/Hartford
1917	9	John Flynn, Lawrence
1918	3	Roy Grimes, Hartford
1919	6	Joe Hauser, Providence
1920	13	Fred Wilder, Springfield
1921	15	John Flynn, Springfield
1922	21	Walter Simpson, Springfield
1923	44	Walter Simpson, Springfield
1924	38	John Roser, Worcester
1925	12	Dolph Schinkle, Albany/Hartford
1926	18	Harold Yordy, Bridgeport
1927	22	Harold Yordy, Albany
1928	27	John Roser, Hartford
1929	41	Bruce Caldwell, New Haven
1930	23	Frank Rogers, New Haven
1931	38	Bruce Caldwell, New Haven
1932	18	Wilbur Davis, Norfolk
	18	Yam Yaryan, New Haven

Eastern League II
1923–present
Called New York-Pennsylvania League, 1923–1937

Year	HR	Player, Club
1923	19	Bill Batch, York
1924	18	Roy Leavitt, Williamsport
1925	33	Joe Munson, Harrisburg
1926	10	John Roseberry, Shamokin
1927	11	Glenn Killinger, Harrisburg
1928	11	Ray Flood, Harrisburg
	11	Bernard Hungling, Syracuse
1929	18	Ray Flood, Harrisburg
	18	Arthur McHenry, Scranton
1930	41	Ken Strong, Hazleton
1931	19	Pat Wright, Wilkes-Barre/Hazleton
1932	19	Jake Plummer, Wilkes-Barre
1933	14	Bob Gibson, Binghamton
1934	26	Horace McBride, Williamsport
1935	18	Roberto Estalella, Harrisburg
1936	19	Morrie Arnovich, Hazleton
	19	Horace McBride, Williamsport
1937	21	Billy Sodd, Wilkes-Barre
1938	22	Bill Nicholson, Williamsport
1939	29	Jack Graham, Binghamton
1940	20	Jack Graham, Binghamton
1941	17	Larry Barton, Wilkes-Barre
1942	14	Ralph Kiner, Albany
1943	10	Bill Nagel, Albany
1944	9	Stan Wentzel, Hartford
1945	7	John Mihalik, Wilkes-Barre
1946	12	Don Manno, Hartford
	12	Nick Picciuto, Utica
1947	24	Bud Heslet, Binghamton
1948	20	Homer Moore, Hartford
1949	31	Harry Simpson, Wilkes-Barre
1950	27	Dale Long, Binghamton
1951	24	Eulas Hutson, Wilkes-Barre
	24	Clint Weaver, Binghamton
1952	27	Jake Crawford, Scranton
1953	28	Rocky Colavito, Reading
1954	16	George Wopinek, Williamsport
1955	34	John Blanchard, Binghamton
1956	22	Andy Rellick, Reading/Syracuse
1957	26	Deron Johnson, Binghamton
1958	23	Don Gile, Allentown
1959	33	Jackie Davis, Williamsport
1960	35	Don Lock, Binghamton
1961	30	George Banks, Binghamton
1962	38	Ken Harrelson, Binghamton
1963	26	Bob Chance, Charleston
1964	15	Bobby Sanders, Williamsport
1965	25	George Scott, Pittsfield
1966	12	Hank McGraw, Williamsport/Elmira
1967	21	Bill Schlesinger, Pittsfield

Year	HR	Player, Club
1968	17	Carmen Fanzone, Pittsfield
1969	26	Angel Mangual, York
1970	34	Richie Zisk, Waterbury
1971	27	Albert Thompson, Pittsfield
1972	31	Albert Thompson, Pittsfield
1973	38	Tom Robson, Pittsfield
1974	27	Jack Baker, Bristol
1975	16	Dick Davis, Thetford Mines
1976	29	Danny Thomas, Berkshire
1977	30	Gary Holle, Holyoke
1978	21	Jeff Yurak, Holyoke
1979	41	Rick Lancellotti, Buffalo
1980	30	Nick Esasky, Waterbury
1981	40	Ron Kittle, Glens Falls
1982	29	Jim Bennett, West Haven
1983	31	Willie Darkis, Reading
1984	24	Pat Adams, Glens Falls
1985	28	Cory Snyder, Waterbury
1986	18	Bernardo Brito, Waterbury
1987	24	Bernardo Brito, Williamsport
1988	17	Chris Hoiles, Glens Falls
	17	Jim Wilson, Vermont
1989	22	Bob Sepanek, Albany
1990	21	Rico Brogna, London
1991	31	Jeromy Burnitz, Williamsport
1992	25	Greg Sparks, London
1993	26	Cliff Floyd, Harrisburg
	26	Glenn Murray, Harrisburg
1994	28	Charles Johnson, Portland
1995	23	Fred McNair, Reading
1996	29	Shane Spencer, Norwich
1997	37	Matt Raleigh, Binghamton
1998	31	Calvin Pickering, Bowie
1999	38	Chris Norton, Portland
2000	31	Adam Hyzdu, Altoona
2001	33	Mike Rivera, Erie
2002	27	Val Pascucci, Harrisburg
2003	24	Jeff Inglin, Reading
2004	39	Mitch Jones, Trenton
2005	34	Dave Duncan, Trenton
2006	27	Chip Cannon, New Hampshire
2007	28	Jeff Larish, Erie
2008	26	Lou Montanez, Bowie

Eastern Canada League
1922–1923

Year	HR	Player, Club
1922	16	Frank Delisle, Montreal / Three Rivers
1923	24	Frank Delisle, Three Rivers / Quebec Canadiens

Eastern Carolina League
1908–1911, 1928–29

Year	HR	Player, Club
1908	3	Clarence Fox, Kinston/Raleigh
1910	2	Walter Steinhouser, Rocky Mount
1928	36	Frank Roscoe, Wilmington
1929	21	Tom Young, Fayetteville/Wilmington

Eastern Championship Association
1881

Year	HR	Player, Club
1881	4	Mike Muldoon, Metropolitan

Eastern Illinois League
1907–1908

Year	HR	Player, Club
1907	10	Andy Lotshaw, Charleston
1908	6	Andy Biltz, Shelbyville

Eastern Inter-State League
1889–1890, 1895

Year	HR	Player, Club
1890	5	Frank Grant, Harrisburg

Eastern Iowa League
1895

Year	HR	Player, Club
1895	13	Leroy Hackett, Burlington

Eastern Michigan League
1912–1913

See Border League

Eastern New England League
1885

See New England League

Eastern Shore League
1922–1928, 1937–1941, 1946–1949

Year	HR	Player, Club
1922	14	Jake Flowers, Cambridge
1923	27	Chick Tolson, Salisbury
1924	24	Roy Zanzalari, Crisfield
1925	25	Charles Fitzberger, Salisbury
	25	Victor St. Martin, Parksley
1926	22	Pete Stack, Parksley
1927	24	Paul Richards, Crisfield
1937	20	Alex Pitko, Centreville
1938	31	Bill Phillips, Federalsburg
1939	29	Henry Schluter, Dover
1940	18	Ed Kobesky, Salisbury
1941	16	Tommy Koval, Cambridge
1946	29	Don Marshall, Dover
1947	29	Ducky Detweiler, Federalsburg
1948	33	Norm Zauchin, Milford
1949	19	Bob Westfall, Federalsburg

Empire State League
1913

See Georgia State League

Evangeline League
1934–1942, 1946–1957

Year	HR	Player, Club
1934	25	Harry Nolan, Rayne
1935	18	Arthur Bartelli, Rayne
	18	Cecil Dunn, Alexandria
1936	47	Cecil Dunn, Alexandria
1937	23	Ken Silvestri, Rayne
1938	18	Robert Hood, Lake Charles
1939	18	Joe Yourkovich, Rayne
1940	24	Woody Fair, New Iberia
1941	13	Woody Fair, New Iberia
1942	3	Clary Hack, Port Arthur
1946	25	Irving Clement, Hammond/Abbeville
1947	22	Dan Seiler, Houma
1948	34	Roy Sanner, Houma
1949	30	Robert Dunn, Hammond
1950	39	Robert Dunn, Hammond
1951	42	Remy LeBlanc, New Iberia
1952	33	Al Meriwether, Crowley
1953	42	Al Meriwether, Crowley
1954	42	Remy LeBlanc, New Iberia
1955	26	Thomas Nerad, Lafayette
1956	20	Eugene Johnson, Lake Charles
1957	26	Dave Irby, Alexandria

Far West League
1948–1951

Year	HR	Player, Club
1948	36	Ray Perry, Redding
1949	45	Ray Perry, Redding
1950	44	Ray Perry, Redding
1951	18	Ray Perry, Redding

Federal League
1913

Not a member of the National Association

Year	HR	Player, Club
1913	9	John Kading, Chicago

Florida–Alabama–Georgia League
1915

Usually called FLAG League. Started season as Georgia State League and changed name at end of May

Year	HR	Player, Club
1915	7	Ben Paschal, Dothan
	7	Jesse Reynolds, Waycross

Florida East Coast League
1940–1942, 1972

Was a Rookie League in 1972

Year	HR	Player, Club
1940	11	Oliver Kelly, Miami
	11	Dale Lynch, Miami Beach
	11	Jack Westley, Fort Lauderdale/Hollywood
1941	21	Joe Murff, Fort Pierce
1942	2	Armando Dominguez, Orlando
	2	Fred Leonhardt, DeLand
1972	10	Randy Bass, Twins

Florida International League
1946–1954

Year	HR	Player, Club
1946	7	Armando Valdes, Havana/West Palm Beach
1947	34	Ned Harris, West Palm Beach
1948	28	Bernardo Fernandez, Miami/Tampa
1949	31	Charles Aleno, Fort Lauderdale
1950	27	Jack Tanner, Lakeland/Fort Lauderdale
1951	19	Jack Tanner, Fort Lauderdale
1952	15	Neb Wilson, St. Petersburg
1953	35	John Davis, Fort Lauderdale
1954	23	Jesse Levan, Greater Miami

Florida Rookie League
1965

See Gulf Coast Rookie League

Florida State League
1919–1928, 1936–1941, 1946–present

Year	HR	Player, Club
1920	10	Elliott Bigelow, St. Petersburg
1921	9	Walter Shannon, Daytona Beach
1922	10	Ernest Burke, Orlando
	10	John Roser, St. Petersburg
1923	14	Al Greene, Orlando
1924	19	Walt Hunter, Orlando
1926	4	Otto Dumas, Sanford
	4	Philip Grandio, Fort Myers
	4	Dick Luckey, St. Petersburg
	4	Rollie Tinker, Orlando
1927	15	Faustin Casaras, Miami
1936	10	George Andrews, Palatka / St. Augustine
	10	Lonnie Smith, Gainesville/Palatka
1937	10	Buster Kinard, Palatka
1938	8	Harry Rice, DeLand
1939	11	Joe Niedson, Daytona Beach
1940	10	Jim Pruitt, Gainesville
1941	11	Fauline Kirkland, Ocala/Gainesville
1946	8	Bill Fuchs, DeLand
	8	Ken Hill, Gainesville
	8	Myril Hoag, Palatka

Florida State League

Year	HR	Player, Club
1947	10	Ben Thorpe, Gainesville
1948	17	Ralph Bartolozzi, Leesburg
1949	18	Lou Bevil, Daytona Beach
1950	33	Ed Levy, Sanford
1951	23	Rocky Colavito, Daytona Beach
	23	Eldon Pichan, Palatka
1952	25	Chuck Aleno, Sanford
1953	20	J. C. Dunn, Sanford
1954	23	Herman Niehaus, Lakeland
1955	20	Inocencio Rodriguez, Cocoa
1956	22	Gene Cockrell, Cocoa
	22	German Pizzaro, Gainesville
1957	16	German Pizzaro, Gainesville
1958	25	German Pizzaro, Gainesville/Tampa
1959	20	Tom Hamilton, St. Petersburg
1960	15	Dave Bristol, Palatka
	15	Miles McWilliams, Palatka
1961	12	Paul Catlo, Palatka
1962	14	Jimmy Wynn, Tampa
1963	12	Rich Littleton, Sarasota
1964	11	Don Pepper, Lakeland
1965	9	Roy Bethell, Cocoa
1966	13	Charles Robinson, Leesburg
1967	18	Joe Keough, Leesburg
1968	16	Nat King, Orlando
1969	14	Wayne Dees, St. Petersburg
1970	22	Moe Hill, Orlando
1971	33	Jim Fuller, Miami
1972	27	Jack Baker, Winter Haven
1973	18	Wayne Cage, Key West
1974	16	Joe Wallis, Key West
1975	14	Jerry Fry, West Palm Beach
1976	18	Dave Koza, Winter Haven
1977	19	John Scoras, West Palm Beach
1978	19	Fay Thompson, Dunedin
1979	26	Steve Balboni, Fort Lauderdale
1980	17	Mark Strucher, Daytona Beach
1981	19	Wes Clements, Daytona Beach
1982	19	Glenn Davis, Daytona Beach
	19	Mark Strucher, Daytona Beach
1983	21	Crestwell Pratt, Tampa
1984	22	Bill Moore, West Palm Beach
1985	16	Steve DeAngelis, Clearwater
1986	18	Jimmy Fortenberry, Clearwater
1987	17	Pat Sipe, West Palm Beach
1988	17	Brian Morrison, Miami
1989	24	Julian Yan, Dunedin
1990	18	Ray Giannelli, Dunedin
1991	14	Ray Noriega, Fort Lauderdale
	14	Jose Oliva, Charlotte
1992	30	Carlos Delgado, Dunedin
1993	20	Rick Holifield, Dunedin
1994	21	Karim Garcia, Vero Beach
1995	21	Dan Held, Clearwater
1996	18	John Curl, Dunedin
1997	26	Adrian Beltre, Vero Beach
1998	26	Shawn Gallagher, Charlotte
1999	23	Morgan Burkhart, Sarasota
2000	29	Rob Stratton, St. Lucie
2001	21	Nick Alvarez, Vero Beach
	21	James Deschaine, Tampa
	21	Mitch Jones, Tampa
2002	23	Leo Daigle, Lakeland
2003	23	Ryan Howard, Clearwater
2004	32	Brandon Sing, Daytona
2005	28	Andrew Wilson, St. Lucie
2006	21	Jesus Flores, St. Lucie
	21	Jay Garthwaite, Sarasota
	21	Brock Peterson, Fort Myers
2007	23	Jacob Butler, Dunedin
2008	29	Ryan Striely, Lakeland

Georgia–Alabama League
1913–1917, 1928–1930, 1946–1951

Year	HR	Player, Club
1914	14	Harry Smith, Newnan
	14	Bill Waldron, LaGrange
1915	15	Don Flynn, Newnan
1916	17	Wilbur Davis, Newnan
1917	2	— Ellis, Talladega
	2	Don Flynn, Griffin
	2	— McGlade, Tri-Cities
	2	Fred Patterson, Tri-Cities
1928	27	Jo-Jo White, Carrollton
1929	25	Charles Knowles, Cedartown
1930	26	George Kelly, Cedartown
1946	30	Jake Daniels, Valley/LaGrange
1947	25	Ken Guettler, Griffin
1948	14	Jim Acton, LaGrange
1949	28	Carl Franson, Newnan
1950	38	Eugene Solt, Carrolltown
1951	26	Claude Shoemake, Rome

Georgia–Florida League
1935–1942, 1946–1958, 1962–1963

YYear	HR	Player, Club
1935	18	Frank Puttman, Albany
1936	16	Lee Johnson, Albany
1937	26	Tom Corbett, Thomasville
1938	8	Ed Hartness, Americus
	8	Pat Riley, Albany
1939	9	Carl Bethmann, Moultrie
1940	14	Dale Alexander, Thomasville
1941	12	Joe Bob Mitchell, Cordele
1942	9	Dave Pluss, Valdosta
1946	22	Ken Rhyne, Moultrie
1947	24	Ken Rhyne, Moultrie
1948	27	Ken Rhyne, Moultrie
1949	21	Harold Shiles, Waycross
1950	15	Robert Fulton, Thomasville
1951	29	Glenn Eury, Moultrie
1952	19	Parnell Ruark, Tifton
1953	21	Jack Paepke, Brunswick

Georgia–Florida League, continued

Year	HR	Player, Club
1954	19	Clarence Buheller, Brunswick
	19	Larry Spinner, Tifton
1955	20	Wayne Davis, Albany
	20	Dick Lubinski, Cordele
1956	30	Bob Wellman, Moultrie
1957	26	Jim Hickman, Albany
1958	32	Bob Boyer, Albany
1962	26	Glen Clark, Dublin
1963	15	Charles Murray, Moultrie

Georgia State League
1906, 1913–1914, 1920–1921, 1948–1956
Called Empire State League in 1913

Year	HR	Player, Club
1913	10	Harry Chancey, Americus
1914	31	Bill Bankston, Cordele
1920	10	Ike Boone, Cedartown
1921	22	Ollie Tucker, Cedartown
1948	11	Truman Connell, Vidalia-Lyons
1949	28	Ralph Burgamy, Eastman/Dublin
1950	39	Parnell Ruark, Dublin
1951	32	Parnell Ruark, Dublin
1952	31	Charles Quimby, Statesboro
1953	44	Van Davis, Douglas
1954	31	Van Davis, Douglas
1955	21	Bob Wellman, Douglas
1956	21	Al Milley, Sandersville

Gulf Coast League
1907–1908, 1926, 1950–1953

Year	HR	Player, Club
1926	6	Bob Fenner, Victoria
1950	24	Charles Harper, Port Arthur
	24	Al Meriwether, Lake Charles
1951	37	Stan Goletz, Brownsville
	37	Bob Moyer, Corpus Christi
1952	45	Walt Sessi, Brownsville
1953	29	Hank Robinson, Galveston

Gulf Coast Rookie League
1964–present
Called Sarasota Rookie League in 1964
Called Florida Rookie League in 1965

Year	HR	Player, Club
1964	3	Michael Mantsch, Braves
1965	3	Larry Hall, Astros
1966	5	Fred Winston, Yankees
1967	7	Bob Storm, Twins
1968	8	Michael Holbrook, Twins
1969	4	Russ Bodkin, Cardinals
	4	Ron McDonald, Twins
	4	Mike Poepping, Twins
1970	6	Bob Gorinski, Twins
	6	Jeff Newman, Indians
	6	Dave Parker, Pirates
1971	8	Dave Revering, Reds
1972	5	Cleo Kilpatrick, White Sox
1973	6	Hector Eduardo, Cardinals
1974	4	Edwin Olszta, White Sox
1975	5	Luis Silverio, Royals
1976	4	Dave Rivera, Rangers
	4	Darrell Vosejpka, Royals
1977	8	Phil Westendorf, Royals
1978	7	Ira Turner, Royals
1979	5	Greg Dikos, Braves
	5	Leon Doak, Royals Gold
	5	Miguel Sosa, Braves
1980	7	Bert Gjesdal, Yankees
1981	10	Tom Thompson, Royals Gold/Royals Blue
1982	9	Fred McGriff, Yankees
1983	8	Dimas Gutierrez, Pirates
	8	Michael Taylor, White Sox
1984	10	Drew Denson, Braves
	10	Mike Smiciklas, Braves
1985	5	Jesus Alvarez, White Sox
1986	9	Eduardo Gonzalez, Yankees
1987	10	Eric Anthony, Astros
1988	8	Steve Lemuth, Expos
1989	7	Ramon Jimenez, Yankees
1990	7	Jim Dismuke, Reds
1991	10	Duane Thomas, Orioles
	6	Juan Thomas, White Sox
1992	6	Chris Burr, Rangers
1993	6	Marc Niethammer, Expos
1994	9	Dan Vasquez, Rangers
1995	11	Gary Coffee, Royals
1996	13	Derrick Bly, Cubs
1997	10	Michael Rivera, Tigers
1998	12	Juan Rivera, Yankees
1999	9	Charlie Dees, Orioles
2000	13	Bryan Barnowski, Red Sox
	13	Tony Blanco, Red Sox
2001	7	Matt Cooper, Red Sox
2002	10	Travis Wong, Reds
2003	8	Steve Doetsch, Braves
	8	Carlos Moreta, Braves
2004	8	Juan Portos, Twins
	8	Maximiliano Ramirez, Braves
	8	Buck Shaw, Phillies
	8	Carlos Torres, Red Sox
2005	9	Angel Reyes, Tigers
2006	11	Christopher Carlson, Tigers
2007	10	John Tolisano, Blue Jays
2008	11	Abner Abreu, Indians

Gulf State League
1976
See Lone Star League

GOING FOR THE FENCES

Illinois–Iowa League
1890–1892
Often called 2I League

Year	HR	Player, Club
1891	8	Mattie McVicker, Joliet
1892	13	Gene Moriarty, Evansville/Jacksonville

Illinois–Missouri League
1908 1914

Year	HR	Player, Club
1908	11	Fred Kommers, Havana
1909	7	Cy Forsythe, Pekin
	7	Fred Johnson, Canton
	7	Will Johnson, Monmouth
1910	5	Al Dean, Pekin/Clinton
1911	29	Andy Lotshaw, Canton
1912	11	Andy Lotshaw, Canton
1913	13	Roy Phillips, Streator
1914	10	Andy Lotshaw, Champaign

Illinois State League
1947–1948

Year	HR	Player, Club
1947	10	Rip Repulski, West Frankfort
1948	8	Paul Deters, Marion

Inter-American League
1979

Year	HR	Player, Club
1979	8	Wayne Tyrone, Miami

Inter-Mountain League
1901

Year	HR	Player, Club
1901	3	Homer Hausen, Ogden

International Association
1877–1880, 1886–1890
Usually called National Association, 1879–1880

Year	HR	Player, Club
1877	1	Ed Caskins, Rochester
	1	Dick Dickson, Maple Leaf
	1	Charles Fulmer, Allegheny
1878	2	George Derby, Hornell/Syracuse
1879	3	Bill McClellan, Washington/Worcester
1880	1	Dan Brouthers, Baltimore/Rochester
	1	Tim Keefe, Albany
	1	Lipman Pike, Albany/Rochester
1886	8	John Fields, Buffalo/Utica
	8	Joe Visner, Rochester
1887	11	Frank Grant, Buffalo
1888	13	Mike Lehane, Buffalo

Year	HR	Player, Club
1889	10	Bill Hoover, Toronto
1890	3	Count Campau, Detroit
	3	Edward Doyle, Saginaw–Bay City
	3	Bill Parks, London
	3	Dan Quinn, Buffalo/Montreal/Detroit

International League I
1898, 1900, 1908

Year	HR	Player, Club
1898	7	Bill Reid, Saginaw
1900	5	Frank Hemphill, London
	5	Charles Jones, London
1908	1	Eight players tied

International League II
1884–87, 1892–present
Called Eastern League through 1911

Year	HR	Player, Club
1884	11	Oyster Burns, Wilmington
1885	16	Dick Johnston, Richmond
1886	10	Oyster Burns, Newark
1887	4	George Wilson, Bridgeport
1892	5	Bill Hoover, Rochester/Providence
	5	Milton West, Albany
1893	16	Frank Bonner, Wilkes-Barre
1894	21	Jake Drauby, Buffalo
1895	14	Jud Smith, Toronto
1896	18	Jake Drauby, Providence
1897	20	Buck Freeman, Toronto
1898	23	Buck Freeman, Toronto
1899	11	Tom Campbell, Springfield
1900	17	Kitty Bransfield, Worcester
1901	12	Reddy Grey, Buffalo/Rochester
	12	Tom Raub, Montreal
1902	14	Pop Foster, Providence/Montreal
1903	9	Ed Atherton, Buffalo
1904	9	Frank Laporte, Buffalo
1905	9	Jim Murray, Buffalo/Toronto
1906	7	Jim Murray, Buffalo
1907	7	Bill Abstein, Providence
	7	Natty Nattress, Buffalo
1908	16	Bill Phyle, Toronto
1909	8	George Simmons, Rochester
1910	11	Albert Shaw, Toronto
1911	20	Tim Jordan, Toronto
1912	19	Tim Jordan, Toronto
1913	8	Del Paddock, Rochester
1914	15	Wally Pipp, Rochester
1915	14	George Whiteman, Montreal
1916	12	George Twombly, Baltimore
1917	16	Harry Damrau, Montreal
1918	5	King Lear, Toronto
1919	15	George Kelly, Rochester
1920	22	Frank Brower, Reading
	22	Michael Konnick, Reading
1921	24	Jack Bentley, Baltimore
1922	34	Red Wingo, Toronto

International League II, continued

Year	HR	Player, Club
1923	22	Max Bishop, Baltimore
	22	Bill Webb, Buffalo
1924	28	Bill Kelly, Buffalo
1925	29	Joe Kelly, Toronto
1926	44	Bill Kelly, Buffalo
1927	31	Del Bissonette, Buffalo
1928	31	Dale Alexander, Toronto
1929	38	Rip Collins, Rochester
1930	63	Joe Hauser, Baltimore
1931	31	Joe Hauser, Baltimore
1932	54	Buzz Arlett, Baltimore
1933	39	Buzz Arlett, Baltimore
1934	32	Woody Abernathy, Baltimore
	32	Vince Barton, Newark
1935	53	George Puccinelli, Baltimore
1936	42	Woody Abernathy, Baltimore
1937	37	Ab Wright, Baltimore
1938	45	Ollie Carnegie, Buffalo
1939	29	Ollie Carnegie, Buffalo
1940	37	Bill Nagel, Baltimore
1941	37	Frank Kelleher, Newark
1942	28	Les Burge, Montreal
1943	18	Ed Kobesky, Buffalo
1944	27	Howie Moss, Baltimore
1945	38	Frank Skaff, Baltimore
1946	38	Howie Moss, Baltimore
1947	53	Howie Moss, Baltimore
1948	33	Howie Moss, Baltimore
1949	42	Russ Derry, Rochester
1950	30	Russ Derry, Rochester
	30	Chet Laabs, Toronto/Jersey City
1951	35	Marv Rickert, Baltimore
1952	30	Frank Carswell, Buffalo
1953	36	Jack Wallaesa, Springfield/Buffalo
1954	31	Rocky Nelson, Montreal
1955	37	Rocky Nelson, Montreal
1956	35	Luke Easter, Buffalo
1957	40	Luke Easter, Buffalo
1958	43	Rocky Nelson, Toronto
1959	37	Pancho Herrera, Buffalo
1960	31	Joe Altobelli, Montreal
1961	32	Boog Powell, Rochester
1962	32	Pancho Herrera, Buffalo
1963	33	Dick Allen, Arkansas
1964	39	Mack Jones, Syracuse
1965	21	Pancho Herrera, Columbus
1966	29	Mike Epstein, Rochester
1967	25	Jim Beauchamp, Richmond
1968	34	Dave Nicholson, Richmond
1969	34	Bob Robertson, Columbus
1970	37	Hal Breeden, Richmond
1971	32	Bobby Grich, Rochester
1972	26	Richie Zisk, Charleston
1973	39	Jim Fuller, Rochester
1974	25	Jim Rice, Pawtucket
1975	19	Bill Nahorodny, Toledo
1976	36	Jack Baker, Rhode Island
1977	30	Terry Crowley, Rochester
1978	25	Hank Small, Richmond
1979	28	Sam Bowen, Pawtucket
1980	23	Marshall Brant, Columbus
1981	33	Steve Balboni, Columbus
1982	32	Steve Balboni, Columbus
1983	35	Brian Dayett, Columbus
1984	28	Jerry Keller, Syracuse
1985	26	Jim Wilson, Maine
1986	28	Ken Gerhart, Rochester
1987	31	Jay Buhner, Columbus
1988	21	Dave Griffin, Richmond
1989	21	Glenallen Hill, Syracuse
1990	33	Phil Plantier, Pawtucket
1991	21	Rick Lancellotti, Pawtucket
1992	26	Hensley Meulens, Columbus
1993	38	Sam Horn, Charlotte
1994	31	Jeff Manto, Norfolk/Rochester
1995	28	Butch Huskey, Norfolk
1996	42	Phil Hiatt, Toledo
1997	33	Russ Morman, Charlotte
1998	35	Brian Daubach, Charlotte
1999	33	Luis Raven, Charlotte
2000	33	Chad Mottola, Syracuse
2001	36	Israel Alcantara, Pawtucket
2002	27	Israel Alcantara, Indianapolis
2003	28	Fernando Seguignol, Columbus
2004	36	Earl Snyder, Pawtucket
2005	30	John-Ford Griffin, Syracuse
2006	36	Kevin Witt, Durham
2007	31	Mike Hessman, Toledo
2008	35	Brad Eldred, Charlotte

International Northwestern League
1919

See Pacific Coast International League

Inter–State Association
1883, 1885, 1890–1891, 1894–1900, 1906

Delaware, New Jersey, New York, and Pennsylvania

Year	HR	Player, Club
1883	6	Frank Fennelly, Camden/Brooklyn

Indiana, Michigan, Ohio, Pennsylvania, and West Virginia

Year	HR	Player, Club
1895	14	Reddy Grey, Findlay
1896	17	John Ganzel, New Castle
1897	17	Dummy Kihm, Fort Wayne
	17	Joe Reiman, Dayton
	17	Joe Werrick, Mansfield
1898	14	Joe Reiman, Dayton
1899	25	Erv Beck, Toledo
1900	18	Ed Bradley, Columbus/Anderson

GOING FOR THE FENCES

Inter-State League
1903, 1905–1908, 1913–1916, 1932, 1939–1952
Not member of the National Association in 1903.

Alabama and Florida

Year	HR	Player, Club
1903	3	Art Wallace, Brewton/Mobile

New York and Pennsylvania

Year	HR	Player, Club
1908	3	Jake Weimer, Olean

Ohio, Pennsylvania, and West Virginia

Year	HR	Player, Club
1913	6	Art Watson, Steubenville

New York and Pennsylvania

Year	HR	Player, Club
1915	3	Frank Moran, Warren
1916	4	John Gilmore, Warren/St. Marys/Wellsville
	4	Frank Gleich, Erie

New Jersey and Pennsylvania

Year	HR	Player, Club
1932	7	Dom Dallesandro, St. Clair
	7	Frank DeManicore, Stroudsburg
	7	Paul Piontek, Stroudsburg

Connecticut, Delaware, Maryland, New Jersey, and Pennsylvania

Year	HR	Player, Club
1939	14	Dave Kelly, Sunbury
1940	21	Arnold Greene, Harrisburg
1941	23	Edward Murphy, Allentown
1942	27	Tom Koval, Allentown
1943	20	Bill Burgo, Wilmington
1944	30	John Cappa, Allentown
1945	21	Rolland Seltz, Allentown
1946	30	Ed Sanicki, Wilmington
1947	37	Ed Sanicki, Wilmington
1948	25	Maurice Cunningham, Trenton
1949	27	Jim Lemon, Harrisburg
1950	24	Fred Marolewski, Allentown
1951	20	Harold Cox, Harrisburg
1952	30	Lou Heyman, Wilmington

Iowa–South Dakota League
1902–1903

Year	HR	Player, Club
1902	21	John Baxter, Sioux City

KOM League
1946–1952
Formal name was Kansas–Oklahoma–Missouri League

Year	HR	Player, Club
1946	10	Larry Singleton, Iola
1947	20	Jim Baxes, Ponca City
1948	13	Joe Beran, Ponca City
	13	Charles Sturnborg, Pittsburg
1949	14	Bob Speake, Carthage
1950	21	Willard Davis, Ponca City
1951	13	Brandy Davis, Bartlesville
	13	Bill Phillips, Bartlesville
1952	24	Don Ervin, Miami

Kansas State League
1887, 1895–1896, 1905–1906, 1909–1911, 1913–1914

Year	HR	Player, Club
1887	6	— Gibbs, Emporia
1896	2	Rube Adams, Chanute
	2	Thomas Leahy, Chanute
1909	6	Pete LaFlambois, Arkansas City
1910	13	Joe Riggert, Lyons

Kitty League
1903–1906, 1910–1914, 1916, 1922–1924, 1935–1942, 1946–1955
Formal name was Kentucky–Illinois–Tennessee League

Year	HR	Player, Club
1906	11	Andy Lotshaw, Jacksonville
1910	4	Rebel Keen, Clarksville
	4	Big Boy Kraft, McLeansboro
1911	10	Ernie Calbert, Harrisburg–Jackson
1912	10	Al Basham, Clarksville
1913	13	P. Vogt, Hopkinsville
1914	14	Dow VanDine, Paducah
1922	19	William Brown, Hopkinsville
1923	10	Tige Garrett, Springfield/Mayfield
1935	10	Lee Keller, Lexington
1936	17	Joe Bestudik, Paducah
1937	13	William Cooper, Fulton
1938	18	Jim E. Poole, Lexington
1939	33	John Newman, Owensboro
1940	34	Edward Urban, Owensboro
1941	30	Melvin Merkle, Jackson
1942	9	Bob Churchill, Bowling Green
	9	Tony Kvedar, Hopkinsville
1946	32	Ray Fletcher, Owensboro
1947	18	Joe Richardson, Hopkinsville
1948	23	John Kall, Hopkinsville
1949	23	Bill Adair, Owensboro
1950	28	Ned Waldrop, Fulton
1951	18	Joe Duhem, Mayfield
1952	21	Jack Hall, Owensboro
1953	26	Austin Knickerbocker, Mayfield
	26	Howard Warrell, Hopkinsville
1954	22	Ned Waldrop, Fulton
1955	24	Paul Bentley, Mayfield

Lone Star League
1927–1929, 1947–1948, 1976–1977
Called Gulf States League in 1976

Year	HR	Player, Club
1927	26	Tom Pyle, Tyler
1928	39	Charles Dorman, Tyler
1929	6	Ed Kallina, Sherman
	6	John King, Tyler
1947	32	John Stone, Henderson
1948	23	John Stone, Henderson
1976	16	Jim Capehart, Corpus Christi
1977	16	Marc Sinovich, Corpus Christi

Longhorn League
1947–1955

Year	HR	Player, Club
1947	37	Bob Cowsar, Sweetwater
1948	34	Ken Peacock, Sweetwater
1949	35	Al Monchak, Odessa
1950	44	Tom Jordan, Roswell
1951	36	Wayne Wallace, San Angelo
1952	50	Joe Bauman, Artesia
1953	53	Joe Bauman, Artesia
1954	72	Joe Bauman, Roswell
1955	46	Joe Bauman, Roswell

Maine State League
1907

Year	HR	Player, Club
1907	7	Henry Roper, Portland

Massachusetts States Association
1884

Year	HR	Player, Club
1884	1	Mike Bradley, Lawrence
	1	Ed Chamberlain, Lynn/Boston
	1	Henry Parry, Waltham

Mexican League
1937–present

Not a member of the National Association in 1937–1954

Year	HR	Player, Club
1937	6	Carlos Galina, Mexico City Petroleros
1938	9	Angel Castro, Tampico
1939	9	Angel Castro, Tampico
1940	12	Cool Papa Bell, Torreon
1941	33	Josh Gibson, Veracruz Blues
1942	20	Monte Irvin, Veracruz Blues
1943	13	Bill Wright, Mexico City
1944	13	Salvador Hernandez, Veracruz Blues
1945	26	Roberto Ortiz, Mexico City
1946	25	Roberto Oritz, Mexico City
1947	22	Roberto Ortiz, Mexico City
1948	19	Roberto Ortiz, Mexico City
1949	13	Jesus Diaz, Torreon
1950	10	Jesus Diaz, Torreon
	10	Angel Castro, Veracruz Blues
1951	22	Angel Castro, Veracruz Blues
1952	21	Rene Gonzalez, Veracruz
1953	13	Hector Lara, Nuevo Laredo
1954	21	Rene Gonzalez, Veracruz
1955	22	Mario Ariosa, Veracruz
1956	28	Alonzo Perry, Mexico City Reds
1957	27	Earl Taborn, Nuevo Laredo
1958	32	Edward Moore, Monterrey
1959	29	Aldo Salvent, Poza Rica
	29	Marv Williams, Mexico City Tigers/ Mexico City Reds
1960	36	Aldo Salvent, Poza Rica
1961	23	Witty Quintana, Veracruz
1962	25	Ronnie Camacho, Puebla
1963	39	Ronnie Camacho, Puebla
1964	46	Hector Espino, Monterrey
1965	39	Bobby Prescott, Poza Rica
1966	41	Bobby Prescott, Poza Rica
1967	41	Elrod Hendricks, Jalisco
1968	27	Hector Espino, Monterrey
1969	37	Hector Espino, Monterrey
1970	33	Rogelio Alvarez, Aguila
1971	23	Humberto Garcia, Tampico
1972	37	Hector Espino, Tampico
1973	26	Romel Canada, Saltillo
1974	32	Byron Browne, Tampico
1975	35	Andres Mora, Saltillo
1976	36	Jack Pierce, Puebla
1977	34	Ismael Oquendo, Saltillo
1978	28	Harold King, Saltillo
1979	24	Luis Alvarez, Leon
	24	Ivan Murrell, Puebla/Leon
1980*	32	Ivan Murrell, Leon
1980*	7	Jack Pierce, Coatzacoalcos
1981	23	Andres Mora, Saltillo
1982	25	Andres Mora, Saltillo/Nuevo Laredo
1983	22	Carlos Soto, Nuevo Laredo
1984	41	Derek Bryant, Tampico
1985	41	Andres Mora, Nuevo Laredo
1986	54	Jack Pierce, Leon
1987	42	Nelson Barrera, Mexico City Reds
1988	36	Leo Hernandez, Union Laguna
1989	39	Leo Hernandez, Campeche
1990	28	Alejandro Sanchez, San Luis Potosi
1991	37	Roy Johnson, Campeche
1992	47	Ty Gainey, Mexico City Reds
1993	38	Matias Carrillo, Mexico City Tigers
1994	30	Marco Romero, Nuevo Laredo
	30	Hector Villanueva, Mexico City Tigers
1995	27	Ty Gainey, Mexico City Reds
1996	30	Sam Horn, Torreon
1997	25	Ty Gainey, Mexico City Red Devils
1998	29	Bubba Smith, Monterrey
1999	28	Mike Meggers, Veracruz/Torreon
2000	45	Eduardo Jimenez, Saltillo

Year	HR	Player, Club
2001	33	Boi Rodriguez, Monclova
	33	Mark Whiten, Veracruz
2002	32	Robert Saucedo, Dos Laredos
2003	28	Guillermo Garcia, Mexico City Tigers
2004	27	Israel Alcantara, Laguna
2005	35	Robert Saucedo, Mexico City
2006	33	Eduardo Rios, Aguascalientes
2007	31	Donny Leon, Puebla
2008	34	Kit Pellow, Saltillo

* Season ended on July 3 due to a players strike. Six clubs did not join the strike and played a new 40-game schedule.

Mexican Center League
1960–1978

Year	HR	Player, Club
1960	23	Saul Villegas, Salamanca
1961	29	Jorge Calvo, Guanajuato
1962	59	Ramiro Caballero, Guanajuato
1963	24	Heriberto Vargas, Guanajuato
1964	35	Ramiro Caballero, Leon
1965	34	Ramiro Caballero, Leon
1966	55	Heriberto Vargas, Guanajuato
1967	26	Felix Alanis, Guanajuato
1968	40	Jose Romellon, Ciudad Madero
1969	20	Juan Martinez, Zacatecas
1970	29	Trinidad Cardona, Ciudad Madero
1971	14	Rafael Ornelas, Ebano
	14	Manuel Parra, San Luis Potosi
1972	15	Manuel Parra, Zacatecas
1973	13	Cruz Espinoza, Ebano
1974	12	Juan Martinez, Ciudad Victoria
	12	Roberto Ornelas, San Pedro
	12	Jose Valenzuela, Durango
1975	12	Jose Luis Quiroz, Leon
1976	15	Roberto Heras, Lagos de Moreno
1977	12	Juan Contreras, Zacatecas
1978	15	Jose Romo, Guanajuato

Mexican National League
1946

Year	HR	Player, Club
1946	—	Manolo Fortes, Juarez

The Sporting News listed Fortes as the leader but did not give his home run total.

Mexican Northern League
1968–1969, 1971

Year	HR	Player, Club
1968	12	Pedro Lozano, San Luis Rio Colorado
1969	23	Romulo Muñoz, Ensenada
1971	19	Rodolfo Hernandez, Mexicali

Mexican Pacific League
1976

Year	HR	Player, Club
1976	6	Oscar Noris, Mazatlan

Mexican Rookie League
1968

Year	HR	Player, Club
1968	18	Marcelino Montoya, Agua Prieta

Mexican Southeast League
1964–1970

Year	HR	Player, Club
1964	15	Celso Oviedo, Puerto Mexico
1965	16	Hector Sanudo, Campeche
1966	17	Celso Oviedo, Puerto Mexico
1967	21	Celso Oviedo, Puerto Mexico
1968	22	Pancho Herrera, Carmen
1969	39	Pancho Herrera, Carmen
1970	14	Luis Peralta, Campeche

Michigan–Ontario League
1919–1926

Commonly called MINT League

Year	HR	Player, Club
1919	13	Andy Lotshaw, Flint/Brantford
1920	12	Frank Wetzel, Flint
1921	15	Frank Emmer, Flint
1922	28	Ernie Calbert, Hamilton
1923	18	Art Jahn, Flint
1924	23	Frank Luce, Flint
1925	18	Guy Froman, Hamilton
1926	5	Karl Weber, Bay City

Michigan State League
1889–1891, 1893–1895, 1897, 1902, 1910–1914, 1926, 1940–1941

Called West Michigan League in 1910

Year	HR	Player, Club
1889	14	Joe Katz, Greenville
1895	25	Jack Daly, Lansing
1910	5	Martin Kubiak, Cadillac
1911	10	Bunny Brief, Traverse City
1912	13	Bunny Brief, Traverse City
1913	14	Grover Prough, Manistee
1914	7	Carl Tennant, Ludington
1926	11	Harry Green, Kalamazoo
1940	20	Joe Wojey, Grand Rapids
1941	35	John Lipon, Muskogen

Middle Atlantic League
1925–42; 1946–51

Year	HR	Player, Club
1925	18	Mike Martineck, Johnstown
1926	28	Jack Smith, Uniontown
1927	16	Edward Conley, Cumberland
1928	20	Bob Holland, Fairmont
1929	21	Fred Lucas, Charleroi
	21	Moose Solters, Fairmont
1930	31	Hal Stricklin, Charleroi
1931	38	Frank Welch, Beckley
1932	29	Fred Sington, Beckley
1933	26	Michael Noonan, Springfield
1934	17	John McCarthy, Dayton
	17	Michael Noonan, Springfield
1935	24	Milt McIntyre, Zanesville
1936	35	Walter Alston, Huntington
1937	34	Frank Scalzi, Springfield
1938	35	Frank Silvanic, Akron
1939	22	Edward Murphy, Portsmouth
1940	28	Walter Alston, Portsmouth
1941	25	Walter Alston, Springfield
1942	12	Walter Alston, Springfield
1946	14	Maurice Cunningham, Butler/Youngstown
1947	26	Maurice Cunningham, Youngstown
1948	26	Earl Littenberger, Vandergrift
1949	36	Joe Beran, Johnstown
1950	21	Harvey Roop, Vandergrift
1951	34	Rudy York, Youngstown–Oil City/New Castle

Middle Texas League
1914–1915

Year	HR	Player, Club
1914	16	Ellis Boggess, Temple
1915	11	Tom Osborne, Temple

Midwest League I
1923–1925

Not a member of the National Association

Year	HR	Player, Club
1923	8	Ed Corey, Racine
1924	15	Bobby Roth, Beloit

Midwest League II
1949–present

Called Mississippi–Ohio Valley League, 1949–1955

Year	HR	Player, Club
1949	17	Arthur Oliver, Paducah
1950	21	Ken Dickens, Vincennes
1951	16	Lewis Bekeza, Centralia
	16	Clint McCord, Paris
1952	20	Jim Zapp, Paris
1953	16	Ken Payne, Paris
1954	26	J. C. Dunn, Hannibal
1955	24	Walt Dixon, Kokomo
1956	30	Carroll Gholson, Paris
1957	22	Don Gordon, Dubuque
1958	29	Gus Sancimino, Kokomo
1959	30	Dale Reichert, Kokomo
1960	26	Art Blunt, Dubuque
1961	30	Bob Lawrence, Waterloo
1962	22	John T. Price, Decatur
1963	28	Lincoln Curtis, Cedar Rapids
1964	24	Rene Lachemann, Burlington
1965	29	Randall Schwartz, Burlington
1966	28	Graig Nettles, Wisconsin Rapids
1967	17	Jim Williams, Quincy
1968	27	Roe Skidmore, Decatur
1969	18	Chris Barkulis, Quincy
	18	Bob Wissler, Wisconsin Rapids
1970	23	Roger Cain, Burlington
1971	31	Gorman Thomas, Danville
1972	26	Lamar Johnson, Appleton
1973	21	Randy Bass, Wisconsin Rapids
1974	32	Moe Hill, Wisconsin Rapids
1975	31	Moe Hill, Wisconsin Rapids
1976	30	Moe Hill, Wisconsin Rapids
1977	41	Moe Hill, Wisconsin Rapids
1978	34	Bill Foley, Burlington
1979	30	Tom Anderson, Waterloo
1980	22	Gary Gaetti, Wisconsin Rapids
1981	35	Glenn Walker, Wausau
1982	42	Jeff Jones, Cedar Rapids
1983	27	Dave Heath, Peoria
1984	30	Joey Meyer, Beliot
1985	29	Bernardo Brito, Waterloo
1986	35	Luis Medina, Waterloo
1987	33	Greg Vaughn, Beliot
1988	22	Steve Davis, Cedar Rapids
	22	Brian Hunter, Burlington
1989	17	Tom Redington, Burlington
1990	22	Fred Cooley, Madison
1991	20	Paul Russo, Kenosha
1992	19	Steve Gibralter, Cedar Rapids
1993	26	Joe Brasucci, Springfield
1994	34	Matt Raleigh, Burlington
1995	34	Jesus Ibarra, Burlington
1996	27	Larry Barnes, Cedar Rapids
1997	33	Joe Frietas, Peoria
1998	27	Buck Jacobsen, Beloit
1999	38	Aaron McNeal, Michigan
2000	27	Austin Kearns, Dayton
2001	28	Samone Peters, Dayton
2002	27	Jason Stokes, Kane County
2003	30	Jason Drobiak, Battle Creek
2004	39	Brian Dopirak, Lansing
2005	24	Ryan Harvey, Peoria
2006	24	Jordan Renz, Cedar Rapids
2007	25	Juan Francisco, Dayton
2008	22	Mike Moustakas, Burlington

MINK League
1910–1913

Formal name was Missouri–Iowa–Nebraska–Kansas League

Year	HR	Player, Club
1912	7	Harvard Marshall, Nebraska City

Minnesota–Wisconsin League
1909–1912

Year	HR	Player, Club
1909	6	Arthur McCrone, Duluth
1910	12	Walter Altermott, Duluth

Mississippi–Ohio Valley League
1949–1955

See Midwest League.

Mississippi State League
1921

See Cotton States League.

Mississippi Valley League
1922–1933

Year	HR	Player, Club
1922	13	Fred Leach, Waterloo
1923	8	Andrew McEwan, Waterloo
1924	20	Stan Keyes, Rock Island
1925	17	Chet Guppy, Moline
1926	20	Les Smith, Ottumwa
1927	20	Len Koenecke, Moline
1928	22	Len Koenecke, Moline
1929	23	Ken Storme, Cedar Rapids/Waterloo
1930	15	Joe Prerost, Waterloo
1931	13	Malcolm Pickett, Moline
1932	9	Larry Wilbanks, Moline
1933	28	Ed Hall, Davenport

Montana State League
1898–1900

Year	HR	Player, Club
1900	19	Bert Schils, Anaconda

Mountain State League
1937–1942

Year	HR	Player, Club
1937	20	Larry Steinbeck, Beckley
1938	26	Murray Franklin, Beckley
1939	26	Edison Guinter, Logan
1940	26	Stan Wentzel, Logan
1941	24	Tennis Mounts, Logan
1942	34	Don Manno, Welch

Mountain States League
1911–1912, 1948–1954

Kentucky, Ohio, and West Virginia

Year	HR	Player, Club
1911	17	Grover Erb, Ashland–Catlettsburg

Kentucky, Tennessee, and West Virginia

Year	HR	Player, Club
1948	12	Eduardo DeHogues, Morristown
	12	Jacob Stirn, Morristown
1949	18	Jack Hall, Jenkins
1950	27	Joe Christian, Harlan
1951	34	Bill Halstead, Pennington Gap
1952	40	Len Cross, Big Stone Gap
1953	37	Walt Dixon, Norton
1954	18	Muscle Shoals, Kingsport

National Colored League
1887

Year	HR	Player, Club
1887	1	— Clark, Louisville
	1	John Evans, New York
	1	Bob Jackson, New York

Naughatuck Valley League
1896

See Connecticut State League.

Nebraska State League
1910–1915, 1922–1923, 1928–1941, 1956–1959

Called Western League, 1939–1941

Year	HR	Player, Club
1910	10	William H. Thompson, Fremont
1911	21	George Harms, York
1914	19	Clint Neff, Beatrice
1922	21	Claude Mitchell, Norfolk
1923	13	Jim Hudgens, Fairbury
1928	19	Walt Cookson, North Platte
1929	15	Joe Smith, Norfolk
1930	15	Mike Kreevich, Norfolk
1931	22	Sebastian Wagner, Norfolk
1932	16	Bill Swinger, Beatrice
1933	19	Howard Moore, Beatrice
1934	14	Bill Swinger, Beatrice
1935	22	Bill Swinger, Beatrice
1936	29	Bill James, Norfolk
1937	22	James Guyman, Mitchell
1938	19	Pete Monahan, Sioux City
1939	17	Bill Morgan, Norfolk
1940	17	Russ Burns, Norfolk
1941	10	Babe Alford, Norfolk
	10	Mel Bergman, Cheyenne
1956	24	Deron Johnson, Kearney
1957	17	Milton Campo, Kearney
1958	12	Keith Williams, North Platte
1959	12	Woody Huyke, Hastings

New California League
1881

See Pacific League.

New England Association
1895

Year	HR	Player, Club
1895	18	Dan Roche, Nashua

New England League
1885–1915, 1919, 1926–1930, 1933–1934, 1946–1949
Called Eastern New England League in 1885
Called Northeastern League in 1934

Year	HR	Player, Club
1885	6	Ernest Ellis, Newburyport
	6	Elmer Foster, Haverhill

Year	HR	Player, Club
1886	11	Ted Scheffler, Portland
	11	Gurdon Whitley, Newburyport/Lynn
	11	George Wilson, Newburyport/Lynn
1887	15	Ed Kennedy, Lowell
1888	14	Mark Polhemus, Lowell
1891	7	John Newell, Portland
1892	10	Abe Lizotte, Lewiston
	10	James Rogers, Portland
1893	25	Abe Lizotte, Lewiston
1894	34	Buck Freeman, Haverhill
1895	16	Harry Davis, Pawtucket
1896	25	Ed Breckinridge, Brockton
	25	George Yeager, Pawtucket
1897	17	Tom News, Pawtucket
1898	9	Tom News, Pawtucket
1899	14	Ed Breckinridge, Brockton
	12	George Noblitt, Portland
1901	14	Nick Wise, Lewiston/Haverhill
1902	12	Jim Murray, Manchester
1903	7	Lou Knau, Manchester
1904	6	Isaac VanZant, Nashua
1905	6	Clarence Lovell, Lynn
1906	4	Fred Klobedanz, New Bedford
	4	Clarence Lovell, Lynn
	4	Simeon Murch, Manchester
1907	4	Harry Billet, Lawrence/Haverhill
	4	Simeon Murch, Brockton
1908	5	Simeon Murch, Lawrence
	5	Gary Wilson, Lawrence
1909	8	Bob Messenger, Fall River
1910	7	Bill McCormick, New Bedford
1911	13	Tony Walsh, Fall River
1912	13	Art DeGroff, Lowell
1913	10	Alban Carlstrom, Lawrence
	10	Art DeGroff, Lowell
1914	9	Bob Conley, Lawrence
	9	William Smith, Lynn/Haverhill
1915	11	Roland Barrows, Lowell
1919	5	Henry Bosse, Lowell/Lewiston
1926	19	Shanty Hogan, Lynn
1927	8	Tony Cuccinello, Lawrence
1928	12	Henry Bosse, Brockton
1929	19	Bernie McHugh, Portland/Lynn
1930	5	John Lehman, Salem
1933	24	Amit Savard, Lowell
1934	17	Amit Savard, Lowell
1946	22	Lucien Belanger, Lawrence
1947	25	Ralph Atkins, Lynn
1948	30	Jim Pokel, Portland
1949	21	Bob Montag, Pawtucket

New Pacific League
1896

Year	HR	Player, Club
1896	13	Count Campau, Seattle

New York–New Jersey League
1913

Year	HR	Player, Club
1913	7	Fred Eley, Middletown
	7	Edward Harrison, Newburgh

New York–Pennsylvania League
1923–1937

See Eastern League II

New York–Pennsylvania League I
1957–1966

Year	HR	Player, Club
1957	22	Tony Gonzalez, Hornell
1958	32	Ray Withrow, Wellsville
1959	22	Bob Bauer, Auburn
1960	22	Larry Daniels, Elmira
1961	36	Robert Sanchez, Batavia
1962	37	Bob Guindon, Olean
1963	32	Byron Browne, Batavia
1964	37	Bill Schlesinger, Wellsville
1965	29	Lewis Dorsch, Wellsville
1966	28	Cito Gaston, Batavia

New York–Pennsylvania League II
1967–present

Year	HR	Player, Club
1967	12	Charles Lelas, Oneonta
1968	14	Tommy Lolos, Auburn
1969	21	Larry Mansfield, Williamsport
1970	14	Pedro Garcia, Newark
1971	18	Mike Poepping, Auburn
1972	14	Cannon Smith, Jamestown
1973	12	Randy Trapp, Batavia
1974	12	Steve Bowling, Newark
1975	9	Greg Anderson, Newark
	9	Sam Jones, Batavia
1976	19	Gary Holle, Newark
1977	21	Tim Glass, Batavia

Year	HR	Player, Club
1978	18	Tom Anderson, Batavia
	18	Ted May, Geneva
1979	10	Tom Grant, Geneva
	10	Randall LaVigne, Geneva
	10	Tommy Martinez, Batavia
	10	Ed Petryschuk, Utica
	10	Jack Upton, Geneva
	10	Matt Winters, Oneonta
1980	15	Tony Stevens, Elmira
1981	19	Bob Gilles, Little Falls
1982	23	John Hennell, Utica
1983	22	Don Jacoby, Utica
1984	19	Bernardo Brito, Batavia
1985	16	Dennis Carter, Erie
1986	15	Julian Yan, St. Catharines
1987	16	Craig Faulkner, Batavia
1988	13	Terry Brown, Erie
	13	Brian Cummings, Batavia
1989	13	Jeff Kent, St. Catharines
1990	16	Sean Ryan, Batavia
1991	12	Felix Colon, Elmira
	12	Osborne Timmons, Geneva
1992	14	Todd Pridy, Erie
1993	17	Wes Shook, Erie
1994	13	Freddy Garcia, St. Catharines
1995	12	Jose Guillen, Erie
1996	15	Will Skett, St. Catharines
1997	14	Andy Dominique, Batavia
	14	Alex Steele, Jamestown
1998	12	Chris Rojas, Watertown
	11	Jared Sandberg, Hudson Valley
1999	22	Dan Grummitt, Hudson Valley
2000	11	Mitch Jones, Staten Island
2001	13	Frank Core, Brooklyn
	13	Walter Young, Williamsport
2002	15	Joey Gomes, Hudson Valley
2003	12	Vito Chiaravolloti, Auburn
	12	
2004	15	Mario Garza, Tri-City
2005	14	Preston Patton, Auburn
2006	8	Mark Hamilton, State College
	8	Kyle Larsen, Staten Island
	8	Ryan Royster, Hudson Valley
	8	Christopher Vinyard, Aberdeen
2007	12	Jason Jacobs, Brooklyn
2008	17	Miguel Fermin, Jamestown

New York State League
1885, 1889–1890, 1894–1895, 1897–1917

Year	HR	Player, Club
1890	6	Andy Costello, Johnstown/Gloversville
1895	7	Cy Lauer, Amsterdam
1898	5	Jim Barrett, Oswego
	5	Tommy Leach, Auburn
1899	9	Edward Hill, Binghamton
1900	9	Lew Whistler, Schenectady
1901	8	Hugh Ahern, Troy
	8	John Rafter, Troy
1902	10	Johnny Evers, Troy
1903	8	Archie Marshall, Troy
1904	6	William Hinchman, Ilion
1905	7	Arthur DeGroff, Troy
	7	Osman Peartree, Troy
1906	7	Arthur DeGroff, Troy
1907	11	Harry Mason, Troy
1908	6	Herbert Grubb, Wilkes-Barre
	6	Charles Miller, Wilkes-Barre
1909	11	Arthur DeGroff, Wilkes-Barre
1910	6	John Carney, Utica
1911	11	Mike O'Neill, Utica
1912	12	Harry McChesney, Elmira
1913	13	Otto Wagner, Troy
1914	13	Otis Johnson, Elmira
1915	16	Joe Ward, Elmira
1916	12	Joe Ward, Elmira
1917	7	Joe Briger, Reading/Scranton
	7	Big Boy Kraft, Wilkes-Barre

North Atlantic League
1946–1950

Year	HR	Player, Club
1946	12	Alex Garbowski, Nyack
1947	34	Carl Sawatski, Bloomingdale
1948	20	Dan Carnevale, Carbondale
1949	18	Alphonse Baselici, Lebanon
	18	Charles McLean, Lebanon
1950	13	Chester Krajeski, Stroudsburg

North Carolina State League
1913–1917, 1937–1942, 1945–1952

Year	HR	Player, Club
1913	18	Bill Schumaker, Winston-Salem
1914	20	Jim Hickman, Winston-Salem
1915	14	Jim Hickman, Asheville
1916	15	Ben Paschal, Charlotte
1917	6	Ray Grimes, Durham
1937	21	Floyd Beal, Shelby
1938	27	Gene Nafie, Gastonia
1939	17	James Hamblen, Salisbury
1940	25	Norm Small, Mooresville
1941	26	Harold Harrigan, Salisbury
1942	32	Norm Small, Mooresville
1945	10	Stephen Lesigonich, Salisbury
1946	18	Norm Small, Mooresville
1947	31	Norm Small, Mooresville
	31	James Thomas, Hickory
1948	33	Harold Harrigan, Salisbury
	33	Norm Small, Mooresville
1949	41	Norm Small, Mooresville
1950	32	Ken Rhyne, Statesville
	32	Norm Small, Mooresville
1951	40	Pud Miller, Hickory
1952	27	Glenn Eury, Salisbury

North Dakota League
1923

Year	HR	Player, Club
1923	6	Henry Oliver, Minot
	6	Albert Wenz, Jamestown

North Texas League
1905, 1907

Year	HR	Player, Club
1905	9	Parker Arbogast, Clarksville
1907	4	Joseph Heigelfort, Terrell

Northeast Arkansas League
1909–1911, 1936–1941

Year	HR	Player, Club
1911	4	Robert Miller, Jonesboro
1936	16	Herbert Naegele, Paragould
1937	22	Jack Grantham, Paragould
1938	16	Pete McHaney, Paragould
	16	George Oldenburg, Paragould
1939	23	Joe Rayne, Paragould
1940	20	Doc O'Neill, Jonesboro
1941	15	John Joyce, Batesville

Northeastern League
1934

See New England League.

Northern Association
1910

Year	HR	Player, Club
1910	7	John Hopkins, Elgin

Northern League
1903–1905, 1908, 1913–17, 1933–42, 1946–71
Operated as a short season league from 1965–1971.

Year	HR	Player, Club
1913	13	Elmer Smith, Duluth
1914	16	Julius DeRose, Fort William
1915	16	Keith Dancy, Fort William
1916	10	Lawrence Miller, Winnipeg
1917	7	Adam Debus, Fargo–Moorhead
1933	18	Gene Corbett, Winnipeg
1934	36	Gus Koch, Fargo–Moorhead
1935	30	Gus Koch, Fargo–Moorhead
1936	48	Cal Lahman, Jamestown
1937	31	Phil Masi, Wausau
1938	31	Mel Wasley, Duluth
1939	31	Joe Schmidt, Duluth
1940	22	Austin Knickerbocker, Wausau
1941	31	Chester Cichosz, Wausau
1942	31	Edmund Mutryn, Wausau
1946	14	Tony Jaros, St. Cloud
1947	19	Harold Schadt, St. Cloud

Year	HR	Player, Club
1948	16	Harry Hannebrink, Eau Claire
	16	William Schumm, Grand Forks
1949	16	George DiPillo, Fargo–Moorhead
1950	22	Howard Boles, Sioux Falls
1951	23	Jake Crawford, Aberdeen
1952	32	Frank Gravino, Fargo–Moorhead
1953	52	Frank Gravino, Fargo–Moorhead
1954	56	Frank Gravino, Fargo–Moorhead
1955	29	Leon Wagner, St. Cloud
1956	26	Orlando Cepeda, St. Cloud
1957	22	Harry Huber, Fargo–Moorhead
1958	24	Julio Gotay, Winnipeg
1959	35	Harold Jones, Minot
	35	Dave Nicholson, Aberdeen
1960	23	Johnny Lewis, Winnipeg
1961	24	Patrick Owens, Grand Forks
1962	18	Mack Kuyendall, St. Cloud
1963	27	Jim Rouse, Aberdeen
1964	28	Andy Kosco, Duluth–Superior/ Bismarck–Mandan
1965	8	Bob Brooks, St. Cloud
	8	Nat King, St. Cloud
1966	13	Roger Freed, Aberdeen
1967	13	Steve Brye, St. Cloud
	13	Roger Freed, Aberdeen
1968	13	Greg Luzinski, Huron
1969	10	Kent Burkick, Sioux Falls
	10	Tom Dittmar, Sioux Falls
1970	17	Jim Stafford, Aberdeen
1971	15	Dennis Silvey, Aberdeeen

Northwest League I
1937–1942, 1946–1965
Called Western International League, 1937–1954.

Year	HR	Player, Club
1937	28	Wes Schulmerich, Lewiston
1938	15	Jim Tyack, Bellingham
1939	37	Morry Abbott, Tacoma
1940	28	Tom Lloyd, Vancouver
1941	34	Pete Hughes, Spokane
1942	17	Morry Abbott, Vancouver
1946	40	Bill Barisoff, Bremerton
1947	36	Jack Harshman, Victoria
1948	33	Bill Wilson, Wenatchee
1949	43	Jim Warner, Wenatchee
1950	36	Dick Greco, Tacoma
1951	24	Will Hafey, Wenatchee
1952	17	Cecil Garriott, Victoria
1953	31	Charlie Mead, Calgary
1954	21	Don Hunter, Calgary/Lewiston
	21	Bob Wellman, Vancouver
1955	27	Bob Duretto, Wenatchee
1956	36	Vince Moreci, Yakima
1957	23	Ellis Burton, Tri-City
1958	26	Larry Helms, Wenatchee
1959	30	Joe Wilson, Salem
1960	29	Bob Nelson, Tri-City

GOING FOR THE FENCES

Year	HR	Player, Club
1961	28	Ray Youngdahl, Tri-City
1962	24	Billy Cowan, Wenatchee
1963	24	Dan Kern, Yakima
1964	37	John Warner, Tri-City
1965	31	Herman Rathman, Tri-City

Northwest League II
1966–present

Year	HR	Player, Club
1966	16	Roy Gleason, Tri-City
1967	16	Nick VanLue, Eugene
1968	12	Joe Ferguson, Tri-City
1969	12	Bruce Hotchkiss, Walla Walla
1970	14	Lloyd Hutchinson, Walla Walla
	14	Dale Sanner, Coos Bay–North Bend
	14	Blas Santana, Walla Walla
1971	14	Robert Davis, Tri-City
	14	Terry Thompson, Bend
1972	17	Jim Buckner, Lewiston
1973	10	Stephen Smith, Tri-City
	10	Gerard Stone, Walla Walla
	10	Gary Walls, Walla Walla
1974	15	Richard Meily, Eugene
1975	15	Don Reynolds, Walla Walla
1976	12	Mike Rodriguez, Boise
1977	16	Juan Delgado, Grays Harbor
	16	Dave Henderson, Bellingham
1978	17	Albert Richmond, Walla Walla
1979	10	Jim Durrman, Medford
	10	Julio Franco, Central Oregon
1980	25	Willie Darkis, Central Oregon
1981	15	Graham Conklin, Bellingham
1982	15	Phil Storm, Medford
1983	15	Oriol Perez, Bellingham
1984	10	Brad Pounders, Spokane
1985	17	Danny Lamar, Tri-Cities
1986	15	John Jaha, Tri-Cities
1987	16	Mark Owens, Everett
1988	17	Bob Hamelin, Eugene
1989	17	Dave Stanton, Spokane
1990	12	Matt Mieske, Spokane
1991	15	Leon Glenn, Bend
1992	15	Larry Sutton, Eugene
1993	15	Todd Greene, Boise
1994	12	Don Denbow, Everett
	12	Derrick Gibson, Bend
1995	14	Ryan Kane, Boise
1996	21	Steve Hacker, Eugene
1997	15	Mike Marchiano, Everett
1998	20	Jason Hart, Southern Oregon
1999	17	Kirk Asche, Southern Oregon
	17	Lamont Matthews, Yakima
2000	14	Chad Santos, Spokane
2001	16	Greg Sain, Eugene
2002	17	Jon Nelson, Everett
2003	15	Brad Vericker, Salem–Keizer
2004	17	Colt Morton, Eugene

Year	HR	Player, Club
2005	12	Freddie Thon, Spokane
	12	Luis Valbuena, Everett
2006	16	Russell Canzler, Boise
	16	Adam Witter, Salem–Keizer
2007	17	Ian Gac, Spokane
2008	11	Collin Cowgill, Yakima

Northwestern League
1879, 1882–1887, 1891, 1905–1917

Illinois, Iowa, Minnesota, and Nebraska

Year	HR	Player, Club
1879	2	William Furlong, Omaha
	2	Jake Goodman, Rockford
	2	Larry Hayes, Davenport
	2	Rudy Kemmler, Davenport
	2	Hugh Nicol, Rockford
	2	Bill Redmond, Rockford
1883	2	Sam Barkley, Toledo
1884	4	Cornelius Doyle, Quincy
	4	Charles Eden, Grand Rapids
1887	17	Elmer Foster, Minneapolis
1891	16	Ed Breckinridge, Grand Rapids

British Columbia, Oregon, Montana, and Washington

Year	HR	Player, Club
1905	7	Joe Marshall, Vancouver
1906	7	Mike Lynch, Tacoma
1907	10	John Clynes, Tacoma/Vancouver
1908	15	Ham Hyatt, Vancouver
1909	15	Ralph Capron, Seattle
1910	11	Charles Swain, Vancouver
1911	27	Art Bues, Seattle
1912	23	Les Mann, Seattle
1913	34	Charles Swain, Victoria
1914	12	Charles Swain, Seattle
1915	10	Bill Brinker, Vancouver
1916	17	Dave Hillyard, Butte
1917	12	Dave Hillyard, Butte

Ohio–Indiana League
1908, 1948–1951

Year	HR	Player, Club
1908	5	Patsy Bauman, Richmond
1948	23	Bob Nieman, Muncie
1949	25	Forrest Rende, Portsmouth
1950	37	Andy Gilbert, Springfield
1951	20	Maxlee Ross, Marion

Ohio–Michigan League
1893

Year	HR	Player, Club
1893	12	Ed McFarland, Akron

Ohio–Pennsylvania League
1905–1912

Year	HR	Player, Club
1908	21	Ray Miller, McKeesport
1910	16	Duke Servatius, McKeesport
1911	23	Hugh Tate, Youngstown
1912	7	Charles Donnelly, East Liverpool

Ohio State League
1887–1889, 1892, 1895, 1897–1898, 1908–1916, 1936–1941, 1944–1947

Year	HR	Player, Club
1887	12	Ed Stapleton, Kalamazoo
1908	12	Frank Foutz, Lima
1909	6	Ed Williams, Marion
1910	6	Frank Nesser, Lima
1911	12	James Kelly, Marion
1912	11	Waldo Jackley, Marion/Ironton
1913	33	Cecil Gray, Charleston
1914	17	Ernie Calbert, Huntington/Charleston
1915	13	Ernie Calbert, Ironton
1916	6	Rube Lindholm, Frankfort
1936	38	John Clements, Tiffin
1937	13	John Barrett, Mansfield
	13	Steve Patias, Mansfield
1938	18	James Geygan, Fremont
1939	18	Hank Edwards, Mansfield
	18	Hubert Wooten, Lima
1940	39	John Cindric, Lima
1941	22	Edmund Mutryn, Mansfield
1944	20	Eddie Volan, Newark
1945	12	Albert Kaiser, Newark
1946	21	Peter Shurman, Middletown
1947	14	Bob Montag, Muncie

Ontario League
1930

Year	HR	Player, Club
1930	8	Paddy Doherty, St. Catharines

Pacific League
1878–1881

Usually called Pacific Coast League in 1878.
Called New California League in 1881.

Year	HR	Player, Club
1880	1	—Allen, San Francisco Renos
	1	Cal McVey, San Francisco Bay Cities
	1	Ed Nolan, San Francisco Bay Cities
	1	Ed Rowen, San Francisco Bay Cities
	1	John Sweeney, San Francisco Bay Cities
1881	1	—Lee, San Francisco Californians
	1	Pete Meegan, San Francisco Mystics
	1	Tom Murray, San Francisco Mystics
	1	Ed Rowen, Oakland

Pacific Coast League I
1898

After playing several weeks into the season, the California League and the Pacific States League merged to form the Pacific Coast League.

Year	HR	Player, Club
1898	3	Al Borland, Sacramento

Pacific Coast League II
1903–present

Not a member of the National Association in 1903.

Year	HR	Player, Club
1903	13	Truck Eagan, Sacramento
1904	21	Truck Eagan, Tacoma
1905	21	Truck Eagan, Tacoma
1906	7	Mike Mitchell, Portland
1907	13	Walter Carlisle, Los Angeles
1908	13	Otis Johnson, Portland
1909	13	Otis Johnson, Portland
1910	30	Ping Bodie, San Francisco
1911	23	Buddy Ryan, Portland
1912	19	Bert Coy, Oakland
1913	18	Bert Coy, Oakland
1914	9	Ty Lober, Portland
1915	20	Biff Schaller, San Francisco
1916	33	Bunny Brief, Salt Lake City
1917	24	Ken Williams, Portland
1918	12	Art Griggs, Sacramento
	12	Earl Sheely, Salt Lake City
1919	28	Earl Sheely, Salt Lake City
1920	33	Earl Sheely, Salt Lake City
1921	22	Paddy Siglin, Salt Lake City
1922	28	Paul Strand, Salt Lake City
1923	43	Paul Strand, Salt Lake City
1924	38	Jim Poole, Portland
1925	60	Tony Lazzeri, Salt Lake City
1926	46	Elmer Smith, Portland
1927	40	Elmer Smith, Portland
1928	45	Smead Jolley, San Francisco
1929	55	Ike Boone, Mission
1930	41	Dave Barbee, Seattle/Hollywood
1931	47	Dave Barbee, Hollywood
1932	38	Fred Muller, Seattle
1933	43	Gene Lillard, Los Angeles
1934	45	Frank Demaree, Los Angeles
1935	56	Gene Lillard, Los Angeles
1936	30	Mike Hunt, Seattle
	30	Fred Muller, Seattle
1937	39	Mike Hunt, Seattle
1938	30	Ted Norbert, San Francisco
1939	26	Rip Collins, Los Angeles
1940	41	Lou Novikoff, Los Angeles
1941	20	Ted Norbert, Portland
1942	28	Ted Norbert, Portland
1943	21	John Ostrowski, Los Angeles
1944	29	Frank Kelleher, Hollywood
1945	23	Ted Norbert, Seattle
1946	26	Loyd Christopher, Los Angeles
1947	43	Max West, San Diego

GOING FOR THE FENCES

Year	HR	Player, Club
1948	48	Jack Graham, San Diego
1949	48	Max West, San Diego
1950	40	Frank Kelleher, Hollywood
1951	43	Joe Gordon, Sacramento
1952	35	Max West, Los Angeles
1953	35	Dale Long, Hollywood
1954	31	Jim Marshall, Oakland
1955	37	Steve Bilko, Los Angeles
1956	55	Steve Bilko, Los Angeles
1957	56	Steve Bilko, Los Angeles
1958	37	Jim McDaniel, Salt Lake City
1959	29	Willie McCovey, Phoenix
1960	37	R. C. Stevens, Salt Lake City
1961	36	Gene Oliver, Portland
1962	33	Stan Palys, Hawaii
1963	33	Deron Johnson, San Diego
1964	36	Costen Shockley, Arkansas
1965	38	Dave Roberts, Oklahoma City
1966	26	Tommy Murray, Oklahoma City
1967	34	Willie Kirkland, Hawaii
1968	24	Clarence Jones, Tacoma
1969	23	Russ Nagelson, Portland
1970	36	Joe Lis, Eugene
1971	43	Adrian Garrett, Tacoma
1972	27	Tom Paciorek, Albuquerque
1973	31	Gene Martin, Eugene/Hawaii
1974	55	Bill McNulty, Sacramento
1975	29	Bob Hansen, Sacramento
1976	28	Bob Gorinski, Tacoma
1977	42	Danny Walton, Albuquerque
1978	29	Willie Aikens, Salt Lake City
1979	30	Ike Hampton, Salt Lake City
1980	26	Tim Hosley, Ogden
1981	34	Mike Marshall, Albuquerque
1982	50	Ron Kittle, Edmonton
1983	32	Sid Bream, Albuquerque
	32	Kevin McReynolds, Las Vegas
1984	31	Rob Deer, Phoenix
1985	43	Danny Tartabull, Calgary
1986	31	Rick Lancellotti, Phoenix
1987	23	Dave Hengel, Calgary
1988	28	Luis Medina, Colorado Springs
1989	27	Denny Gonzalez, Colorado Springs
1990	25	Bernardo Brito, Portland
1991	27	Bernardo Brito, Portland
	27	Luis Medina, Colorado Springs
1992	29	Tim Salmon, Edmonton
1993	27	Charles Phillips, Phoenix
1994	37	Billy Ashley, Albuquerque
1995	25	Harvey Pulliam, Colorado Springs
1996	28	Todd Walker, Salt Lake City
1997	37	Paul Konerko, Albuquerque
1998	46	Chris Hatcher, Omaha
1999	41	Charles Phillips, Colorado Springs
2000	36	Phil Hiatt, Colorado Springs
2001	44	Phil Hiatt, Las Vegas
2002	35	Ivan Cruz, Memphis
2003	34	Graham Koonce, Sacramento
2004	36	Kevin Witt, Memphis
2005	31	Luke Scott, Round Rock
2006	32	Jon Knott, Portland
2007	34	Valentino Pascucci, Albuquerque
2008	42	Dallas McPherson, Albuquerque

Pacific Coast International League
1918–1922

Called Internatnioal northwestern League in 1919
Called Western International League in 1922

Year	HR	Player, Club
1918	4	Bill Fisher, Portland
1919	9	Carl Hinkle, Victoria
1920	19	Lee Dempsey, Victoria
1921	15	Ed Handley, Victoria
1922	6	Bob Snyder, Tacoma

Pacific National League
1901–1905

Called Pacific Northwest League, 1901–1902

Year	HR	Player, Club
1901	15	Joe Marshall, Spokane
1902	6	Joe Marshall, Butte
1903	25	Joe Marshall, Butte
1904	13	Ralph Frary, Spokane
1905	5	Hugh Kellacky, Boise

Pacific Northwest League
1890–1892

Year	HR	Player, Club
1890	12	Tom Turner, Spokane
1891	13	Tom Turner, Spokane
1892	7	Ed Cartwright, Tacoma

Pacific Northwest League
1901–1902

See Pacific National League.

Pacific States League
1898

After playing for several weeks in 1898, the league merged with the California League to form the Pacific Coast League.

Year	HR	Player, Club
1898	1	Nine players tied*

*Truck Eagan of Oakland was the only player of the nine who was relatively well known.

Palmetto League
1931

Year	HR	Player, Club
1931	11	Charlie English, Florence

Panhandle Pecos Valley League
1923

See West Texas League.

Pennsylvania State Association
1886–1887, 1934–1942

Year	HR	Player, Club
1886	8	John McKee, Lancaster/Wilkes–Barre
1887	7	Ed Sales, Wilkes-Barre
1934	15	Tommy Henrich, Monessen
1935	14	Harry Craft, Monessen
1936	24	William Fuchs, Monessen
1937	24	Edward Urban, Beaver Falls
1938	22	Harold Bush, Greensburg
1939	16	Dick Sisler, Washington
1940	22	Steve Greble, Butler
1941	38	Howard Muderski, Johnstown
1942	25	Don Bollweg, Washington

Pennsylvania State League
1890–1896, 1901–1902

Not a member of the National Association in 1902

Year	HR	Player, Club
1892	4	William Rhodes, Danville
1893	10	George Carey, Altoona
	10	Asa Stewart, Easton
1894	21	Henry Cote, Altoona/Lancaster
1895	13	Oscar Hill, Pottsville/Allentown/ Hazleton
1896	7	Bob Cargo, Carbondale/Pottstown
1902	2	Bill Blakley, Scranton
	2	Charles Jordan, Reading
	2	Pat Rollins, Lebanon

Pennsylvania–West Virginia League
1908–1909

Year	HR	Player, Club
1908	11	Robert Conoway, Clarksburg
1909	11	Joe Phillips, Uniontown

Piedmont League
1920–1955

Year	HR	Player, Club
1920	16	Doc Smith, Greensboro
1921	26	Jim Holt, High Point
1922	11	Edward Regan, Danville
	11	Floyd Trexler, Danville
1923	24	Carr Smith, Raleigh
1924	27	Dave Harris, Greensboro
	27	Arnold Townsend, High Point
1925	25	Otis Cashion, Salisbury
1926	29	Dave Barbee, Greensboro
1927	24	Charlie Wade, Winston-Salem
1928	38	Danny Boone, High Point
1929	46	Danny Boone, High Point
1930	39	Tom Wolfe, Durham
1931	21	Frank Packard, Charlotte
1932	19	Parker Perry, High Point/Wilmington
1933	25	Jim Bucher, Greensboro
1934	30	Jim Bryan, Norfolk
1935	26	Buddy Rosar, Norfolk
1936	38	Jim Bryan, Norfolk
1937	33	Bobby Estalella, Charlotte
1938	38	Bobby Estalella, Charlotte
1939	40	Russ Derry, Norfolk
1940	30	Jim Maynard, Richmond
1941	13	Luis Olmo, Richmond
1942	10	Jim Matthews, Winston-Salem
	10	Luis Olmo, Richmond
1943	8	Jack Phillips, Norfolk
1944	9	Duke Snider, Newport News
1945	12	Elwood Grantham, Portsmouth
	12	Wayne Maxie, Lynchburg
1946	17	Chuck Connors, Newport News
1947	20	Len Morrison, Richmond
	20	Vern Shetler, Portsmouth
1948	20	Steve Bilko, Lynchburg
1949	29	Charley Maxwell, Roanoke
1950	23	Bob Mosakoski, Roanoke
1951	30	Ken Guettler, Portsmouth
1952	28	Ken Guettler, Portsmouth
1953	30	Ken Guettler, Portsmouth
1954	27	Willie Tasby, York
1955	41	Ken Guettler, Portsmouth

Pioneer League I
1939–1942, 1946–1963

Year	HR	Player, Club
1939	58	Tony Robello, Pocatello
1940	22	Joe Egnatic, Boise
	22	Walt Lowe, Boise
	22	Tony Robello, Salt Lake City
1941	15	Joe Egnatic, Boise
1942	20	Tony Robello, Twin Falls
1946	29	Bud Heslet, Twin Falls
1947	22	Walt Lowe, Boise
1948	25	Albert Neil, Pocatello
1949	21	Bill Renna, Twin Falls
1950	32	Ray Posipanka, Twin Falls
1951	24	Ron Harrison, Ogden
1952	31	Dick Stuart, Billings
1953	28	John Moskus, Salt Lake City
1954	27	Bernie Mateosky, Idaho Falls
1955	32	Dick Stuart, Billings
1956	28	Mike Coppola, Pocatello
1957	30	Dick Greco, Missoula
1958	35	Chuck Weatherspoon, Missoula
1959	24	Jim Campbell, Idaho Falls
	24	Bruno Terilli, Boise
1960	37	Ray Reed, Boise
1961	40	Bobby Sanders, Magic Valley

Year	HR	Player, Club
1962	37	Hank Allen, Magic Valley
	37	Felix DeLeon, Billings
1963	35	Alex Johnson, Magic Valley

Pioneer League II
1964–present

Year	HR	Player, Club
1964	12	Johnny Smith, Pocatello
1965	15	Gary Cortopassi, Treasure Valley
1966	11	Paul Campbell, Idaho Falls
	11	Fred Rodriguez, Treasure Valley
1967	7	John Lung, Caldwell
1968	20	Steve Garvey, Ogden
1969	10	Pedro Garcia, Billings
1970	12	Marc Mengo, Magic Valley
1971	14	John Balaz, Idaho Falls
1972	11	Randolph Wilson, Idaho Falls
1973	10	Phillip Robinson, Billings
1974	8	Dan Daniel, Ogden
	8	Steve Henderson, Billings
1975	13	Andre Dawson, Lethbridge
1976	13	John Scoras, Lethbridge
1977	21	Michael Zouras, Lethbridge
1978	20	Edward Packard, Idaho Falls
1979	20	Willie Darkis, Helena
1980	9	Gerald Miller, Butte
1981	10	Tom Fettig, Calgary
	10	Glen Stackert, Calgary
1982	20	Cecil Fielder, Butte
1983	20	Tom Krupa, Calgary
1984	17	Darryl Landrum, Medicine Hat
1985	11	Peter Callas, Idaho Falls
1986	16	Greg Vaughn, Helena
	16	Jeff Weiss, Idaho Falls
1987	12	Mike Malinak, Salt Lake City
1988	17	Armando Verdugo, Salt Lake City
1989	13	Ramces Guerrero, Idaho Falls
1990	13	Mike Busch, Great Falls
1991	11	Rick Hirtensteiner, Salt Lake City
1992	16	Tim Unroe, Helena
1993	16	Willie Brown, Lethbridge
1994	14	Nick Morrow, Billings
	14	Chris Priest, Lethbridge
1995	13	Sean Watkins, Idaho Falls
1996	17	David Hayman, Lethbridge
	17	Darron Ingram, Billings
	17	Miguel Rodriguez, Ogden
1997	23	Greg Morrison, Medicine Hat
1998	19	Jay Gibbons, Medicine Hat
1999	19	Troy Schada, Idaho Falls
2000	20	John Woodward, Idaho Falls
2001	16	Jesus Cota, Missoula
	16	Jesse Gutierrez, Billings
2002	19	Ryan Shealy, Casper
2003	12	Casey Fuller, Casper
	12	Walter Olmstead, Billings
2004	19	Robert Mosby, Billings
2005	15	Christopher Cook, Casper

Year	HR	Player, Club
2006	15	Christopher Carter, Great Falls
2007	20	Brandon Waring, Billings
2008	15	Luis Jimenez, Orem

Pony League
1939–1956

Formal name was Pennsylvania–Ontario–NewYork League.

Year	HR	Player, Club
1939	17	Arthur Strott, Niagara Falls
1940	25	Lawrence Mancini, Olean
1941	29	John Newman, Jamestown
1942	27	John Newman, Jametown
1943	11	Carl Petroziello, Hornell
1944	14	George Shuba, Olean
1945	13	Lee Riley, Bradford
	13	Carl Sawatski, Bradford
1946	21	Joe Abreu, Wellsville
	21	Dick Kokos, Batavia
1947	28	Jim Pokel, Bradford
1948	18	Joe Fromuth, Wellsville
1949	24	Carmen Links, Batavia
1950	23	Don Zimmer, Hornell
1951	27	Ray Reed, Wellsville
1952	20	Tom McDonald, Olean
1953	37	Ted Sepkowski, Wellsville
1954	45	Ted Sepkowski, Wellsville
1955	19	Dale Bennetch, Bradford
1956	32	George Lewis, Corning

Potomac League
1916

Year	HR	Player, Club
1916	6	Paul Cobb, Lonaconing/Cumberland

Provincial League
1935–1940, 1944–1955, 1958–1970

Not a Member of the National Association, 1935–1939, 1944–1949, 1958–1970.
Called Quebec Provincial League in 1940.

Year	HR	Player, Club
1938	14	Joe Cicero, St. Hyacinthe
1939	11	Howie Moss, Granby
1940	17	James Walsh, Granby
1945	3	Yvon Bazinet, St. Hyacinthe
1947	11	Roger Bedard, Granby
1948	31	Joe Atkins, Farnham
	31	Bus Clarkson, St. Jean
1949	23	Quincy Barbee, St. Jean
1950	21	Silvio Garcia, Sherbrooke
1951	42	Frank Gravino, St. Jean
1952	30	Al Pinkston, St. Hyacinthe
1953	26	Robert Diers, Sherbrooke
1954	27	Bill Williamson, Sherbrooke
1955	24	Bill Causion, St. Jean
1960	7	Jacques Monette, Three Rivers
	7	Claude Saint Vincent, Waterloo
1961	16	Jacques Monette, Sherbrooke

Provincial League, continued

Year	HR	Player, Club
1962	17	Jacques Monette, Sherbrooke
1963	14	— Carter, Acton Vale
1964	7	Jacques Monette, Sherbrooke
	7	Ernest Sawyer, Drummondville
1965	12	John Sell, Granby
1966	12	Chuck Klymchuck, Longueil
	12	—— McKinley, Acton Vale
1967	15	John McKee, Thetford Mines
1968	14	Renald Grenald, Granby
1969	19	Renald Grenald, Granby
1970	13	Larry Haggett, Three Rivers

Quebec–Ontario–Vermont League
1924

Year	HR	Player, Club
1924	15	Buck Fraser, Rutland/Quebec

Quebec Provincial League
1940
See Provincial League.

Rio Grande Valley Association
1915

Year	HR	Player, Club
1915	10	Frank Huelsman, Albuquerque

Rio Grande Valley League
1931, 1949–1950

Year	HR	Player, Club
1931	8	Harry Bonds, McAllen
1949	28	Don Petschow, Brownsville
1950	53	Jesse McClain, Harlingen

San Joaquin Valley League
1910–1911
Not a member of the National Association in 1911

Year	HR	Player, Club
1910	2	Slim Bath, Tulare
	2	Roy Kuhn, Coalinga
	2	Walter Kuhn, Tulare
1911	2	George Porterfield, Coalinga

Sarasota Rookie League
1964
See Gulf Coast Rookie League.

Sooner State League
1947–1957

Year	HR	Player, Club
1947	11	Paul Richardville, Ada
	11	Howard Weeks, Lawton
1948	19	Howard Martin, McAlester
1949	23	Bill Milligan, Seminole/Ada
	23	Daryl Spencer, Pauls Valley
1950	39	Steve Molinari, Ada
1951	30	Dan Demby, Pauls Valley
	30	Donnie Williamson, Pauls Valley
1952	22	Bob Hertel, McAlseter
	22	Donnie Williamson, Pauls Valley
1953	31	Bob Norden, Ada
	31	Ron Slawski, Ada
1954	34	Gene Green, Ardmore
1955	21	James Brown, Ardmore
1956	39	Gene Oliver, Ardmore
1957	25	Bob Beattie, Paris

Sophomore League
1958–1961

Year	HR	Player, Club
1958	27	Ken Clark, Hobbs
1959	34	Gilbert Carter, Carlsbad
1960	23	Lewis Bishop, Carlsbad
1961	35	Jose Cardenal, El Paso

South Atlantic Association
1926–1930
See Southern League

South Atlantic League
1904–1917, 1919–1925, 1936–1942, 1946–1963
See Southern League

South Atlantic League
1980–present
Commonly known as Sally League

Year	HR	Player, Club
1980	26	Dave Kable, Gastonia
1981	29	Tom Dodd, Greensboro
1982	23	Randy Braun, Asheville
1983	27	Tracy Dophied, Asheville
1984	20	Wilmer Caraballo, Columbia
	20	John DiGioia, Savannah
1985	28	Peter Mueller, Asheville
1986	26	Cameron Drew, Asheville
1987	39	Mike Simms, Asheville
1988	29	Eric Anthony, Asheville
1989	22	Doug Cronk, Gastonia
1990	18	Cliff Brannon, Savannah
1991	26	Butch Huskey, Columbia
1992	25	Shane Andrews, Albany
1993	24	Derek Hacopian, Columbus
1994	28	Nate Holdren, Asheville
	28	Ruben Rivera, Greensboro
1995	32	Derrick Gibson, Asheville
	32	Ron Wright, Macon
1996	40	Russell Branyan, Columbus
1997	33	Steve Hacker, Macon
1998	37	Marcus Giles, Macon
1999	28	Travis Hafner, Savannah
2000	23	James House, Hickory
2001	30	Jason Kinchen, Greensboro

Year	HR	Player, Club
2002	25	Walter Young, Hickory
2003	29	Jeff Salazar, Asheville
2004	32	Joe Benick, Hickory
2005	36	Joseph Koshansky, Asheville
2006	22	Eric Campbell, Rome
2007	30	Ryan Royster, Columbus
2008	39	Michael Stanton, Greensboro

South Dakota League
1920–1923
Called Dakota League, 1921–1922

Year	HR	Player, Club
1920	18	Pete Turgeon, Aberdeen
1921	9	Albert Wenz, Madison
1922	17	Lyman Nason, Wahpeton–Breckenridge
1923	10	Wesley Clemons, Aberdeen

South Michigan League
1906–1909
See Southern Michigan Association

South Texas League
1903–1906

Year	HR	Player, Club
1904	18	Dick Latham, Galveston
1906	5	Pat Newnam, Houston

Southeastern League
1897, 1910–1912, 1926–1930, 1932, 1937–1942, 1946–1950

Year	HR	Player, Club
1897	11	John Flournoy, Knoxville
1910	3	Sephia Silvers, Knoxville
1911	18	Tommy Long, Gadsden
1912	12	John Cochran, Bessemer/Anniston
1926	28	Clay Parrish, Columbus
1927	34	Clay Parrish, Columbus
1928	17	Sam Stuart, Columbus
1929	12	Parker Perry, Selma
1930	15	Rip Radcliff, Selma
1932	6	Fred Sington, Columbus
1937	20	Fred Stroble, Meridian
1938	26	Prince Oana, Jackson
1939	39	Prince Oana, Jackson
1940	22	Norm DeWeese, Pensacola
1941	25	Fred Stroble, Meridian
1942	18	Al Simononis, Mobile
1946	33	Roy Pinkston, Gadsden
1947	27	Bill Johnson, Gadsden
1948	24	Ken Guettler, Montgomery/Gadsden
1949	19	Harold Summers, Meridian
1950	35	Neb Wilson, Pensacola

Southern Association
1885–1889, 1892–1896, 1898–1899, 1901–1961
Formal name was the Southern League through 1899 and was still often called that in the early 1900s

Year	HR	Player, Club
1885	6	Walt Andrews, Columbus
	6	John Cahill, Atlanta
	6	Walton Goldsby, Atlanta
	6	Charlie Levis, Chattanooga/Macon
	6	Denny Lyons, Columbus
1886	8	Blondie Purcell, Atlanta
1887	28	Walt Andrews, Memphis
1888	5	Perry Werden, New Orleans
1889	5	Mark Polhemus, New Orleans
1892	6	Pat Meaney, Memphis
1893	19	Bones Ely, Atlanta
1894	11	Count Campau, New Orleans
1895	26	Hercules Burnett, Evansville
1896	10	Newton Fisher, Mobile
1898	4	Jim Jones, Charleston
1899	4	Ed Pabst, New Orleans
	4	Frank Weikart, Mobile
1901	11	Jim Ballantyne, Nashville
1902	11	Frank Weikart, Shreveport
1903	18	Lew Whistler, Montgomery
1904	7	Frank Weikart, Shreveport/New Orleans
1905	7	Frank Weikart, Shreveport
1906	5	Charles Babb, Memphis
1907	6	Dode Paskert, Atlanta
1908	6	Jake Daubert, Nashville
	6	Harry Lord, New Orleans
1909	5	Frank Huelsman, New Orleans
1910	5	Jake Weimer, New Orleans
1911	11	Roy Moran, Atlanta/Chattanooga
1912	7	Del Young, Nashville
1913	11	Dave Robertson, Mobile
1914	15	Bill Jacobson, Chattanooga
1915	11	Fred Thomas, New Orleans
1916	9	Joe Harris, Chattanooga
1917	14	Fred Bratschi, Memphis
1918	7	Fred Bratschi, Memphis
1919	8	Tex McDonald, Nashville
1920	19	Bing Miller, Little Rock
1921	22	Dutch Bernsen, Birmingham
1922	12	Joe Connolly, Little Rock
	12	Emil Huhn, Mobile
	12	John Schulte, Mobile
1923	19	Danny Clark, Birmingham/Atlanta
1924	26	John Anderson, Chattanooga
1925	30	Nick Cullop, Atlanta
1926	20	Yam Yaryan, Birmingham
1927	19	Elliott Bigelow, Birmingham
1928	24	Dick Wade, Nashville
1929	33	Jim Poole, Atlanta/Nashville
1930	50	Jim Poole, Nashville
1931	23	Moose Clabaugh, Nashville
1932	35	Stan Keyes, Nashville
1933	23	Dutch Prather, Nashville
1934	17	Prince Oana, Atlanta

Southern Association, continued

Year	HR	Player, Club
1935	17	Doug Taitt, Nashville
1936	20	Doug Taitt, Nashville
	20	Earl Webb, Knoxville
1937	19	Willie Duke, Nashville
1938	24	Tom Hafey, Knoxville
1939	23	Bill Nicholson, Chattanooga
1940	22	Gus Dugas, Nashville
	22	Dutch Meyer, Knoxville
1941	38	Les Burge, Atlanta
1942	29	Chuck Workman, Nasville
1943	19	Cecil Dunn, Knoxville
1944	16	Mel Hicks, Nashville
1945	16	Gil Coan, Chattanooga
1946	15	Ted Pawelek, Nashville
1947	24	Al Flair, New Orleans
1948	52	Chuck Workman, Nashville
1949	45	Carl Sawatski, Nashville
1950	36	Bill Wilson, Memphis
1951	47	Jack Harshman, Nashville
1952	35	Frank Thomas, New Orleans
1953	34	Ralph Atkins, Little Rock
	34	Bill Wilson, Memphis
1954	64	Bob Lennon, Nashville
1955	29	Bob Hazle, Nashville
1956	39	Johnny Powers, New Orleans
1957	29	Harmon Killebrew, Chattanooga
1958	34	Kent Hadley, Little Rock
1959	30	Gordy Coleman, Mobile
1960	32	Jim McManus, Shreveport
1961	30	Bill Gabler, Macon

Southern League
1885–1889, 1892–1896, 1898–1899
See Southern Association.

Southern League
1904–1917, 1919–1930, 1936–1942, 1946–present
Called South Atlantic League, 1904–1925, 1936–1942, and 1946–1963
Called South Atlantic Association, 1926–1930
Commonly called Sally League through 1963

Year	HR	Player, Club
1904	5	Chris Miller/Columbia/Augusta/Savannah
1905	5	James Fox, Macon
1906	6	Wilbur Murdock, Macon
1907	8	Fred Wohleben, Macon
1908	6	Fred Wohleben, Macon
1910	5	William Hille, Columbus
1912	8	Walton Cruise, Macon
1913	6	John Dowell, Savannah
	6	Robert Prysock, Macon
1915	11	Harry Chancey, Macon
1916	14	Felix Clare, Montgomery/Charleston
1919	11	Red Wingo, Greenville
1920	14	Norm McMillan, Greenville
1921	19	Gus Felix, Charleston
1922	18	Ben Paschal, Charlotte
1923	26	Ben Paschal, Charlotte
1924	28	Clarence McCrone, Asheville
1925	29	Pete Daniels, Greenville
1926	35	Roy Moore, Greenville
1927	39	William Barrett, Knoxville
1928	33	Tilly Walker, Greenville
1929	29	Frank Welch, Greenville
1930	39	Jim Hudgens, Greenville
1936	18	Dee Moore, Macon
1937	21	Nick Etten, Savannah
1938	17	Dan Pavlovic, Augusta/Macon/Spartanburg/Savannah
1939	19	Dan Pavlovic, Savannah
1940	21	Beverly Ferrell, Greenville
1941	17	Clyde Vollmer, Columbia
	17	James Walsh, Jacksonville
1942	13	Vic Bradford, Jacksonville
1946	16	Robert Erps, Columbus
1947	19	William Hockenbury, Savannah
	19	Lloyd Lowe, Columbus
1948	28	Harold Summers, Augusta
1949	19	Ray Cash, Macon
1950	20	Jim Dickey, Columbus
1951	33	Dick Greco, Montgomery
1952	24	Dick Greco, Montgomery
1953	24	Tom Giordano, Savannah
1954	28	Jim Dickey, Macon
	28	Clarence Riddle, Jacksonville
1955	28	Wiley Williams, Savannah/Jacksonville
1956	27	Ed Barbarito, Jacksonville
1957	25	Jacques Monette, Knoxville/Jacksonville
1958	22	Carl Warwick, Macon
1959	32	Cliff Cook, Savannah
1960	28	Donn Clendenon, Savannah
1961	25	Gary Rushing, Asheville
1962	36	Dick Means, Charlotte/Asheville
1963	21	Jim Hicks, Macon/Lynchburg
	21	Fred Loesekam, Lynchburg
1964	29	Dick Kenworthy, Lynchburg
1965	22	Orlando McFarlane, Asheville
1966	32	Bob Robertson, Asheville
1967	19	Rogelio Alvarez, Knoxville/Evansville
	19	Graig Nettles, Charlotte
1968	26	Wayne Redmond, Montgomery
1969	23	Bob Brooks, Birmingham
1970	21	Jim Covington, Jacksonville
1971	37	Ken Hottman, Asheville
1972	30	Mike Reinbach, Asheville
1973	35	Terry Clapp, Asheville
1974	23	Bob Gorinski, Orlando
	23	Mike Poepping, Orlando
1975	27	Jim Obradovich, Orlando
1976	21	Jim Obradovich, Orlando
1977	17	Tom Chism, Charlotte
	17	Alfredo Javier, Columbus
	17	Jerry Keller, Savannah
1978	25	Eddie Gates, Memphis

GOING FOR THE FENCES

Year	HR	Player, Club
1979	33	Alan Knicely, Columbus
1980	34	Steve Balboni, Nashville
1981	42	Tim Laudner, Orlando
1982	37	Mike Fuentes, Memphis
1983	25	Glenn Davis, Columbus
	25	Larry Sheets, Charlotte
1984	33	Dan Pasqua, Nashville
1985	34	Mark Funderburk, Orlando
1986	31	Glenallen Hill, Knoxville
1987	39	Rondal Rollin, Birmingham
1988	25	Matt Winters, Memphis
1989	28	Eric Anthony, Columbus
1990	24	Luis Gonzalez, Columbus
	24	Terrell Hansen, Jacksonville
1991	24	Elvin Paulino, Charlotte
1992	28	Tim Costo, Chattanooga
1993	25	Carlos Delgado, Knoxville
1994	23	Mark Johnson, Carolina
1995	31	Ivan Cruz, Jacksonville
1996	34	Derrick Lee, Memphis
1997	30	Mike Coolbaugh, Huntsville
	30	Luis Raven, Birmingham
	30	Kevin Witt, Knoxville
1998	28	Gabe Kapler, Jacksonville
1999	26	Javier Cardona, Jacksonville
2000	25	Alejandro Friere, Jacksonville
2001	31	Josh Phelps, Tennessee
2002	20	Dave Kelton, West Tennessee
	20	Pete LaForest, Orlando
2003	31	Bucky Jacobsen, Tennessee
2004	28	Greg Sain, Mobile
2005	26	Brandon Sing, West Tennessee
	26	Christopher Young, Birmingham
2006	26	Jerry Gil, Tennessee
2007	24	Brendan Katin, Huntsville
2008	27	Michael Wilson, West Tennessee

Southern California League
1899, 1910, 1913

Called Southern California Trolley League in 1910

Year	HR	Player, Club
1899	4	Elmer Gibbs, San Diego
	4	Tom Works, San Diego
	4	Babe Whaling, San Bernardino/Los Angeles
1910	1	Six players tied

Southern California Trolley League
1910

See Southern California League

Southern Michigan Association
1906–1915

Called South Michigan League, 1906–1909.

Year	HR	Player, Club
1907	6	John Cocash, Flint
	6	Fred Merkle, Tecumseh

Year	HR	Player, Club
1908	11	Jim Bowser, Flint
1910	14	Jim Bowser, Flint
1911	19	Big Boy Kraft, Flint
1912	25	Bull Durham, Bay City/Lansing
1913	10	Cecil Coombs, Adrian
1914	12	Edward Hoffman, Flint
1915	7	Edward Hoffman, Flint

Southern New England League
1885

Year	HR	Player, Club
1885	4	Ed Mulligan, Springfield
	4	Ed Toohey, Bridgeport

Southwest International League
1951–1952

See Sunset League

Southwest Texas League
1910–1911

Year	HR	Player, Club
1911	9	Harry Sweet, Bay City

Southwest Washington League
1903–1905

Year	HR	Player, Club
1903	2	Ira Harmon, Centralia

Southwestern League
1904, 1921–1926, 1956–1957

Kansas and Oklahoma

Year	HR	Player, Club
1921	22	Glenn Wright, Independence
1922	23	George Wetzel, Muskogee
1923	49	Moses Solomon, Hutchinson
1924	28	Fuzzy Hufft, Arkansas City
1925	28	Ed Yuna, Arkansas City
1926	28	Dick Wykoff, Salina

New Mexico and Texas

Year	HR	Player, Club
1956	60	Frosty Kennedy, Plainview
1957	34	Ray Patterson, Carlsbad

Sunset League
1947–1952

Called Southwest International League, 1951–1952

Year	HR	Player, Club
1947	52	Cal Felix, Las Vegas
1948	42	Dick Wilson, Mexicali
1949	24	Pete Hughes, Las Vegas
1950	26	Ron Johnson, Las Vegas
1951	23	Herman Lewis, Phoenix
1952	28	Refugio Bernal, Mexicali
	28	Pete Hughes, Tijuana

Tar Heel League
1939–40, 1953–1954

Year	HR	Player, Club
1939	27	Hooper Triplett, Gastonia
1940	16	Frank Shone, Lenior
	16	Woody Traylor, Hickory
1953	21	Carl Miller, Marion
1954	5	Joe Crestello, Rutherford County
	5	Harold Kollar, Shelby

Tennessee–Alabama League
1903–1904

Not a member of the National Association.

Year	HR	Player, Club
1903	5	Sox Sorber, Decatur
1904	5	W. C. Kyle, Knoxville

Texas Association
1923–1926

Year	HR	Player, Club
1923	22	Don Flynn, Waco/Austin
1924	27	Stephen Barrett, Corsicana
1925	28	Stan Keyes, Terrell
1926	29	Norman Peterson, Austin

Texas League
1888–1890, 1892, 1895–99, 1902–42, 1946–present

Sometimes called the Texas–Southern League, 1895–1896.
Sometimes called the North Texas League, 1903–1906.

Year	HR	Player, Club
1888	5	Lew Whistler, San Antonio / Houston
1889	18	Bill Joyce, Houston
1890	5	Jake Stenzel, Galveston
	5	Bill Works, Galveston
1892	6	Ollie Smith, Houston
1895	15	Charles Meyers, Sherman / Galveston
1896	18	Mike O'Connor, Denison / San Antonio
1898	9	Tom Turner, Galveston
1899	16	Fred Houtz, Galveston
1902	12	Mike O'Connor, Corsicana
1903	13	Clyde Bateman, Paris–Waco
	13	Roland Wolfe, Paris–Waco
1904	10	Otis Johnson, Dallas
1905	5	Ben Shelton, Temple
	5	Sam Stovall, Austin/Waco
1908	18	Pat Newnam, San Antonio
1907	17	Frank Weikart, Galveston
1909	18	Dick Hoffman, Waco/Galveston
1910	11	Hank Gowdy, Dallas
	11	George Stinson, San Antonio
	11	Harry Storch, Dallas
1911	22	Frank Metz, San Antonio
1912	21	Frank Metz, San Antonio
1913	12	Fred Wohleben, Waco
1914	10	Eddie Edmonson, Beaumont
1915	8	Berton James, Waco
	8	Otto McIver, Fort Worth
	8	Harry Storch, Dallas
	8	Fred Wohleben, Waco
1916	9	Al Nixon, Beaumont
1917	18	Roy Leslie, Waco
1918	9	John Mokan, Waco
1919	16	Jewel Ens, Dallas
	16	Roy Leslie, Waco/Houston
1920	12	Dave Callahan, Galveston
1921	35	Henry Eibel, Shreveport
1922	32	Big Boy Kraft, Fort Worth
1923	32	Big Boy Kraft, Fort Worth
1924	55	Big Boy Kraft, Fort Worth
1925	41	Ed Konetchy, Fort Worth
1926	30	Charles Miller, Dallas
1927	32	Del Pratt, Waco
1928	27	Tom Jenkins, Wichita Falls
1929	33	George Blackerby, Waco
1930	43	Larry Bettencourt, Wichita Falls
1931	19	Joe Medwick, Houston
1932	39	Hank Greenberg, Beaumont
1933	24	Zeke Bonura, Dallas
1934	29	Paul Easterling, Tulsa
1935	32	Rudy York, Beaumont
1936	27	Jim Stroner, Dallas
1937	33	Cecil Dunn, Beaumont
1938	25	Stan Schino, Tulsa
1939	25	Nick Cullop, Houston
1940	23	Carl Jorgenson, Oklahoma City/San Antonio
1941	24	Jake Jones, Shreveport
1942	27	Merv Connors, Dallas/Fort Worth
1946	24	Bob Moyer, Dallas
1947	28	Nick Gregory, Shreveport
1948	26	Russ Burns, Tulsa
1949	50	Jerry Witte, Dallas
1950	39	Jim Lemon, Oklahoma City
1951	38	Jerry Witte, Houston
1952	31	Bud Heslet, San Antonio
1953	41	Bud Heslet, Shreveport
1954	42	Bus Clarkson, Beaumont/Dallas
1955	33	Prentice Brown, Shreveport
1956	62	Ken Guettler, Shreveport
1957	30	Keith Little, Oklahoma City/Houston
1958	39	Mike Lutz, Corpus Christi
1959	35	Carl Warwick, Victoria
1960	32	Duke Ducote, San Antonio
1961	27	Craig Sorenson, San Antonio
1962	36	Jerry Robinson, El Paso
1963	41	Arlo Engel, El Paso
1964	40	Chuck Harrison, San Antonio
1965	26	Leo Posada, Amarillo
1966	25	Winston Llenas, El Paso
	25	Larry Stubing, Arkansas
1967	28	Nate Colbert, Amarillo
1968	28	Jim Spencer, El Paso
1969	24	Adrian Garrett, San Antonio
1970	29	Adrian Garrett, San Antonio
1971	20	Larry Fritz, Memphis
1972	26	Gorman Thomas, San Antonio
1973	30	Hector Cruz, Arkansas
1974	29	Jerry Tabb, Midland
	29	Wayne Tyrone, Midland

Year	HR	Player, Club
1975	23	Gary Alexander, Lafayette
	23	Jack Clark, Lafayette
	23	Mitchell Page, Shreveport
1976	30	Willie Aikens, El Paso
1977	28	Karl Pagel, Midland
1978	31	Bobby Clark, El Paso
1979	28	Mark Brouhard, El Paso
1980	33	Mike Bishop, El Paso
1981	32	Greg Brock, San Antonio
1982	34	Darryl Strawberry, Jackson
1983	35	Rob Deer, Shreveport
1984	31	Ralph Bryant, San Antonio
1985	37	Joey Meyer, El Paso
1986	30	Kevin King, Midland
1987	30	Stan Holmes, Midland
	30	Doug Jennings, Midland
	30	Joe Redfield, Midland
1988	28	Greg Vaughn, El Paso
1989	25	Dean Palmer, Tulsa
1990	28	Henry Rodriguez, San Antonio
1991	30	John Jaha, El Paso
1992	24	Billy Ashley, San Antonio
1993	29	Trey McCoy, Tulsa
1994	28	Scott Talanoa, El Paso
1995	30	George Arias, Midland
1996	32	Bubba Smith, Tulsa
1997	26	Dan Collier, Tulsa
1998	37	Tyrone Horne, Arkansas
1999	39	Adam Piatt, Midland
2000	35	Alex Cabrera, El Paso
2001	40	Brandon Berger, Wichita
2002	24	Graham Koonce, Midland
2003	27	Daniel Johnson, Midland
2004	29	Ryan Shealy, Tulsa
2005	31	Michael Napoli, Arkansas
2006	34	Nate Gold, Frisco
2007	29	Colby Rasmus, Springfield
2008	26	Kila Ka'aihue, Northwest Arkansas
	26	Corey Smith, Arkansas

Texas–Oklahoma League
1911–1914, 1921–1922

Year	HR	Player, Club
1911	16	Cliff Weatherspoon, Wichita Falls
1912	9	Fred Morris, Wichita Falls
1914	7	C. H. O'Neill, Texarkana
1921	11	G. C. Rainey, Graham–Mineral Wells/Sherman
1922	21	Ed Seeley, Greenville

Texas–Southern League
1888

Year	HR	Player, Club
1888	2	Joe Masran, Galveston

Texas–Southern League
1895–1896

See Texas League.

Texas Valley League
1927–1928, 1938

Year	HR	Player, Club
1927	17	Jack Holloway, Mission
1938	20	Manuel Cortinas, Corpus Christi
	20	Kirby Jordan, McAllen
	20	Bill McClaren, Harlingen
	20	Leo Najo, McAllen

Three I League
1901–1917, 1919–1932, 1935, 1937–1942, 1946–1961
Formal name was Indiana–Illinois–Iowa League

Year	HR	Player, Club
1901	27	Frank Roth, Evansville
1902	16	Charles Buelow, Rockford
1908	9	Charles Buelow, Rockford
1909	10	Elmer Johnson, Springfield
1910	6	Paul Meloan, Springfield
	6	Biff Schaller, Springfield
1913	12	Frank Lofton, Springfield
1914	10	Howard Wakefield, Springfield
1915	7	Otto Jacobs, Rockford
1916	10	Fred Beck, Peoria
	10	Rhino Williams, Rockford
1917	8	Norman Glockson, Rockford
1919	8	Fred Foelsch, Rockford
1920	11	Norman Glockson, Rock Island
	11	Earl Sykes, Bloomington
1921	17	Howard Jones, Moline
1922	20	Frank McCue, Moline
1923	18	Ernie Calbert, Decatur
	18	Harry Rice, Danville
1924	18	Paddy Reagan, Evansville
1925	20	Joe Bratcher, Peoria
	20	Frank McGee, Peoria
1926	30	Al Maderas, Springfield
1927	23	Ted Menze, Springfield
	23	Bill Mizeur, Peoria
1928	19	Rip Collins, Danville
	19	Marucis Duffy, Peoria
1929	21	Marucis Duffy, Peoria
1930	30	Moose Clabaugh, Quincy
1931	16	Ollie Bejma, Quincy
1932	15	Hal Trosky, Quincy
1935	24	Chet Laabs, Fort Wayne
1937	13	Bert Haas, Clinton
1938	25	Frank Piet, Springfield
1939	21	Fred Stroble, Springfield
1940	29	Chuck Workman, Cedar Rapids
1941	23	Hank Edwards, Cedar Rapids
1942	33	Pat Seerey, Cedar Rapids
1946	14	Jim Christie, Terre Haute
	14	Bill Sanders, Terre Haute
1947	22	Edwin Ehlers, Quincy
Year	HR	Player, Club
1948	22	Don Lenhardt, Springfield
	22	John Novosel, Springfield
1949	15	Lloyd Lowe, Decatur
	15	Emil Tellinger, Quincy

Year	HR	Player, Club
1950	25	Allen Thomas, Waterloo
1951	26	Bill Renna, Quincy
1952	27	Robert Erps, Waterloo
1953	30	Marv Throneberry, Quincy
1954	35	Ed Barbarito, Quincy
1955	38	John Romano, Waterloo
1956	27	Clyde McNeal, Cedar Rapids
1957	31	Jim Koranda, Cedar Rapids
1958	37	Frank Howard, Green Bay
1959	27	Cal Emery, Des Moines
1960	23	Billy Joe Dashner, Topeka
	23	Manly Johnston, Lincoln
1961	23	Barry Morgan, Cedar Rapids

Tobacco State League
1946–1950

Year	HR	Player, Club
1946	30	Orville Nesselrode, Sanford
1947	32	Orville Nesselrode, Sanford
1948	27	Orville Nesselrode, Sanford
1949	15	John Helms, Fayetteville
	15	Joe Stern, Clinton/Lumberton
1950	14	Michael Milosevich, Lumberton

Tri-State League
1888–1891, 1894, 1904–1914, 1924–1926, 1946–1955
Not a member of the National Association, 1904–1906

Michigan, Ohio, Pennsylvania, and West Virginia

Year	HR	Player, Club
1888	13	George Rooks, Lima
1890	14	Frank Motz, Akron

Delaware, New Jersey, and Pennsylvania

Year	HR	Player, Club
1906	14	Bob Unglaub, Williamsport
1907	7	Kip Selbach, Harrisburg
1908	9	Charles Johnson, Johnstown
1909	10	Mert Whitney, Harrisburg
1910	10	Scotty Ingerton, Altoona
1911	12	George Cockill, Reading
1912	15	Mert Whitney, Trenton
1913	7	Harry Fritz, Wilmington
1914	7	Charles Miller, Harrisburg

Arkansas, Mississippi, and Tennessee

Year	HR	Player, Club
1925	14	Bill Akers, Jonesboro
	14	C. T. Swafford, Jonesboro
1926	9	Duncan Doty, Jonesboro

North Carolina, South Carolina, and Tennessee

Year	HR	Player, Club
1946	19	Pud Miller, Spartanburg
1947	27	Al Simononis, Anderson
1948	29	Len Cross, Spartanburg
1949	43	Harold Harrigan, Anderson
1950	33	Albert Neil, Knoxville
1951	44	Albert Neil, Spartanburg

Year	HR	Player, Club
1952	27	Juan Perez, Anderson
1953	26	Lamar Bowden, Spartanburg
1954	22	Albert Neil, Knoxville
1955	18	Paul Jones, Spartanburg

Twin Ports League
1943

Year	HR	Player, Club
1943	1	John Norlander, Duluth Dukes
	1	Dick Seltz, Duluth Dukes
	1	Joe Shouts, Duluth Heralds

Union Association
1911–1914

Year	HR	Player, Club
1911	17	Frank Huelsman, Great Falls
1912	14	Henry Spencer, Salt Lake City
1913	22	Frank Huelsman, Salt Lake City
1914	23	Frank Huelsman, Salt Lake City

United States League
1912–1913
Not a member of the National Association

Year	HR	Player, Club
1912	8	Herman McFarland, Richmond
1913	1	— Alexander, Baltimore
	1	Wallace Clements, Washington
	1	— McGrath, Lynchburg
	1	Harry Sentz, Baltimore
	1	—Wiley, Reading

Utah–Idaho League
1926–1928
Sometimes called Timber League

Year	HR	Player, Club
1926	20	Laman Cox, Ogden
1927	24	Wally Berger, Pocatello
1928	26	Ed Coleman, Boise/Twin Falls

Venezuelan Summer League
1997–Present

Year	HR	Player, Club
1997	7	Yibert Salinas, Guacara
1998	7	Julio Cordido, Brewers
1999	14	Angel Chavez, Giants
2000	15	Darwin Aristigueta, Chino
2001	10	Carlos Levi, LaPradera
2002	10	Vladimir Balentien, Aguirre
2003	7	Trino Aguilar, Mariara
2004	9	Jesus Garcia, Ciudad Alianza
	9	Jonel Pacheco, Tronconero 2
2005	12	Alfredo Bompart, Marlins/Nationals
2006	10	Francisco Murillo, Phillies
2007	12	Alexis Espineza, Tigers
2008	8	Jonathan Quinoney, Rays

Virginia League
1886, 1894–1896, 1900, 1906–1928, 1939–1942, 1948–1951

Year	HR	Player, Club
1895	19	Bob Berryhill, Lynchburg
	19	Charlie McIntyre, Lynchburg
1896	16	Joe Dolan, Lynchburg
	16	Ruben Stephenson, Norfolk/Portsmouth/Petersburg
	16	Zeke Wrigley, Roanoke
1900	11	Jim Murray, Portsmouth
1906	5	Willie Fetzer, Danville
1907	8	Jacob Henn, Danville
1908	8	Jacob Henn, Danville
1909	5	Frank Shaughnessy, Roanoke
1910	3	Joe Holland, Roanoke
	3	Clarence Munson, Norfolk
	3	Watt Powell, Roanoke
1911	9	Ralph Mattis, Richmond
1912	12	Luis Castro, Portsmouth
1913	7	Jim Barnett, Petersburg
	7	Ducky Eberts, Richmond
	7	Jim Tennant, Portsmouth
1914	8	Pryor McElveen, Portsmouth
1915	15	Cecil Gray, Rocky Mount
1916	15	Rasty Walters, Newport News
1917	2	Brook Crist, Newport News
	2	Jack Orr, Portsmouth
	2	Joe Stanley, Lynchburg
1918	3	Curt Daughton, Newport News
1919	5	Jack Ballinger, Norfolk
1920	8	Lee Gooch, Richmond
	8	Luke Stewart, Richmond
	8	Pie Traynor, Portsmouth
1921	17	Joe Kelly, Norfolk
1922	13	Elmer Yoter, Portsmouth
1923	19	Hack Wilson, Portsmouth
1924	33	Ed Konetchy, Petersburg
1925	38	Blackie Carter, Richmond
1926	44	Stan Stack, Richmond
1927	24	Stan Stack, Richmond
	24	George Thomas, Portsmouth
1928	7	Bill Hohman, Richmond
1939	10	Louis Cipalla, Harrisonburg/Lynchburg
1940	16	Crawford Howard, Lynchburg
1941	21	Noel Casbier, Salem–Roanoke
1942	31	Wes Ferrell, Lynchburg
1948	31	Morris Aderholt, Emporia

Year	HR	Player, Club
1949	25	John Garrison, Emporia
1950	32	Ken Hatcher, Petersburg
1951	34	Ken Hatcher, Colonial Heights/Petersburg

Virginia–North Carolina League
1901

Year	HR	Player, Club
1901	10	Joe Stanley, Raleigh

Washington State League
1910–1912

Year	HR	Player, Club
1910	6	Edward Kennedy, Raymond
1911	8	C. D. Wineholt, Raymond/Chehalis
1912	2	— Kinkelon, Hoquiam

West Dixie League
1934–1935

Year	HR	Player, Club
1934	40	Lou Frierson, Paris–Lufkin
1935	29	Merv Connors, Palestine

West Michigan League
1910

See Michigan State League.

West Texas League
1920–1923, 1928–1929

Called Panhandle–Pecos Valley League in 1923

Year	HR	Player, Club
1920	9	Jim Galloway, Ranger
1921	17	Ed Conkrite, San Angelo
1922	21	Sam Langford, Lubbock
1923	19	Edward Shaw, Amarillo
1928	35	Bob Sanguinett, Midland
1929	44	Ed Kallina, Midland

West Texas–New Mexico League
1937–1942, 1946–1955

Year	HR	Player, Club
1937	30	Robert Hood, Wink
1938	31	Mal Stevens, Lubbock
	31	Jake Suytar, Midland
1939	44	Gordon Nell, Pampa
1940	40	Gordon Nell, Borger
1941	28	Gordon Nell, Borger
1942	22	Frank Hargrove, Amarillo
1946	48	Joe Bauman, Amarillo
1947	57	Bill Serena, Lubbock
1948	69	Bob Crues, Amarillo
1949	52	Pud Miller, Lamesa
1950	37	Crawford Howard, Amarillo
1951	35	Les Mulcahy, Amarillo
1952	47	Merv Connors, Amarillo
1953	50	Jim Matthews, Amarillo
1954	35	Frosty Kennedy, Amarillo
1955	44	Lincoln Boyd, Clovis

Western Association I
1888–1891, 1894–1899

Year	HR	Player, Club
1888	16	John Carroll, St. Paul
1889	27	Charlie Reilly, St. Paul
1890	21	John Carroll, Minneapolis
1891	18	Dell Darling, Minneapolis
1894	33	Joe Strauss, Jacksonville

Western Association I, continued

Year	HR	Player, Club
1895	12	Buck Ebright, Lincoln
	12	Bill Krieg, Rockford
	12	Mattie McVicker, Des Moines
	12	Sam Mertes, Quincy
	12	Joe Visner, Rockford
1896	15	Bill Krieg, Rockford
1897	31	Jim Williams, St. Joseph
1898	3	Jay Andrews, Cedar Rapids/ Rock Island/St. Joseph
1899	2	Harry Bay, Rock Island
	2	Charles Lutenberg, Rockford
	3	Elmer Stricklett, Rock Island

Western Association II
1901

Year	HR	Player, Club
1901	14	Tuck Turner, Toledo

Western Association III
1905–1911, 1914–1917, 1920–1932, 1934–1942, 1946–1954

Year	HR	Player, Club
1905	9	Henry Gehring, Wichita
1906	9	Jerry Downs, Topeka
1908	16	Milt Porkorney, Webb City
1909	11	Wilder Gray, Springfield
	11	Tex Jones, Enid
1910	11	Henry Goodrich, Sapulpa
1914	21	Ed Palmer, Muskogee
1915	34	Otto Besse, McAlester
1916	22	Pete Adams, Fort Smith
	22	Ed Hopper, Tulsa/Muskogee
	22	Henry Moore, Tulsa
1917	43	Ernie Calbert, Muskogee
1920	15	Dave Williams, Okmulgee
1921	20	Frank Reiger, Enid
1922	31	Frank Reiger, Enid
1923	36	Chili McDaniel, Enid
1924	51	Stormy Davis, Okmulgee
	51	Wilbur Davis, Okmulgee
1925	34	Leon Najo, Okmulgee
1926	36	John Reider, Springfield
1927	26	John King, Joplin
1928	36	Paul Richards, Muskogee
1929	25	Bill Hooton, Springfield
1930	27	Gordon Nell, Joplin/Muskogee
1931	44	Gordon Nell, Muskogee
1932	22	Ival Goodman, Bartlesville
1934	16	Ed Gray, Muskogee
1935	19	Buster Adams, Springfield
	19	Tony Masucci, Muskogee
1936	31	Ted Jennings, Muskogee
1937	30	Al Mele, Muskogee
1938	24	Russ Derry, Joplin
1939	38	Harry Goorabian, Topeka
1940	24	Glenn Peters, Muskogee
1941	26	Stan Musial, Springfield
1942	20	Mal Stevens, Muskogee
1946	18	Peter Deem, Muskogee
1947	29	Butch Nieman, Topeka
1948	34	Butch Nieman, Topeka
1949	26	Butch Nieman, Topeka
1950	28	Butch Nieman, Topeka
1951	28	Butch Nieman, Topeka
1952	30	John Blanchard, Joplin
1953	37	Joe Beran, Hutchinson
1954	37	Al Kubski, Blackwell

Western League I
1885–1888, 1892–1893

Year	HR	Player, Club
1885	3	Jim Keenan, Indianapolis
1886	11	Perry Werden, Lincoln
1887	16	Jake Beckley, Leavenworth/Lincoln
	16	Bug Holliday, Topeka
1892	18	Ed Breckinridge, Columbus
1893	4	Andrew Costello, Lawrence

Western League II
1894–1900

Called American League in 1900 and became the major league American League in 1901.

Year	HR	Player, Club
1894	43	Perry Werden, Minneapolis
1895	45	Perry Werden, Minneapolis
1896	18	Bill Schriver, Minneapolis
	18	Perry Werden, Minneapolis
1897	19	Bill Grey, Indianapolis
1898	12	Frank Shugart, St. Paul
1899	8	Bob Stafford, Milwaukee
1900	9	Socks Seybold, Indianapolis
	9	Perry Werden, Minneapolis

Western League III
1900–1937

Year	HR	Player, Club
1900	10	Tim Hoy, Omaha
1901	13	Dave Brain, St. Paul
1902	15	Emil Frisk, Denver
1903	8	Mike Jacobs, Kansas City
1904	10	Del Howard, Omaha
1905	10	Bill Shipke, Omaha
1906	11	George Noblitt, Sioux City
1907	9	John Thomas, Lincoln
1908	7	Ira Belden, Denver
	7	Ham Patterson, Pueblo
	7	John Thomas, Lincoln
1909	13	Fred Hunter, Sioux City
1910	22	John Thomas, Lincoln
1911	12	John Thomas, Lincoln
1912	18	John Beall, Denver
1913	26	Les Channell, Denver

GOING FOR THE FENCES

Year	HR	Player, Club
1914	21	Bill Fisher, Denver
1915	16	Bill McCormick, Denver
1916	16	Ben Dyer, Denver
1917	13	Hank Butcher, Denver
1918	8	Bob Murphy, Des Moines
1919	12	Yam Yaryan, Wichita
1920	41	Yam Yaryan, Wichita
1921	35	Fred Beck, Wichita
1922	35	Yank Davis, Tulsa
1923	37	Jim McDowell, Wichita
1924	48	Mule Washburn, Tulsa
1925	33	Leo Payne, Wichita
1926	49	Guy Sturdy, Tulsa
1927	32	Joe Munson, Tulsa
1928	42	Jim Stroner, Wichita
1929	36	Jack Burns, Tulsa
1930	35	Stan Keyes, Des Moines
1931	38	Stan Keyes, Des Moines
1932	30	Dick Goldberg, Wichita
1933	22	Victor Shiell, Topeka
1934	24	Vern Johnson, Sioux City
1935	20	Hugh Willingham, Sioux City
1936	22	Dutch Prather, Rock Island
1937	22	Cal Lahman, Cedar Rapids

Western League
1939–1941
See Nebraska State League

Western League IV
1947–1958

Year	HR	Player, Club
1947	24	Tony Jaros, Sioux City
1948	29	Carl Sawatski, Des Moines
1949	29	Lou Limmer, Lincoln
1950	44	Pat Seerey, Colorado Springs
1951	32	Howard Boles, Des Moines/Denver
1952	35	Bill Pinckard, Denver
1953	34	Jim Gentile, Pueblo
1954	30	Bill White, Sioux City
1955	40	Willie Kirkland, Sioux City
1956	66	Dick Stuart, Lincoln
1957	43	Len Williams, Topeka
1958	37	Dan Lynk, Sioux City

Western Canada League
1907, 1909–1914, 1919–1921

Year	HR	Player, Club
1910	10	Ted Smith, Calgary
1911	8	Mark Freer, Winnipeg

Year	HR	Player, Club
1912	5	Jim Flanagan, Calgary
1913	13	Brad Hollis, Calgary
1914	12	Ken Williams, Edmonton
1921	9	Heinie Manush, Edmonton

Western Carolinas League
1948–1952, 1960–1979
Called Western Carolina League through 1962.

Year	HR	Player, Club
1948	43	Floyd Yount, Newton–Conover
1949	22	Carl Miller, Lincolnton
1950	27	Bob Featherstone, Lenior
1951	24	Bordie Waddle, Morganton
1952	19	Ken Paschal, Rutherford County
1960	23	Paul Roberts, Salisbury
1961	15	Dick Simpson, Statesville
1962	9	Frank Petrellis, Shelby
	9	J. C. Snead, Statesville
	9	Steve Whitaker, Shelby
1963	21	Dave McDonald, Shelby/Statesville
1964	20	Bill Parlier, Salisbury
1965	32	Bob Robertson, Gastonia
1966	35	Luis Lagunas, Thomasville
1967	18	John Jeter, Gastonia
1968	24	Zelman Jack, Gastonia
1969	33	Earl Williams, Greenwood
1970	18	Roy Gibson, Anderson
1971	25	Dave Criscione, Anderson
	25	Lloyd Hutchinson, Spartanburg
1972	19	Ken Caldwell, Greenville
1973	19	Doug Ault, Gastonia
1974	28	John Guarnaccia, Spartanburg
1975	25	Gary Begnand, Spartanburg
1976	24	Pat Putnam, Asheville
1977	26	David Rivera, Asheville
1978	18	Jim Barbe, Asheville
1979	31	Hediberto Vargas, Shelby

Western International League
1922
See Pacific Coast International League

Western International League
1937–1942, 1946–1954
See Northwest League

Western Inter-State League
1890, 1895

Year	HR	Player, Club
1890	12	George McVey, Terre Haute
1895	3	Bill Geiss, Bloomington
	3	A. M. Gifford, Terre Haute/Hammond
	3	Bill Raffert, Lafayette
	3	Ed Riley, Aurora

Western New York and Pennsylvania League
1890–1891

Year	HR	Player, Club
1890	11	Sam Gillen, Erie
1891	16	Fred Miller, Erie

Western Tri-State League
1912–1914

Year	HR	Player, Club
1913	16	Henry Martini, Walla Walla
1914	11	Earl Sheely, Walla Walla

Wisconsin Association
1905–1906

Year	HR	Player, Club
1905	2	George Perring, Beloit
	2	Frank Schneiberg, Freeport
	2	Tom Sullivan, Freeport
1906	2	Frank Baker, Eau Claire
	2	William Gleason, Oshkosh
	2	Fred Goldsmith, Eau Claire

Wisconsin–Illinois League
1908–1914

Year	HR	Player, Club
1908	12	Hank Butcher, Rockford
1912	12	Earl Smith, Green Bay
1913	26	Bull Durham, Oshkosh
1914	25	Bull Durham, Oshkosh

Wisconsin State League
1940–1942, 1946–1953

Year	HR	Player, Club
1940	20	Rudy Novak, Green Bay
1941	31	Pat Seerey, Appleton
1942	22	Cliff Aberson, Janesville
1946	20	Elwood Grantham, Janesville
1947	20	James Adlam, Fond du Lac
1948	32	Fred Collins, Fond du Lac
1949	18	Edward Fenelon, Sheboygan
1950	30	Ray Shearer, Sheboygan
1951	23	David Garcia, Oshkosh
1952	21	Paul Bentley, Oshkosh
1953	28	Joe Tuminelli, Fond du Lac

Notes

Facts about home run title holders

- Ray Perry led his league in home runs for seven consecutive seasons, a minor league record. Perry led the Far West League every year the league was in existence from 1948 through 1951. In 1952 he won in the Cotton States League then moved back west where he led the California League in 1953 and 1954. During that seven-year stretch, Perry hit a total of 232 homers, including one in the Pacific Coast League where he appeared in a few games for the San Diego Padres early in the 1952 season.

- Buck Freeman led the majors in home runs twice: the National League in 1899 and the American League in 1903. Freeman also won five minor league home run crowns: the New England League in 1894, the Eastern League in 1897 and 1898 and the American Association in 1907 and 1908.

- Nephew of golfing legend Sam Snead, J. C. Snead, led the Western Carolinas League in home runs in 1962. He then went on to join the PGA Tour and later the Seniors Tour, and was a success on both.

- Rip Collins tied with Mel Ott for the National League home run crown in 1934. He also tied for the crown in 1928 in the Three I League. Collins won outright home run titles in the International League (1929) and the Pacific Coast League (1939).

- In 1973, Romel **Canada**, an **American** hailing from Philadelphia, Pennsylvania, led the **Mexican** League in home runs…which was over twenty years before the three countries ratified **NAFTA**.

- At least five pitchers have won home run titles. Two deadball-era pitchers led the California State League: Benny Henderson took the league title in 1907 with three home runs and pitcher-outfielder Eddie Householder did it in 1910 with nine. Then in 1921, Jack Bentley led the International League. He compiled a stunning 12–1 record in 119 innings for the Baltimore club. Five years later, in 1926, Dick Wykoff of Salina in the Southwestern League hit a league-leading 26 round trippers which complimented his 25–6 record very nicely. Roy Sanner, playing for Houma in the Evangeline League, arguably had the finest combined batting-pitching year ever by a moundsman. He won the 1948 Evangeline League triple crown with 34 home runs, 126 RBI and a .386 batting average. As a pitcher, he had a gaudy 21–2 record, with 251 strikeouts and a 2.58 ERA. Those are figures of which legends are made.

- Frank Roth, who played for Evansville of the Three I League in 1901, was credited with hitting 36 home runs. The figure was not only good enough to lead the Three I League but also all the minor leagues that season. Years later, however, an exhaustive search of the two Evansville newspapers revealed that Frank Roth had only socked 27 that year. The good news is that he still had the most home runs in the minors that year.

Players Who Led Two Different Leagues in the Same Season

Charles "Count" Campau hit three home runs for Detroit of the International Association in 1890. The league folded in early July and Campau's three homers turned out to be good enough to tie him for the league lead. Shortly before the league folded, Detroit sold him to St. Louis of the American Association, then a major league. In his second game with the Browns, he hit a homer and he went on to lead the league with nine.

Lew Whistler led the Texas League in home runs in 1888 while playing for San Antonio and Houston. Late in the season, the league reorganized by adding New Orleans and played a short schedule under the name Texas–Southern League. Whistler appeared for both Houston and Galveston in the new league and tied for the league lead with two home runs.

Ed Kallina of Sherman was tied for the league lead with six home runs when the Lone Star League folded on May 16, 1929. He then joined Midland of the West Texas League and led that league with 44 homers.

Fred Sington, playing for Columbus of the Southeastern League, was leading the league in home runs when the league went out of business on May 23, 1932. Sington then hooked on with Beckley of the Middle Atlantic League and won league home run honors with 29.

Sington was an All-American tackle at the University of Alabama and is a member of the College Football Hall of Fame. Three fellow members of the College Football Hall of Fame led a league in home runs. Larry Bettencourt led the Texas League in 1930, Ken Strong led the Eastern League in 1930 and Beattie Feathers led the Appalachian League in 1943.

Hall of Fame Players Who Have Led a Minor League in Home Runs

Player	Year	HR	Team, League
Jake Beckley	1887	16	Leavenworth/Lincoln, Western League
Orlando Cepeda	1956	26	St. Cloud, Northern League
Roger Connor	1898	5	Waterbury, Connecticut State League
Johnny Evers	1902	10	Troy, New York State League
Hank Greenberg	1932	39	Beaumont, Texas League
George Kelly	1919	15	Rochester, International League
Harmon Killebrew	1957	29	Chattanooga, Southern Association
Ralph Kiner	1942	14	Albany, Eastern League
Tony Lazzeri	1925	60	Salt Lake City, Pacific Coast League
Willie McCovey	1959	29	Phoenix, Pacific Coast League
Joe Medwick	1931	19	Houston, Texas League
Stan Musial	1941	26	Springfield, Western Association
Jim Rice	1974	25	Pawtucket, International League
Duke Snider	1944	9	Newport News, Piedmont League
Pie Traynor	1920	8	Portsmouth, Virginia League
Ted Williams	1938	43	Minneapolis, American Association
Hack Wilson	1922	30	Martinsburg, Blue Ridge League
Hack Wilson	1923	19	Portsmouth, Virginia League

Major League Season Home Run Leaders Who Also Led a Minor League in Home Runs

Player	Major League	Minor League
Dick Allen	American, 1972, 1974	International, 1963
Fred Beck	National, 1910	Three I, 1916
		Western, 1921
Adrian Beltre	National, 2002	Florida State, 1997
Wally Berger	National, 1935	Utah–Idaho, 1927
Dave Brain	National, 1907	Western, 1901
Dan Brouthers	National, 1881, 1886	International Association, 1880
Oyster Burns	National, 1890	Eastern, 1884, 1886
Count Campau	American Association, 1890	International Association, 1890
		Southern, 1894
		New Pacific, 1896
Orlando Cepeda	National, 1961	Northern, 1956
Rocky Colavito	American, 1959	Florida State, 1951
		Eastern, 1953
		American Association, 1954
Rip Collins	National, 1934	Three I, 1928
		International, 1929
		Pacific Coast, 1939
Roger Connor	Players, 1890	Connecticut State, 1898
Gavvy Cravath	National, 1913–1915, 1917–1919	American Association, 1910–1911
Harry Davis	American, 1904–1907	New England, 1895
Andre Dawson	National, 1987	Pioneer, 1975
Nick Etten	American, 1944	South Atlantic, 1937
Cecil Fielder	American, 1990–1991	Pioneer, 1982
Buck Freeman	National, 1899	New England, 1894
	American, 1903	Eastern, 1897–1898
		American Association, 1907–1908
Juan Gonzalez	American, 1992–1993	American Association, 1990
Hank Greenberg	American, 1935, 1938, 1940, 1946	Texas, 1932
Bug Holliday	American Association, 1889	Western, 1887
	National, 1892	
Frank Howard	American, 1968, 1970	Three I, 1958
Ryan Howard	National, 2006, 2008	Florida State, 2003
Tim Jordan	National, 1906, 1908	Eastern, 1911
	International, 1912	
George Kelly	National, 1921	International, 1919
Harmon Killebrew	American, 1959, 1962–1964, 1967, 1969	Southern Association, 1957
Ralph Kiner	National, 1946–1952	Eastern, 1942
Tommy Leach	National, 1902	New York State, 1898
Harry Lumley	National, 1904	American Association, 1902
Willie McCovey	National, 1963, 1968–1969	Pacific Coast, 1959
Fred McGriff	American, 1989	Gulf Coast Rookie, 1982
	National, 1992	
Mark McGwire	American, 1987, 1996	California, 1985
	National, 1998–1999	
Joe Medwick	National, 1937	Texas, 1931
Graig Nettles	American, 1976	Midwest, 1966
		Southern, 1967
Bill Nicholson	National, 1943–1944	Eastern, 1938
		Southern Association, 1939
Lipman Pike	National, 1877	International Association, 1880
Wally Pipp	American, 1916–1917	International, 1914
Manny Ramirez	American, 2004	Appalachian, 1991

Player	Major League	Minor League
Jim Rice	American, 1977–1978, 1983	International, 1974
Dave Robertson	National, 1916–1917	Southern Association, 1913
Al Rosen	American, 1950, 1953	Canadian–American, 1946
Jimmy Ryan	National, 1888	Central, 1905
George Scott	American, 1975	Eastern, 1965
Socks Seybold	Atlantic, 1897–1899	American, 1902
Roy Sievers	American, 1957	Central Association, 1947
Duke Snider	National, 1956	Piedmont, 1944
Darryl Strawberry	National, 1988	Texas, 1982
Gorman Thomas	American, 1979, 1982	Midwest, 1971
		Texas, 1972
Tilly Walker	American, 1918	South Atlantic Association, 1928
Ken Williams	American, 1922	Western Canada, 1914
		Pacific Coast, 1917
Ted Williams	American, 1941–1942, 1947, 1949	American Association, 1938
Hack Wilson	National, 1926–1928, 1930	Blue Ridge, 1922
		Virginia, 1923
Rudy York	American, 1943	Texas, 1935
		Middle Atlantic, 1951
Gus Zernial	American, 1951	Carolina, 1946

Buck Freeman led a minor league five times as well as leading both the National League and the American League.

Socks Seybold led a minor league four times while three *C*'s—Campau, Colavito, and Collins—each led three times.

Rudy York led a minor league two times but waited sixteen years to capture his second title.

Moses Solomon

Moses Solomon was given the name "The Rabbi of Swat" when being compared to Babe Ruth, "The Sultan of Swat." Solomon ruled supreme for one brief and brilliant year. He hit 49 round-trippers in 1923 for Hutchinson in the Southwestern League. This was the highest total ever recorded in the minor leagues. He would have hit a nice round number of 50, but one was rained out on August 26.

The 23-year-old slugger was to all appearances the answer to John McGraw's quest for a "Jewish Babe Ruth." McGraw was anxious to compete with the Yankees in the heavily Jewish residential areas of the Bronx and upper Manhattan. Moses was a native of New York City, which also whetted McGraw's enthusiasm. The Giants paid $4,500 for Solomon.

Solomon was brought up to the Giants at the tail end of the 1923 season. He was joined by two other rookies, the not so well-known Bill Terry and Hack Wilson. Each of the three played in several games. Terry hit .143 and Wilson hit .200, while Solomon hit .375.

But then what happened? The king abdicated. The clouting collapsed. His fielding was atrocious. He couldn't catch. He was soon exiled to the minors.

He did have a fairly good minor-league career, with a career batting average over .300. He whacked more homers in his one year at Hutchinson than he did for the rest of his combined career. He quit in 1930 at 30 years of age. He then moved into the real-estate game, where he became richer and happier.

Condensation of article "Moses Solomon, the Rabbi of Swat," by Howard Lavelle, which appeared in SABR's 1976 *Baseball Research Journal*.

Joe Hauser

Joe Hauser is the only minor-league player with two 60–home run seasons, He hit 63 for Baltimore in the International League in 1930 and bettered that mark with 69 while playing for Minneapolis of the American Association in 1933. Joe finished his career with 399 home runs in the minors. It's too bad that he couldn't just hit one more—.400 looks so much more impressive than 399.

Joe had a promising major-league career ruined by a broken leg during spring training in 1925. This caused him to miss the entire season. In his first three seasons in the majors, with the Philadelphia A's, Joe hit .304 with 52 home runs. He came back after his injury and played for three more years in the majors but was never the same hitter.

However, he went on to have a long outstanding minor-league career, mostly in the high minors. He led his league in homers for four consecutive years, from 1930 through 1933. He had a minor-league career batting average of .299. Joe was always falling one short.

Joe is well remembered by SABR members at the 1988 SABR convention in Minneapolis. He was one of our guests. He stayed in the hotel lobby late one night regaling members with stories and answering questions. He was 89 years old at the time and still had a sharp mind.

Joe Bauman

Joe Bauman was one of the greatest minor-league sluggers of all time. He passed away several years ago at age 83. He lived just long enough to see his Organized Baseball season record of 72 home runs broken by Barry Bonds. In a way, it would have been nice if he had gone a little earlier knowing that he still owned the record.

Joe had his 72-homer year in 1954 while playing for Roswell in the Longhorn League. To go along with his home runs, he hit an even .400, scored 188 runs, hit 35 doubles, and had 224 RBI. He was walked 150 times and was plunked with 9 pitched balls with only 99 strikeouts. All of this in only 498 at-bats. (The Longhorn League played a 140-game schedule.) You would have to call that a fairly good season.

Skeptics might say, "Yea, but he was playing in one of those post World War II leagues in the Southwest where they used a juiced-up ball." The eight-team league hit 930 home runs. Thus, Joe hit 7.7 percent of all the league homers. The skeptics will then say, "Well, he probably played in a bandbox park." Jim Day, with 14, had the second-highest total on the team. The second-highest total for a lefty teammate (Joe batted left) was 8, by Pat Stasey.

Bauman hit 337 home runs during his minor-league career. However, he missed seven years during what should have been his prime playing time. He retired at age 34 due to a nagging ankle injury.

Joe started his pro career with Newport of the Northeast Arkansas League in 1941, and he moved up to Little Rock of the Southern Association for three games at the end of the season. With the war getting into full swing in 1942, Joe took a defense job with Beechcraft in Wichita, Kansas. Beechcraft sponsored a baseball team in a fast semipro league and Joe, naturally, played on the team. He joined the navy in 1943 and spent the next three years mostly playing for navy baseball teams.

After the war in 1946, Joe signed with Amarillo, of the West Texas–New Mexico League and he hit 48 homers to lead the league. He returned to Amarillo in 1947. He was promoted to Milwaukee of the American Association, a Boston Braves farm club, in 1948. After one game with Milwaukee, the Braves sent him down to Hartford of the Eastern League, where he spent the season. At this point in his career, his record was not overly impressive.

He was very unhappy with the contract offered him for the 1949 season, so he decided to stay home and run a gas station. He also joined a strong semipro team, the Elk City Elks. Most of the players on the team had played minor-league ball at some time. The strong opposition included a number of Negro teams featuring such players as Cool Papa Bell, Buck O'Neill, and Ernie Banks. Over three years with the Elks, Joe hit 78 home runs in 786 at-bats.

After the 1951 season, Bauman was talked into returning to pro ball. The Artesia club of the Longhorn League purchased the rights to Joe from the Braves and signed him for $500 per month. Joe played for Artesia in 1952 and 1953, leading the league in home runs both years with 50 and 53, respectively.

Bauman then bought out his contract for $200 and signed with nearby Roswell in the same league for a bonus of $1,000 plus $1,000 per month. After his great season in 1954 with Roswell, Joe "slumped" to 46 homers with a .336 average and 132 RBI in 1955. He wound up his career with Roswell in 1956 after 52 games.

He continued to live in Roswell for the rest of his life.

The information in this article regarding Bauman's career outside of Organized Baseball is taken from an excellent article "The Lost Years of Home Run King Joe Bauman," by Royse Parr, *NINE* 14, no. 2 (spring 2006).

Join SABR today!

If you're interested in baseball — writing about it, reading about it, talking about it — there's a place for you in the Society for American Baseball Research.

SABR was formed in 1971 in Cooperstown, New York, with the mission of fostering the research and dissemination of the history and record of the game. Our members include everyone from academics to professional sportswriters to amateur historians and statisticians to students and casual fans who merely enjoy reading about baseball history and occasionally gathering with other members to talk baseball.

SABR members have a variety of interests, and this is reflected in the diversity of its research committees. There are more than two dozen groups devoted to the study of a specific area related to the game — from Baseball and the Arts to Statistical Analysis to the Deadball Era to Women in Baseball. In addition, many SABR members meet formally and informally in regional chapters throughout the year and hundreds come together for the annual national convention, the organization's premier event. These meetings often include panel discussions with former major league players and research presentations by members. Most of all, SABR members love talking baseball with like-minded friends. What unites them all is an interest in the game and joy in learning more about it.

Why join SABR? Here are some benefits of membership:

- Two issues of the *Baseball Research Journal*, which includes articles on history, biography, statistics, personalities, book reviews, and other aspects of the game.
- One issue of *The National Pastime*, which focuses on baseball in the region where that year's national convention is held (in 2013, it's Philadelphia)
- Regional chapter meetings, which can include guest speakers, presentations and trips to ballgames
- "This Week in SABR" e-newsletters every Friday, with the latest news in SABR and highlighting SABR research
- Online access to back issues of *The Sporting News* and other periodicals through Paper of Record
- Access to SABR's lending library and other research resources
- Online member directory to connect you with an international network of passionate baseball experts and fans
- Discount on registration for our annual conferences
- Access to SABR-L, an e-mail discussion list of baseball questions and answers that many feel is worth the cost of membership itself
- The opportunity to be part of a passionate international community of baseball fans

SABR membership is on a "rolling" calendar system; that means your membership lasts 365 days no matter when you sign up!
Enjoy all the benefits of SABR membership by signing up today at SABR.org/join or by clipping out the form below and mailing it to SABR, 4455 E. Camelback Rd., Ste. D-140, Phoenix, AZ 85018.

SABR 2013 MEMBERSHIP RENEWAL FORM
2013 dues payable by check, money order, Visa, MasterCard or Discover Card; online at: http://store.sabr.org; or by phone at (602) 343-6455

	Annual	3-year	Senior	3-yr Sr.	Under 30
U.S.:	☐ $65	☐ $175	☐ $45	☐ $129	☐ $45
Canada/Mexico:	☐ $75	☐ $205	☐ $55	☐ $159	☐ $55
Overseas:	☐ $84	☐ $232	☐ $64	☐ $186	☐ $55

Add a Family Member: $15 each family member at same address (list on back)
Senior: 65 or older before 12/31/2013
All dues amounts in U.S. dollars or equivalent

Participate in Our Donor Program!
I'd like to designate my gift to be used toward:
☐ General Fund ☐ Endowment Fund ☐ Research Resources ☐ _____
☐ I want to maximize the impact of my gift; do not send any donor premiums
☐ I would like this gift to remain anonymous.

Note: Any donation not designated will be placed in the General Fund.
SABR is a 501 (c) (3) not-for-profit organization & donations are tax-deductible to the extent allowed by law.

Name _____

Address _____

City _____ ST_____ ZIP_____

Home Phone _____ Birthday _____

E-mail: _____
(Your e-mail address on file ensures you will receive the most recent SABR news.)

Dues $_____
Donation $_____
Amount Enclosed $_____

Do you work for a matching grant corporation? Call (602) 343-6455 for details.
☐ Check/Money Order Enclosed   ☐ VISA, Master Card, Discover Card

Card#_____

Exp Date_____ Signature _____

Mail to: SABR, 4455 E. Camelback Rd., Ste. D-140, Phoenix, AZ 85018

10/13

www.ingramcontent.com/pod-product-compliance
Lightning Source LLC
Chambersburg PA
CBHW051409070526
44584CB00023B/3350